Modeling
Mathematical Ideas

Modeling Mathematical Ideas

Developing Strategic Competence in Elementary and Middle School

Jennifer M. Suh
and Padmanabhan Seshaiyer

ROWMAN & LITTLEFIELD
Lanham • Boulder • New York • London

Executive Editor: Susanne Caravan
Associate Editor: Carlie Wall
Marketing Manager: Karin Cholak
Cover Designer: Paul Josowitz
Production Editor: Elaine McGarraugh

Credits and acknowledgments for material borrowed from other sources, and reproduced with permission, appear on the appropriate page within the text.

Published by Rowman & Littlefield
A wholly owned subsidary of The Rowman & Littlefield Publishing Group, Inc.
4501 Forbes Boulevard, Suite 200, Lanham, Maryland 20706
www.rowman.com

Unit A, Whitacre Mews, 26-34 Stannary Street, London SE11 4AB

British Library Cataloguing in Publication Information Available

Library of Congress Cataloging-in-Publication Data
Names: Suh, Jennifer M., 1971- | Seshaiyer, Padmanabhan, 1972-
Title: Modeling mathematical ideas : developing strategic competence in elementary and
    middle school / Jennifer M. Suh and Padmanabhan Seshaiyer.
Description: Lanham : Rowman & Littlefield, [2017] | Includes bibliographical references and
    index.
Identifiers: LCCN 2016042051 (print) | LCCN 2016043048 (ebook) | ISBN 9781475817584
    (cloth) | ISBN 9781475817591 (pbk.) | ISBN 9781475817607 (ebook)
Subjects: LCSH: Mathematics—Study and teaching (Elementary) | Mathematics—Study and
    teaching (Middle school) | Cognition in children.
Classification: LCC QA135.6 .S84 2017 (print) | LCC QA135.6 (ebook) | DDC 372.7—dc23
LC record available at https://lccn.loc.gov/2016042051

∞™ The paper used in this publication meets the minimum requirements of American National Standard for Information Sciences—Permanence of Paper for Printed Library Materials, ANSI/NISO Z39.48-1992.

Printed in the United States of America

Contents

Preface

This book is for preservice and in-service teachers' teaching elementary and middle-school mathematics. The focus of our book is to develop mathematical ideas by sharing ways students respond to modeling mathematical ideas and allowing teachers to discuss student strategies through case scenarios from lesson studies taken from the elementary and middle-grade classrooms.

With the recent release of the Common Core State Standards (CCSS) (NGACBP & CCSSI, 2010), researchers and mathematics educators are looking at the standards to help teachers map out the learning progression that will guide the sequence of mathematical concepts crucial in building mathematical understanding. Learning progression extends "previous learning while avoiding repetition and large gaps" (Hunt Institute, 2012, p. 8) and guides "a path through a conceptual corridor in which there are predictable obstacles and landmarks" (Confrey, 2012, p. 4).

Understanding the learning progression is important for teachers for it serves as the guiding post for analyzing student learning and tailoring their teaching sequence. This essential instructional practice leads to important professional development focused on vertical articulation around important math concepts and worthwhile tasks with cognitive demand at multiple levels. Teachers need to be engaged in understanding the learning progression across standards. Our proposed book will provide the support with the focus on the learning progression for grades 3–8 by presenting rich problem-solving tasks that model mathematics across the vertical progression. We hope this book will provide a guide for navigating through the mathematics learning progression through meaningful conceptual tasks and formative and summative assessments.

All of the Lesson Study Vignettes are from our past lesson studies with classroom teachers in the past eight years. These lesson studies were supported in part by the Virginia Department of Education, State Council for Higher Education in Virginia, and the National Science Foundation through a variety of Mathematics Science Partnership grants. We have conducted multiple professional development courses focused on these important math practices and strands and essential themes including computational fluency, building number sense, rational numbers and proportional reasoning, STEM in high schools and have used this curriculum.

We want to thank all the teachers who participated in our professional development institutes and lesson study over the eight years. We have learned a great deal about students' mathematical thinking, and how teachers can skillfully incorporate rich tasks in their classrooms to develop mathematical hearts and minds. We also would like to express gratitude to all our school partnership mathematics professional development leaders (Patti Freeman, Spencer Jamieson, Kim Leong, Katherine Meints, Theresa Wills, Linda Gillen, Mimi Corcoran, and Courtney Baker) whom we have had the fortunate opportunities to work with. Finally, we would not be able to do this kind of work without the support of our graduate students and our doctoral students (Lesley King, Sara Birkhead, Kathleen Matson, Monique Williams, Terrie Galanti, Dasha Gerasimova, and Kim Fair) who have dedicated countless hours on observing and supporting lesson studies.

Chapter 1

Developing Strategic Competence through Modeling Mathematical Ideas

Text Box 1.1   A Math Happening 1a: The Handshake Problem

At a neighborhood party, there were a total of 25 guests. All 25 guests shook hands to introduce themselves. How many distinct handshakes happened at this party? Show the different ways you can represent your thinking.

The problem above is one of the classic problem-solving tasks called the "handshake problem." It is one that we always start within any workshop. One reason is not only because it allows us to introduce ourselves to other members in the room but also because it illustrates one of the most important teaching practices (NCTM, 2013) that we focus on throughout this book, which is *Implementing tasks that promote reasoning and problem solving across grade levels.*

> Effective teaching of mathematics engages students in solving and discussing tasks that promote mathematical reasoning and problem solving and allow multiple entry points and varied solution strategies. (p. 3)

The handshake problem is one of the best examples of a task that has multiple entry points and varied solution strategies.

In this book, we explore how students and teachers at all levels can engage and challenge in an inquiry-based learning environment through interactive modeling approaches in mathematics. Such opportunities with rich mathematical tasks require the use of higher-level critical-thinking strategies and self-monitoring problem-solving skills. This book presents approaches that will engage the reader in the modeling of real-world problems across the curriculum and discusses teaching and learning opportunities that will benefit students and teachers. In addition, we focus on the learning progression across grades 3–8 by presenting rich problem-solving tasks that model mathematics across the learning progression that aligns to the standards.

With the recent release of the Common Core State Standards (CCSS) (NGACBP & CCSSO, 2010), researchers and mathematics educators are looking at the standards to help teachers unpack the learning progressions that is crucial in building mathematical

1

understanding and guiding the sequence of mathematical concepts. Learning progression extends "previous learning while avoiding repetition and large gaps" (Hunt Institute, 2012, p. 8) and guides "a path through a conceptual corridor in which there are predictable obstacles and landmarks" (Confrey, 2012, p. 4).

Understanding the learning progression is important for teachers because it serves as the critical markers for analyzing student learning and tailoring their teaching sequence. This essential instructional practice leads to the vital professional development that focused on vertical articulation around essential math concepts and worthwhile tasks. In each chapter, we use the learning progressions to map out student learning outcomes as they advance through different grade levels and provide standards for formative and summative assessments.

Think about it!

Try the Handshake problem. How is the "Classic Handshake Problem" an accessible and rich problem?

1.1   DEVELOPING STRATEGIC COMPETENCE THROUGH MODELING MATHEMATICAL IDEAS

Modeling mathematical ideas include real-world problems in mathematics and have different interpretations at multiple levels of learning. For example, modeling mathematics in elementary grades can simply refer to writing number sentences or multistep equations using the four basic operations to describe mathematical situations involving addition, subtraction, multiplication, and division. In addition, modeling mathematics can be used to mean employing mathematics to analyze a real-world problem in their school and community.

At the secondary-school level, modeling mathematics can refer to using principles from geometry to create an architectural design or using calculus to obtain marginal cost and revenue in economics. At the college or university level, modeling typically helps students to research an important problem in their field that can impact society. To develop students to become mathematically and conceptually proficient in modeling, it is important to teach them how to: apply their prior knowledge to observe and theorize from a situation; make suitable assumptions and formulate a problem; identify essential inputs and outputs to describe the problem; make educated approximations to simplify complex problems and perform related analysis; implement the approximated problem via simulations and validate against benchmark solutions; and validate the model by comparing with true experimental data that can help predict the evolution of a more efficient model.

The process described above for modeling can be implemented using the National Council of Teachers of Mathematics (NCTM) process standards, which include problem solving, reasoning and proof, communication, representations, and connections. Related to these process standards is the framework called the *Five Strands of Mathematical Proficiency* described by the National Research Council's (2001) report called *Adding It Up*. The five strands of mathematical proficiency include conceptual understanding, procedural fluency, strategic competence, adaptive reasoning, and productive disposition (National Research Council, 2001). These strands are interwoven to represent the interconnectedness of these proficiency strands (see Figure 1.1).

In particular, the strands of *conceptual understanding and procedural fluency are* essential for students in all grade levels in order to comprehend the mathematical concepts, perform operations, and identify appropriate relationships. Strategic competence and adaptive reasoning are especially important when students make sense of mathematical ideas as they problem solve, problem pose, and justify one's reasoning. One of the last but most essential strands of mathematical proficiency is having a productive disposition toward mathematics. This is something that we refer to as *developing students' mathematical hearts and minds*. That means, mathematics should be a sense-making experience that is positive where students feel exhilaration from discovering and making mathematical connections marked by the "Aha" and Eureka moments. Many of our former pre-service teachers, who reflect on their elementary and middle-school mathematics, recount how they started disliking mathematics later in middle and high school because mathematics became a series of senseless steps of operations and rules that they memorized without constructing meaning.

Each of the strands of mathematical proficiency discussed above connects directly to the Standards for Mathematical Practice. Standard 4 of Common Core State Standards in Mathematics (CCSS-M) (NGACBP & CCSSO, 2010) describes mathematically proficient students who can apply what they know to simplify a complicated

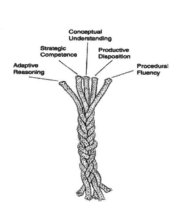

(1) *Conceptual understanding* refers to the "integrated and functional grasp of mathematical ideas," which "enables them [students] to learn new ideas by connecting those ideas to what they already know." A few of the benefits of building conceptual understanding are that it supports retention and prevents common errors.

(2) *Procedural fluency* is defined as the skill in carrying out procedures flexibly, accurately, efficiently, and appropriately.

(3) *Strategic competence* is the ability to formulate, represent, and solve mathematical problems.

(4) *Adaptive reasoning* is the capacity for logical thought, reflection, explanation, and justification.

(5) *Productive disposition* is the inclination to see mathematics as sensible, useful, and worthwhile, coupled with a belief in diligence and one's own efficacy. (NRC, 2001, p. 116)

Figure 1.1   Five strands of math proficiency. National Research Council, 2001.

Table 1.1   Common Core Mathematical Practices (NGA Center and CCSSO, 2010, p. 6) with question prompts for encouraging mathematical practices (Suh & Seshaiyer, 2014)

Mathematical Practices	*Questioning Prompts*
(MP1) Make sense of problems and persevere in solving them.	Does the problem make sense? What do you need to find out? What information do you have? What strategies are you going to use? Does this problem require you to use your numeric ability, spatial reasoning, and/or logical reasoning? What can you do when you are stuck?
(MP2) Reason abstractly and quantitatively.	What do the numbers in the problem mean? What is the relationship among the numbers in the problem? How can you use number sense to help you check for reasonableness of your solution? What operations or algorithms are involved? Can you generalize the problem using symbols?
(MP3) Construct viable arguments and critique the reasoning of others.	How can you justify or prove your thinking? Do you agree with your classmate's solution? Why or why not? Does anyone have the same answer but a different way to explain it? How are some of your classmates strategies related and are some strategies more efficient than others?
(MP4) Model with mathematics.	How is this math concept used in a real-world context? Where have you seen similar problems happening in everyday life? Can you take a real-world problem and model it using mathematics? What data or information is necessary to solve the problem? How can you formulating a model by selecting geometric, graphical, tabular, algebraic, or statistical representations that describe relationships between the variables?
(MP5) Use appropriate tools strategically.	What tools or technology can you use to solve the problem? Are certain manipulatives or representations more precise, efficient, and clear than others? How could you model this problem situation with pictures, diagrams, numbers, words, graphs, and/or equations? What representations might help you visualize the problem?
(MP6) Attend to precision.	What specific math vocabulary, definitions, and representations can you use in your explanation to be more accurate and precise? What are important math concepts that you need to include in your justification and proof to communicate your ideas clearly?
(MP7) Look for and make use of structure.	What patterns and structures do you notice in the problem? Are there logical steps that you need to take to solve the problem? Is this problem related to a class of problems (i.e., multi-step, work backwards, algebraic, etc.)? Can you use a particular algorithmic process to solve this problem?
(MP8) Look for and express regularity in repeated reasoning.	Do you see a repeating pattern? Can you explain the pattern? Is there a pattern that can be generalized to a rule? Can you predict the next one? What about the last one?

situation and who can "apply the mathematics ... to solve problems in everyday life." In addition to modeling with mathematics as described in the standards, the process of selecting and using tools to visualize and explore the task connects with CCSS-M standard 5: use appropriate tools strategically. Furthermore, as students struggle to make sense of their task by translating within and among multiple representations, they develop an important aspect of strategic competence in mathematics. To help us discuss the important ways that modeling mathematical ideas support teachers' and students' strategic competence, we created the visual in Figure 1.2 to show how all these different modeling activities support the "ability to formulate, represent, and solve mathematical problems" (NRC 2001, p. 116).

In one of our chapters entitled, *Developing Strategic Competence by Teaching through Mathematical Practice*s (Suh & Seshaiyer, 2014), we discussed what strategic competence means for teachers. We defined strategic competence for teachers to include the ability to (a) formulate, represent, and solve problems; (b) model mathematical ideas using engaging real-life problems; and (c) demonstrate representational fluency by translating and connecting within and among students' multiple representations and strategies with accuracy, efficiency, and flexibility. One of the ways that teachers can help students advance their mathematical reasoning is through explicit use of questioning and mathematical discourse. To bring out the Common Core Mathematical Practices, we developed some questions that teachers could use in their classroom to prompt their students (see Table 1.1).

These question prompts can help students *make sense of problems and persevere in solving them (MP1)* and sustain students' interest in the problem-solving process by engaging them in mathematics conversation where they can *discuss the reasoning of their classmates (MP3)*. Teachers can focus on having students' *reason abstractly and quantitatively (MP2)* so that they can better connect the conceptual understanding with the procedural fluency. Students model mathematics by *visualizing the problem situation and relating the problems to real-life scenarios (MP4)* while using *appropriate tools to represent their thinking (MP5)*.

Students use *mathematical structures (MP7)* in computational work, data analysis, algebraic, and geometric structures to *look for patterns and methods in the repeated reasoning (MP8)*. To develop these important mathematical practices, teachers need to provide time and space for students to reason, critique classmates' reasoning, and value different perspectives to problem solving.

In addition, teachers need to develop their own strategic competence as they evaluate strategies *and judiciously select the strategies as pedagogical content tools* (Rasmussen & Marrongelle, 2006) to help advance students' mathematical thinking. Developing proficiency in teaching mathematics with a focus on eliciting students' strategic competence requires more than the analysis of students' diverse strategies; more time and space is needed for students to reason through by sharing, arguing, and justifying their strategic thinking as well.

Think about it!

What are some classroom strategies you use to promote mathematics proficiency as shown in the Five Strands for Math Proficiency?

1.2 PROMOTING MATHEMATICAL PROFICIENCY AND PRACTICES

There is a great need to promote the awareness of modeling mathematical ideas across the curriculum in order for students to gain conceptual understanding of the methods employed to solve real-world problems. What does modeling mathematical ideas mean to elementary and middle-grade teachers and students? The term "model" is used in many different ways in our everyday language and also has many interpretations within our academic vocabulary.

The release of the CCSS-M has also drawn a lot of attention to the word model and modeling. Some of the ways in which models and modeling are used are from the specific grade-level standards, for example, from the third-grade CCSS-M standard, *3.OA. develop an understanding of the meanings of multiplication and division of whole numbers through activities and problems involving equal-sized groups, arrays, and area models* and another, 3.NF.3 *recognize and generate simple equivalent fractions, for example, 1 / 2 = 2/4, 4 / 6 = 2 / 3. Explain why the fractions are equivalent, for example, using a visual fraction model.*

The term "model" is used differently in the fourth Standard for Mathematical Practice, "Model with Mathematics" and also in the high-school content standard, "Mathematical Modeling." To understand the CCSS-M, let us take a look at the description for the mathematical practices standard 4: model with mathematics:

Text Box 1.2   Model with Mathematics. From Standard 4 of CCSS-M

Mathematically proficient students can apply the mathematics they know to solve problems arising in everyday life, society, and the workplace. In early grades, this might be as simple as writing an addition equation to describe a situation. In middle grades, a student might apply proportional reasoning to plan a school event or analyze a problem in the community. By high school, a student might use geometry to solve a design problem or use a function to describe how one quantity of interest depends on another. Mathematically proficient students who can apply what they know are comfortable making assumptions and approximations to simplify a complicated situation, realizing that these may need revision later. They are able to identify important quantities in a practical situation and map their relationships using such tools as diagrams, two-way tables, graphs, flowcharts, and formulas. They can analyze those relationships mathematically to draw conclusions. They routinely interpret their mathematical results in the context of the situation and reflect on whether the results make sense, possibly improving the model if it has not served its purpose. (NGACBP & CCSSO, 2010)

"Model with mathematics" calls for an important mathematical practice to connect between real-world scenarios and mathematical representations to solve problems where students "can apply the mathematics that they know to solve problems arising in everyday life, society, and the workplace." In the description, it also states, "They are able to identify important quantities in a practical situation and map their relationships using such tools as diagrams, two-way tables, graphs, flowcharts, and formulas."

While we worked on defining what strategic competence was for our teachers, we noticed that there were many parallels with the recently released Mathematical Practices from the CCSS (NGACBP & CCSSO, 2010). In particular, we saw a direct connection to standard 4: model with mathematics and standard 5: use appropriate tools strategically. As students develop their algebraic habits of mind, they need to be encouraged to effectively communicate mathematical ideas using language efficient tools, appropriate units, and graphical, numerical, physical, or algebraic mathematical models.

As we consider all the important and different ways that we model mathematical ideas in elementary and middle grades, we offer *Developing Strategic Competence in Modeling Mathematical Ideas* as a balanced approach to teaching and learning mathematics. *Developing Strategic Competence in Modeling Mathematical Ideas* (see Figure 1.2), as we define it in our book, includes (1) the important representational models, tools, technology, and manipulatives that bring mathematical thinking visibly

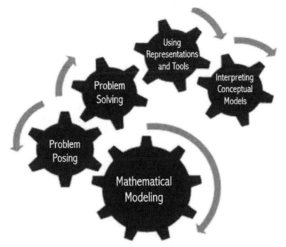

Figure 1.2   **Developing strategic competence in modeling mathematical ideas.** *Source*: Authors.

as student communicate their mathematical understanding; (2) the interpretative models of mathematical ideas critical to understanding a specific mathematics concept; (3) the application of mathematics for problem solving; (4) problem posing; and (5) mathematical modeling (more about it in chapter 3).

In the figure above, we use a metaphor of gears that must work together, because the different models and modeling must all work together to provide students' mathematical understanding, fluency, and mathematical power.

One of the ways that we discuss developing strategic competence in modeling mathematics ideas is through **problem solving**. According to the NCTM, *problem solving* refers to mathematical tasks that have the potential to provide intellectual challenges that can enhance students' mathematical development. Such tasks can promote students' conceptual understanding, foster their ability to reason and communicate mathematically, and capture their interests and curiosity (Van de Walle, Karp, & Bay-Williams, 2014).

Throughout our book, we engage our readers in a math happening, which is a simple yet powerful mathematical routine to include in a mathematical classroom to bring mathematics closer to each individual's daily life. Math happenings present a realistic problem that can happen to an individual in their immediate world (see Appendix MMI Toolkit 4—Sharing Math Happenings).

For students, they may encounter a math happening when deciding on which cell phone plan works best for their family's usage, or when calculating their statistics for their favorite athlete or game. Polya's (1945) famous book *How to Solve It* introduced the dynamic, cyclic nature of problem solving, where a student may begin with a problem and engage in thought and activity to understand it. The student attempts to make a plan and in the process may discover a need to understand the problem better. Or when a plan has been formed, the student may attempt to carry it out and be unable to do so.

The next activity may be attempting to make a new plan, or going back to develop a new understanding of the problem, or posing a new (possibly related) problem to work on. Schoenfeld's (1985) work on problem solving described and demonstrated the importance of metacognition, an executive, or monitor component to his problem-solving theory. His problem-solving courses included explicit attention to a set of guidelines for reflecting about the problem-solving activities in which the students were engaged. Effective problem-solving instruction must provide the students with an opportunity to reflect during problem-solving activities in a systematic and constructive way.

The second way, we discuss developing strategic competence in modeling mathematics ideas, is through the use of important **representational models**, tools, technology, and manipulatives that bring mathematical thinking visibly as students' problem solving and communicate their mathematical understanding. We use the five star representations (see Figure 1.3) to reinforce the notion that having representational fluency, being able to translate a mathematical idea among these representations, strengthens one's strategic competence and conceptual understanding.

This particular meaning for modeling mathematics ideas relates to the Common Core Mathematical Practice Standard 5: use tools appropriately, as outlined in the description, "When making mathematical models, they [students] know that technology can enable them to visualize the results of varying assumptions, explore consequences, and compare predictions with data." An example would be using the virtual coin toss simulator to generate outcomes to discuss the difference between experimental and theoretic probability, taking advantage of technology's ability to generate large sets of trials in an efficient manner to reveal the "law of large numbers." Developing representational fluency is important for a mathematics teacher and learner. Representations is an important mathematical process in the NCTM (2000) standard:

> *Mathematical ideas can be represented in a variety of ways: pictures, concrete materials, tables, graphs, number and letter symbols, spreadsheet displays, and so on. The ways in which mathematical ideas are represented is fundamental to how people understand and use those ideas. Many of the representations we now take for granted are the result of a process of cultural refinement that took place over many years. When students gain access to mathematical representations and the ideas they express and when they can create representations to capture mathematical concepts or relationships, they acquire a set of tools that significantly expand their capacity to model and interpret physical, social, and mathematical phenomena.* (NCTM, 2000, p. 4)

A way to think about representations is that they allow for construction of knowledge from "models *of* thinking to models *for* thinking" (Gravemeijer, 1999). The Association of Mathematics Teacher Educator's standards for Pedagogical Knowledge for Teaching Mathematics includes the ability to "construct and evaluate multiple representations of mathematical ideas or processes, establish correspondences between representations, understand the purpose and value of doing so, and use various instructional tools, models, technology, in ways that are mathematically and pedagogically grounded" (AMTE, 2010, p. 4).

Throughout our book, we will focus on strengthening representational fluency through visible thinking strategies in the classroom that will offer opportunities for students to use representations, tools, technology, and manipulatives to show their mathematical thinking.

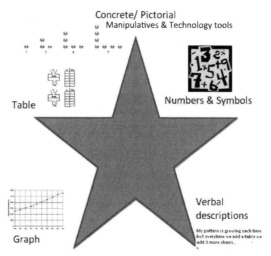

Figure 1.3   Five star representations and math tools. *Source*: Authors.

The third way, we discuss developing strategic competence in modeling mathematics ideas, is understanding and interpreting important **conceptual models** within and between mathematics topics. For example, we discuss the different interpretations within division when we give examples of partitive and measurement division.

Partitive division would be a story problem about fair share to see how many items each person gets, whereas the measurement division model would be a story problem about repeated subtraction or measuring off a number of items to find out the number of groups. Another example would be used when teaching fractions and exposing students to the region model, set model, measurement model, and the area model for fractions. In addition, in rational-number conceptual models, Lesh, Laudau, and Hamilton (1983) cited an example of how a youngster's rational-number conceptual model can have a within-concept network associated with each rational-number sub-construct, for example, ratio, number line, part whole, operator, rate, and quotient model. An example of a between-concept systems links rational-number ideas with other concepts such as measurement, whole-number division, and intuitive geometry concepts related to areas and number lines. In our book, we will visit these important conceptual models and interpretations within and between concepts by delving deeply in understanding the learning progressions of mathematical ideas.

Finally, but one of the most important ways that we focus on developing strategic competence in modeling mathematics ideas is by introducing elementary and middle-grade students to the nature of **mathematical modeling** that involves **problem posing** through real-world problem scenarios (more in chapter 3). These authentic mathematical modeling tasks involve students engaging in unique stages of the mathematical modeling process. The following six steps were modified from the steps as defined by the Society for Industrial and Applied Mathematics (SIAM)—Moody's Mega Math Challenge—which is a national mathematical modeling contest for high-school students sponsored by The Moody's Foundation (see http://m3challenge.siam.org/resources/modeling-handbook).

1. **Posing the Problem Statement:** Is it real-world and does it require math modeling? What mathematical questions come to mind?
2. **Making Assumptions to Define, and Simplify the Real-world Problem:** What assumptions do you make? What are the constraints that help you define and simplify the problem?
3. **Considering the Variables:** What variables will you consider? What data/information is necessary to answer your question?
4. **Building Solutions:** Generate solutions.
5. **Analyzing and Validating their Conclusions:** Does your solutions make sense? Now, take your solution and apply it to the real-world scenario. How does it fit? What do you want to revise?
6. **Presenting and Justifying the Reasoning for Your Solution:** (From Bliss, K.M., Fowler, K.R., & Galluzzo, B.J. (2014). Math Modeling. Getting Started & Getting Solutions. SIAM: Society for Industrial and Applied Mathematics.)

In the following chapters, we share how these important ways models and modeling are used in teaching and learning mathematics through our research lessons, and we consider how teachers, students, math educators, researchers, and mathematicians use models and modeling to understand mathematics teaching and learning. Using this holistic approach allows one to appreciate all the different facets of modeling math ideas.

Think about it!

A close look at our national and state standards and you will see the word "model" appears throughout these documents. Take the time to search for the word model within your grade level standard. What are some examples from your current grade/standards that address these different and important ways to model mathematical ideas? Cite the specific standards and give an example.

1.3 PROBLEM SOLVING AND MATHEMATICAL MODELING IN THE ELEMENTARY AND MIDDLE GRADES

Problem solving is central to mathematics and can challenge students' curiosities and interest in mathematics. Polya's (1945) seminal book, *How to Solve It* stated,

> *A teacher of mathematics has a great opportunity. If he fills his allotted time with drilling his students in routine operations he kills their interest, hampers their intellectual development and misuses opportunity. But if he challenges the curiosity of his students by setting them problems proportionate to their knowledge, and helps them to solve their problems with stimulating questions, he may give them a taste for, and some means of independent thinking.* (Polya, 1945, p. v)

Polya suggested four steps to problem solving, which included (1) understanding the problem; (2) devising a plan; (3) carrying out the plan; and (4) looking back. Problem solving is also one of the important NCTM mathematical process standards along with communication, representations, connections, and reasoning. The NCTM (2000) defined problem solving as:

Engaging in a task for which the solution method is not known in advance. In order to find a solution students must draw on their knowledge, and through this process, they will often develop new mathematical understandings. Solving problems is not only a goal of mathematics but also a major means of doing so. (p. 52)

The Common Core State Standards for Mathematics (CCSSM) encourages a problem-solving approach to teaching the standards in order to develop mathematically proficient students and emphasizes the importance of developing students' metacognition, self-monitoring, and self-reflection.

Mathematically proficient students start by explaining to themselves the meaning of a problem and looking for entry points to its solution...[They] check their answers to problems using a different method, and they continually ask themselves, "Does this make sense?" They can understand the approaches of others to solving complex problems and identify correspondences between different approaches. (NGACBP & CCSSO, 2010, p. 9)

Think about the many ways that you can encourage the use of models and math modeling in your teaching. Some examples may include finding the height of a monument or finding the mass of the earth or estimating the population of a town in 50 years. In each case, "modeling the physical situation" would involve identifying the appropriate variables to work with that represent known and unknown quantities in the problem; establishing relationships between the variables identified and finally be able to solve for the unknown under some given constraints.

For example, one may try to express the height of the monument in the first example in terms of some distance and angles, which can be measured on ground. For finding the mass of the earth, one may employ masses of known objects that are similar in shape to the earth and invoke proportional reasoning arguments. To estimate population, one can extrapolate from a previous census or possibly develop a model expressing the population of the town as a function of time.

Polya's Four Steps to Problem Solving have similar processes that are employed as big ideas in mathematical modeling. The first idea involves *observation*, which helps us to recognize the problem. In this step, the variables describe the attributes in the problem as well as any implicit or explicit relationships between the variables. The second idea includes the *formulation* of the mathematical model. In this step, one makes the necessary approximations and assumptions under which one can try to obtain a reasonable model for the problem.

These approximations and assumptions may be based on experiments or observations and are often necessary to develop, simplify, and understand the mathematical model. The third idea addresses *computation* that involves solving the mathematical model for the physical problem formulated. It is then important as a final step to then perform *validation* of the solution obtained that helps to interpret the solution in the context of the physical problem. If the solution is not reasonable, then one can attempt to modify any part of the three steps including observation, formulation, and computation, and continue to validate the updated solution until a reasonable solution to the given physical problem is obtained. *Mathematical modeling* is a very distinct class of problems that are very open (example of a mathematical modeling research lesson in chapter 3).

In any given mathematics classroom, problems might be presented along a continuum ranging from the mathematics being presented in a structured word problem to the mathematics being presented in an unstructured real-world problem. The difference along this continuum can be seen as the degree of open-ness (unstructured) or closed-ness (structured) of the application. Each of these different types of problems along the continuum has its place in the mathematics classroom.

Depending on the specific learning goals, teachers may want to use a variety of problem types for different purposes. When learning about the different multiplication and division structures and interpretations, one might use structured word problems to be able to distinguish from equal group problems and multiplicative comparison problems. For example, *Zachary has 3 bags with 4 apples in each bag. How many apples does Zachary have?* versus *Jeremy has 3 apples and Zachary has 4 times more than Jeremy. How many apples does Zachary have?* Learning multiple interpretations for multiplication can help students be flexible in the way that they use these operations with meaning.

On the other hand, one may pose a rich task like the handshake problem to teach problem-solving strategies and the notion of algebraic reasoning in finding a pattern of the number of handshakes given any number of people. Furthermore, one might use an open-ended real-world problem for students to see how they go through the process of defining the variables, making assumptions to build a mathematical model or solution to a nonroutine problem. There are several unique affordances of mathematical modeling problems that are important to consider.

Mathematical modeling requires reasoning about several ideas or quantities simultaneously. It requires thinking about situations in relative rather than absolute terms. For example, if the number of students in a middle school grows from 500 to 800 and another middle school grows from 300 to 600, a student thinking in absolute terms (or additively) might answer that both schools had the same amount of increase. On the other hand, a student that is taught to think in relative terms might argue that the second middle school saw *more* increase since it doubled the number of students unlike the first school which would have needed to end up with 1000 students to grow by the same relative amount. While both answers seem reasonable, it is the relative multiplicative thinking that is essential for proportional reasoning. This ability to think and reason proportionally is very important in the development of a student's ability to understand and apply mathematical modeling to real-world problem solving.

The goal for the lesson can determine what type of problems that students are working through. It is important for educators to support students in the discovery of connections that help them comprehend the applications of mathematical concepts to real-world problems in a way that is beyond what is taught in a traditional classroom.

Making such connections in the middle grades would require the teachers to begin a process of investigation, which may take multiple forms. Such forms may include anything from random guessing to a more systematic and organized approach, but inherent to this problem-solving investigation process would be to make algebraic connections between these various forms. Good problems are those that are mystifying and interesting. They are mystifying when they are not easy to solve using traditional textbook formulas and approaches. The *handshake problem* is a prime example of a task that can engage students in a rich problem-solving investigation and algebraic thinking process as they make important connections through various models.

1.4   MULTIPLE REPRESENTATIONS AND STRATEGIES AS TOOLS TO CULTIVATE VISIBLE THINKING IN MATHEMATICS

One of the major benefits of orchestrating a lesson with an inquiry approach is that it provides opportunities for students' visible thinking to take center stage in our math classrooms. Visible thinking (Ritchhart & Perkins, 2011) is a systematic, research-based approach to integrating the development of students' thinking with content learning across subject matters. Researchers and authors, Ron Ritchhart and David Perkins, stated that visible thinking provides opportunities to cultivate students' thinking skills and dispositions, and to deepen content learning while stimulating greater motivation for learning and positive disposition toward learning. This shift in classroom culture toward a community of enthusiastically engaged thinkers and learners is further explored at their website (http://www.visiblethinkingpz.org) and see Appendix MMI Toolkit 5—Visible Thinking Strategies in mathematics.

In our research lessons, we promote visible thinking through **Poster Proofs**, which encourages students to publish their mathematics strategies for others to evaluate just as mathematicians justify their thinking. Having students display their thinking through different representations makes thinking visible and allows for teachers to better assess whether a student or a group of students conceptually understands a problem.

To distinguish representations used by teachers and students, Lamon (2001) stated that representations can be "both presentational models (used by adults in instruction) and representational models (produced by students in learning), which can play significant roles in instruction and its outcomes" (p. 146). A teacher who has strategic competence can use these representations as "pedagogical content tools, devices such as graphs, diagrams, equations, or verbal statements that teachers intentionally use to connect students thinking while moving the mathematical agenda forward" (Rasmussen & Marrongelle, 2006, p. 388).

Another way to integrate visible thinking routine in problem solving is to use *Same and Different Venn Diagrams* where students use a think-pair-share strategy to actively explain, reason, and agree to disagree their thinking while looking for similarities and differences in their approaches to a problem. We encourage students to create *Poster Proofs* with their solutions as another visible thinking activity that they display through a *Math Gallery Walk*, to encourage students to explore diverse perspectives and multiple strategies. Finally, one of our favorite routines is to ask students to write an exit pass using the prompt, *I used to think … but now I think …* which is a visible thinking routine for reflecting on how and why our thinking has changed (see Appendix MMI Toolkit 5—Visible Thinking Strategies).

The modeling activity can begin by asking the students sitting at the various tables to introduce themselves by shaking hands and at the same time asking them how many different handshakes happened at their table. It is very common to hear about

Pictorial Approach

- Handshake with three people
  2 + 1 = 1 + 2 = 3

- Handshake with four people
  3 + 2 + 1 = 1 + 2 + 3 = 6

- Handshake with five people
  4 + 3 + 2 + 1 = 1 + 2 + 3 + 4 = 10

Figure 1.4   Pictorial approach. *Source:* Authors.

misconceptions that may involve the total number of handshakes at the table being twice of what it should be or the total number being the square of the number of people.

For instance, a table of three students may instantly say, since there are three people and since it takes two people to shake hands, the answer is three times two, which is six. Another response might be that the answer is three squared, which is nine. Such misconceptions introduce great teaching moments. For example, one can ask the table of three students to stand up and start shaking their hands, while the rest of the class keeps a count. They will quickly realize that they are engaged in *an active-learning exercise* that helps to identify that they had double counted the number of handshakes.

As reinforcement, another geometric connection can be made at this point by drawing three dots that would refer to the students at the table. If an edge between the dots would represent a handshake, then it is easy to connect to the numerical answer obtained through the active-learning process to the number of edges in the picture (see Figure 1.4).

Another useful approach to help the students think about the problem would be to create an organized list to record the handshakes, which illustrates the fine difference between a permutation and a combination. The active-learning exercise where the students physically shook hands, the geometric approach of drawing dots with edges indicating handshakes, as well as creating the organized list brings out another important approach, which is verbalizing the process. For instance, saying that the first person shook hands with two people and then the second person shakes only one more mathematically translates to the total number of handshakes being 2 + 1.

This *verbal reasoning* not only helps the students to make a connection to the active-learning, geometry, and organized list approaches, but also helps them to think ahead and start seeing a pattern when there are more people at the table. For instance, a table with four students may immediately notice that this pattern leads to 3 + 2 + 1. This then could lead to a *tabular approach* where one could record the relationship between the number of students at a table and the corresponding handshake count as a sum of natural numbers (see Figure 1.5).

Although we want the students to ultimately converge upon the fact that there is some hidden formula that this investigation process is going to lead them to, we want to help them discover this through their mathematical work. Naturally, we want them

Tabular Approach

Number of People	Number of Handshakes	
1	0 ◦	
2	1 o———•	1
3	3 △	1 + 2 = 3
4	6 ⊠	1 + 2 + 3 = 6

Figure 1.5   Tabular approach. *Source*: Authors.

Algebraic Approach

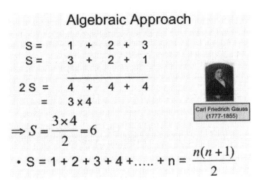

$$S = 1 + 2 + 3$$
$$S = 3 + 2 + 1$$
$$\overline{2S = 4 + 4 + 4}$$
$$= 3 \times 4$$
$$\Rightarrow S = \frac{3 \times 4}{2} = 6$$
$$\bullet\ S = 1 + 2 + 3 + 4 + \ldots + n = \frac{n(n+1)}{2}$$

Carl Friedrich Gauss
(1777-1855)

Figure 1.6   Algebraic approach. *Source*: Authors.

to next *abstract from the computation* that they have worked out. For instance, we next ask how many different handshakes happen if the room had 25 people in it.

The students at this point recognize the importance of being able to learn how to abstract. It is common to see them verbalize or argue that the answer is the sum of all the natural numbers 1 + 2 + 3 + ... + 24, but not knows how to go about computing this. This is a good place to help them learn and discover *triangular numbers* and their connection to the Gauss formula through efficient algebraic approaches (see Figure 1.6).

Even after, it is evident by applying this formula to the original problem with 25 people, resulting in a solution of (24 × 25) / 2, teachers have the opportunity to talk about taking advantage of important arithmetic operations that can help compute such answers without having to rely on a calculator. For instance, talking about associative property of multiplication helps us to think of one half times (24 × 25) as (½ × 24) times 25, which yields the final answer of 12 × 25.

At this point, we once again help the students to make a real-world connection to what they are computing. For example, 12 × 25 could be thought of as 12 quarters, which by proportional reasoning up and down can be seen to be $3.00 or 300 cents (since four quarters is a dollar). Such simplicity in solving problems helps teachers

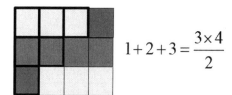

$$1+2+3 = \frac{3 \times 4}{2}$$

Figure 1.7   Picture proof. *Source*: Authors.

to recognize the power of using real-world examples to reinforce computation. Along with simplicity, it is also important for students to learn to appreciate and use mathematical formulas to help provide greater insight into solving complex problems.

Revisiting this newly discovered formula for the original example of three people yields $1 + 2 + 3 = (3 \times 4) / 2$. While this equation may seem obvious, it provides a natural challenge to prove that an additive representation on the left side of the equation equals a multiplicative representation on the right-hand side. One may think of proving this using mathematical induction for the general case, but how does one convince students that this equation makes sense using a simple mathematical model?

Consider the illustration shown that denotes a pictorial proof. If each addend on the left can be thought of as a square, the $1 + 2 + 3$ is denoted by the group of squares on the left that have boundary denoted by solid lines. Adding an exact copy to this makes a rectangular grid whose area is 3×4, and since we only wanted the sum of one of those copies, we can divide this area by 2. Such simple pictorial illustrations not only help to provide a simple proof of the mathematical statement, but also provide opportunity for students to test hypotheses by doing the mathematics using manipulatives (see Figure 1.7).

While the approaches that we have taken so far to solve the handshake problem may seem elementary, one can also take advantage of advanced concepts students learn in middle school and beyond involving combinations to solve this problem. For example, the handshake problem can be simply solved with some basic knowledge of combinations, as it only takes two people to shake hands, and since there are n people to choose these two people from, the answer is the formula, which may also be referred to as the number of combinations of n people selected two at a time. Note that in order to increase the cognitive demand of the task, the students may be asked to make predictions on the function that represents the number of handshakes from the values obtained from the tabular approach.

One approach to accomplish this may be to plot the set of ordered pairs obtained from the tabular approach on a graph to determine the nature of the function (see Figure 1.8). This will later lead to connections to high-school standards, where one may also combine this with observations of the change in the y-values, which can then help to determine the quadratic function for H(n) that we are looking for via finite differences as shown in Figure 1.9. Having such flexibility in problem solving not only helps the students to engage in multiple representations in problem solving, but also helps the teachers to scaffold the task to accommodate cognitive demand at multiple levels.

Once the students are taken through the journey of doing the problem and abstracting from computation, it is important to also teach them the skill of *undoing a problem*. For example, we go on to ask the following question: "*If you were at a party*

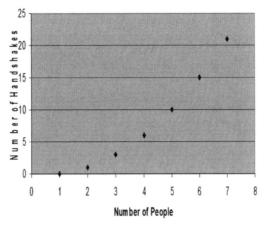

Figure 1.8   Graphical approach. *Source*: Authors.

n	H(n)	First Difference	Second Difference
1	0		
2	1	1	
3	3	2	1
4	6	3	1
5	10	4	1
6	15	5	1
7	21	6	1

$$H(n) = an^2 + bn + c$$

$$H(1) = a(1)^2 + b(1) + c = 0$$
$$H(2) = a(2)^2 + b(2) + c = 1$$
$$H(3) = a(3)^2 + b(3) + c = 3$$

$$a = \frac{1}{2}, \ b = -\frac{1}{2}, \ c = 0$$

Figure 1.9   Finite difference approach that appears later in high-school topics. *Source*: Authors.

where 190 different handshakes happen, how many people were there?" At this point, the students recognize that the answer to the handshake problem is given and they must now work backward to find out the number of people in the room. Going through this, they recognize the power of being able to work backward to solve problems, which is a very powerful problem-solving strategy.

The work in Figure 1.10 is based on reflection from a teacher from a professional development that we offered along with a poster their team created that summarizes the discussion on the multiple solution strategies to the handshake problem where the star was used as a way to assess their representational fluency.

As mentioned earlier, the choice of the problem that we want the students to grapple with should not only be mystifying but also be interesting. This means that besides learning multiple approaches to solving the handshake problem, it is important to discuss related problems where such triangular number patterns naturally emerge. For example, as a follow-up to our discussion, we introduce the following Christmas song,

After organizing the data in a table it was possible to find the rule. The rule written in the form of a formula is used to find a given number to determine the handshakes. The rule consists of Symbolic representation

n(n-1)/2=h

where n is the number of people shaking hands and h the total number of handshakes. The 1 is subtracted from the number since there will be no handshake by one person. When the class consists of 20 students the rule makes it easier to calculate the number of handshakes rather than drawing pictures or filling in the numbers in a chart. Over all, the formula shortens the continuous computation of numbers. For example,

n(n-1)/2=h

20(20-1) =h

20 (19) =h

380/2 =h

When there are 20 students there are 190 handshakes.

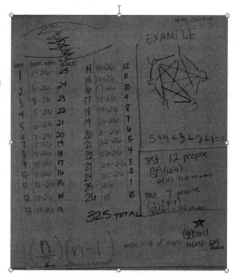

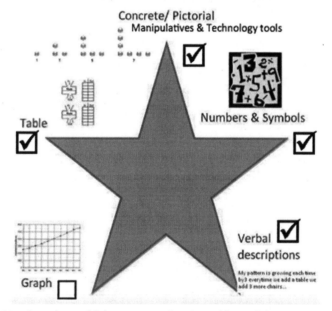

Figure 1.10   Assessing multiple representations in problem solving. *Source*: Authors.

The 12 days of Christmas. The first few lines are as follows: *On the first day of Christmas, my true love sent to me, A partridge in a pear tree. On the second day of Christmas, my true love sent to me, Two turtle doves, and a partridge in a pear tree. The song continues with three French hens* on the 3rd day, four calling birds on the 4th day, five golden rings on the 5th, and so on, up to the 12th day. As the teachers read through this problem, they seem to immediately notice a connection to the triangular number patterns. These connections can also be seen in the Pascal's triangle (see Figure 1.11).

The Pascal's Triangle

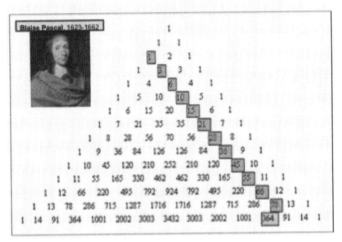

Figure 1.11   Pascal's triangle. *Source*: Authors.

As shown here, the handshake problem is a great example of a task that not only engages the participants whether they are students or teachers in rich problem solving, but also helps them to expand their algebraic habits of minds, namely doing and undoing, building patterns from representations, and abstracting from computation (Driscoll, 1999). For educators, it also provides the opportunity to learn about five practices (Smith & Stein, 2011) including:

- Anticipating: The teacher can anticipate the type of strategies that students might employ, along with misconceptions that can be turned into opportunities.
- Monitoring: It is important for teachers to provide their students with the opportunity to engage in problem solving, to monitor students to identify the various strategies that are discussed, and to understand how students think as they solve the problem.
- Selecting: This step requires teachers to select the order in which the strategies will be shared so everyone benefits from learning all strategies.
- Sequencing: This allows the teacher to sequence the approaches being presented, whether that be from simple to complex or in a sequence that supports the lesson agenda. This might mean starting with the acting out strategy, moving to looking for patterns, and concluding with finding an algebraic formula, or it might mean starting with a common misconception so that students can repair their understanding.
- Connecting: As a last step, the teacher has the opportunity to facilitate a discussion that helps to connect all of the various strategies displayed and shared during the discussion. This helps students to see connections not only within and across the strategies, but also to related problems. For example, this problem could be changed to accommodate the distribution of valentine cards in an elementary classroom or to find the number of diagonals of n-sided regular polygon.

1.5   IMPORTANCE OF UNDERSTANDING THE VERTICAL LEARNING PROGRESSION TO DEEPEN STUDENTS' MATHEMATICAL UNDERSTANDING OF CONCEPTUAL MODELS

One way to deepen one's conceptual understanding is to make connections among important conceptual models within and between mathematics topics by unpacking the vertical learning progressions. Learning progression describes students' reasoning as it becomes more sophisticated, and as "...hypothesized descriptions of the successively more sophisticated ways student thinking about an important domain of knowledge or practice develops as children learn about and investigate that domain over an appropriate span of time" (Corcoran, Mosher & Rogat, 2009, p. 37). In mathematics education, the notion of learning trajectories has been important in trying to understand the progression of mathematical concepts and how students' learning progresses and becomes more advanced and sophisticated.

To better understand how student come to understand concepts, mathematics education researchers have focused on hypothetical learning trajectories, which include "the learning goal, the learning activities, and the thinking and learning in which the students might engage" (Simon, 1995, p. 133). These goals provide direction for teachers as they plan learning activities and are critical for teachers to predict the potential reasoning, misconceptions, and learning of students. Clements and Samara's work (2004, 2009) takes on a curriculum developers' stance as they use learning trajectories to develop a specific set of sequenced instructional activities focused on early geometric reasoning in young children.

These research-based tasks are designed to promote the child's construction of the skills and concepts of a particular level with a set of sequenced instructional activities hypothesized to be a productive route (Clements & Samara, 2009). Confrey and her colleagues (2009) define a learning trajectory as "a researcher conjectured, empirically supported description of the ordered network of constructs a student encounters through instruction (i.e., activities, tasks, tools, forms of interaction and methods of evaluation), in order to move from informal ideas, through successive refinements of representation, articulation, and reflection, toward increasingly complex concepts over time (Confrey et al., 2009, p. 347)."

Understanding the learning trajectory requires an understanding of the components of the learning progression that are important for teachers as they plan instruction, anticipate students' responses, differentiate for diverse learners, and assess students' learning. The work with learning trajectories also supports *vertical teaming* by teachers, for it "allows an exciting chance for teachers to discuss and plan their instruction based on how student learning progresses. An added strength of a learning trajectories approach is that it emphasizes why each teacher, at each grade level along the way, has a critical role to play in each student's mathematical development" (Confrey, 2012, p. 3). For example, there may be many ways to implement and interpret the CCSS or even the district-created teaching and assessment standards.

Teachers may understand them, initially, at a surface level, as the big ideas or list of objectives on which to base their lessons. However, deeper understanding of how these standards are implemented and interpreted in different grade levels is quite a complex task. According to the Confrey (2012, pp. 7–8), there are five elements that can help unpack a learning trajectory. Teachers need to understand: (1) the conceptual principles and the development of the ideas underlying a concept; (2) strategies, representations, and misconceptions; (3) meaningful distinctions, definitions, and multiple models; (4) coherent structure—recognizing that there is a pattern in the development of mathematical ideas as a concept becomes more complex; (5) bridging standards—understanding that there may be gaps between standards and knowing what underlying concepts are in between in order to bridge any gaps between that exist. The complexity of unpacking standards mirrors the complexity of teaching. Understanding the learning progression across grade levels requires the collaboration of teachers through meaningful vertical articulation and professional development.

A great resource for teachers is the website TurnonCC https://turnonccmath.net/. The website describes and offers learning trajectories of how concepts, and student understanding, develop over time by connecting the Common Core Standards across the vertical grades and providing examples and activities for educators. In our work

Table 1.2   Mapping the learning progression for the handshake problem

Learning progression for the handshake problem

Benchmark Problem: At a neighborhood party, there were a total of 25 guests. All 25 guests shook hands to introduce themselves. How many distinct handshakes happened at this party? Show the different ways you can represent your thinking.

Grades 3–4	Grades 5–6	Grades 7–8
Use the four operations with whole numbers to solve problems.	Analyze patterns and relationships.	Solve real-life and mathematical problems using numerical and algebraic expressions and equations.
Related problems:	Related problems:	Related problems:
Every student in the second-grade classroom exchanged a valentine card with each other. If there were 30 students, how many valentine cards were exchanged?	If everyone in your class (30 students) shakes hands with everyone else, how many handshakes would there be?	There are nine justices on the Supreme Court. How many handshakes occur if each of them shakes hands with every other justice exactly once?
How many handshakes do you have in at your table groups of 3, 4, and 5 friends?	Use words, pictures, numbers, and express the pattern or rule for the problem.	At a birthday party, each guest shakes hands with every guest. If 190 different handshakes take place, how many guests were at the party?

Strategies, representations, and misconceptions

To introduce the Handshake Problem across the vertical grades, teachers in grades 3–4 might begin with the related problem of the Valentine Exchange. This is a real-world scenario that most students can relate to regardless of the holiday. It is a problem about each student (30) giving something/item to each person (29) in the class. The problem begs for a multiplication problem structure of 30×29 because you do not have to give yourself a card or something. The simpler problem is of course to start with a smaller number of guests at the party to see if there is a pattern. As shown in the various examples above from Figures 1.4 to 1.12, there are a variety of strategies and approaches to this rich problem. The common misconception for the handshake problem is sometimes counting oneself or double counting which is allowed in the Valentine Exchange because there is a give and take of the cards, whereas in the handshake, the give and take of the shake is counted as one.

with lesson study with vertical teams, we used the tools on TurnonCC to help our teachers look across the learning trajectory to describe a "typical student conceptual growth, from prior knowledge and informal ideas, through intermediate understandings, to increasingly complex understandings, over time."

In addition to this great resource, we have used the progressions documents for the Common Core Math Standards from University of Arizona. The progression documents explain why "standards are sequenced the way they are, point out cognitive difficulties and pedagogical solutions, and give more detail on particularly knotty areas of the mathematics" (http://math.arizona.edu/~ime/progressions).

The deep understanding of the mathematical learning progressions involves important aspects of mathematical knowledge for teaching. Mathematics knowledge for teaching (Hill, Sleep, Lewis & Ball, 2007) includes understanding of general content but also having domain-specific knowledge of students. More specifically, mathematical knowledge for teaching includes practice-based knowledge of "being able to pose meaningful problems, represent ideas carefully with multiple representations, interpret and make mathematical and pedagogical judgments about students' questions, solutions, problems, and insights (both predictable and unusual)" (Ball, 2003, p. 6). Understanding students' learning trajectories in different content domains can help teachers develop the specific knowledge of students and the pedagogical content knowledge necessary for high-leverage teaching.

Each chapter will zoom in on a learning progression and share a lesson study vignette to illustrate how teachers can design instruction of important mathematical concepts with strategies and tasks for modeling the mathematical ideas (see Table 1.2).

Think about it!

Pick an important concept you teach at your grade level. Unpack the learning trajectory in terms of development of the ideas underlying a concept; strategies, representations, and misconceptions; and the underlying concepts are in between to bridge the gaps between the standards.

1.6   TECHNOLOGY INTEGRATION IN PROBLEM SOLVING

Technology should be used to "amplify the mathematics," bring out the mathematics concepts to the forefront, using specific affordances. Specific opportunities that technology rich mathematics environments afford teachers and students are the abilities to: (a) build representational fluency by making connections among multiple representations; (b) experiment and test out conjectures which efficiently develop reasoning and proof; and (c) facilitate the communication of mathematical ideas through problem solving (Suh, 2010).

In the handshake applet discussed later, we see how one can employ technology to enhance the understanding of the solution approaches to the handshake problem. We will now describe an applet that has been custom created that can be employed as a tool to discover the associated pattern. A technology tool is also helpful to generalize a pattern observed for larger numbers.

Let us consider seven members shaking hands with each other. The technology tool allows students to enter the number seven for the "number of people" and as they proceed to solve for the handshakes, the tool can help prompt the steps in the process. For instance, the illustration in figure 1.12 shows that the first person has performed six handshakes (denoted by yellow bold lines), and the last one by red bold line. Note that besides a visual confirmation of the handshakes on the left, the number of hand-shakes is recorded as circles in the center and also as a part of the lower row in the 6×7 rectangle shown in the right.

As the student continues to navigate through the process, one can obtain interme-diate steps like the one shown in figure 1.12 that helps the student to make a con-nection between the representations and guess a growing pattern. Eventually, as the students go through the process, they would observe not only the connections but also build a representation that makes sense algebraically. The final step is shown in figure 1.12.

For more practice with the technology tool, the students may be encouraged to visit: http://completecenter.gmu.edu/java/handshake/index.html

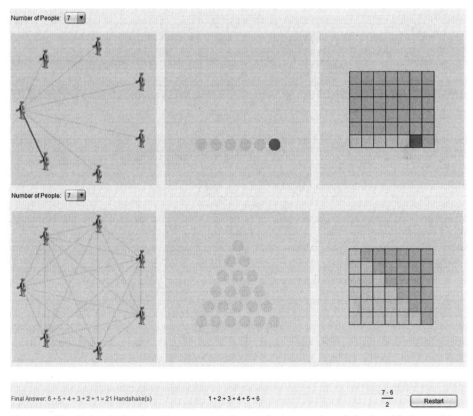

Figure 1.12 Using technology to represent the worked examples of the handshake problem. *Source*: Authors.

1.7 MORE RELATED RICH PROBLEMS TO EXPLORE

1. Thirty people at a party shook hands with each other. How many handshakes were there altogether?

2. At a party, everyone shook hands with everybody else. There were 45 handshakes. How many people were at the party?

3. Every student in the second-grade classroom exchanged a valentine card with each other. If there were 30 students, how many valentine cards were exchanged?

4. Twenty people are sitting in a circle. Each person shakes hands with everyone but his/her neighbors. How many handshakes have been exchanged?

5. Two ten-member volleyball teams play a game. After the game, each of the members of the winning team shakes hands once with each member of both teams. How many handshakes take place?

6. Eight students of different heights are at a party. Each student decides to only participate in a handshake with another student shorter than himself or herself. How many handshakes take place?

7. Each person at a graduation party shook hands with everyone else. John shook hands with three times as many men as women. John's wife shook hands with four times as many men as women. How many men and women were there at the party?

8. Find the number of diagonals of a 12-sided polygon?

9. If you build a staircase with cubes that is 10 steps high, how many cubes will you need?

10. At a party, each man shook hands with everyone except his spouse, and no handshakes took place between women. If 13 married couples attended, how many handshakes were there among these 26 people?
    (A) 78   (B) 185   (C) 234   (D) 312   (E) 325

11. (AMC8 2012) In the BIG N, a middle-school football conference, each team plays every other team exactly once. If a total of 21 conference games were played during the 2012 season, how many teams were members of the BIG N conference?
    (A) 6   (B) 7   (C) 8   (D) 9   (E) 10

12. (AMC12 2011) At a twins and triplets convention, there were nine sets of twins and six sets of triplets, all from different families. Each twin shook hands with all the twins except his/her siblings and with half the triplets. Each triplet shook hands with all the triplets except his/her siblings and with half the twins. How many handshakes took place?
    (A) 324   (B) 441   (C) 630   (D)648   (E) 882

Chapter 2

Setting Math Norms to Promote
Math Reasoning and Modeling
Developing Mathematical Hearts and Minds

Learning is a cultural activity that is facilitated by the social interaction among the members in the learning community. One of the most important ways to impact the teaching and learning of mathematics is by creating the optimal learning environment and classroom culture by setting the norms for math learning. Our framework for setting norms is called "Developing Mathematical Hearts and Minds" because it is equally important to develop a productive disposition for mathematics in our "hearts" as it is important to develop a mathematical "mind." We asked teachers what norms were important in their classroom, and the top eight norms were as follows:

1. Be respectful when working individually and collaboratively.
2. Share your strategy and try another person's strategy.
3. Persevere through problem solving.
4. Embrace mistakes as springboards to understanding.
5. Reflect and think about your thinking metacognition.
6. Be accountable for your work.
7. Ask questions.
8. Justify your answer.

The following chapter will describe the important practices that develop teachers' and students' productive dispositions toward mathematics and at the same time deepen their mathematical proficiency in teaching and learning mathematics.

2.1 DEVELOPING PERSISTENT PROBLEM SOLVERS WITH A PRODUCTIVE DISPOSITION TOWARD MATHEMATICS

Good problem solvers are flexible and resourceful, demonstrating many ways to think about problems (Suh, Graham, Ferranone, Kopeinig, and Bertholet, 2011). They have "alternative approaches if they get stuck, ways of making progress when they hit road-blocks, of being efficient with (and making use of) what they know. They also have a certain kind of mathematical disposition—a willingness to pit themselves against difficult mathematical challenges under the assumption that they will be able to make progress on them, and the tenacity to keep at the task when others have given up" (Schoenfeld, 2007, p. 60).

In addition, research has linked mathematics anxiety to decreased performance on mathematics exams. Problem solvers experience a range of emotions associated with different stages in the solution process. Dweck (2006), a Stanford University psychologist with research on achievement and success, shares that there are two mindsets about learning: a *growth mindset* and a *fixed mindset*. A growth mindset holds that your basic qualities are things that you can cultivate through your efforts, whereas a fixed mindset holds that your qualities are "carved in stone" (i.e., your intelligence is something you cannot change very much).

When facing challenging problems, children who believe that effort drives intelligence tend to do better than children who believe that intelligence is a fixed quality that they cannot change. According to the research on competence and motivation (Elliot and Dweck, 2005; Weiner, 2005), students can attribute their successes and failures to ability (e.g., "I am just [good/bad] at mathematics"), effort (e.g., "I [worked/did not work] hard enough"), luck, or powerful people (e.g., "the teacher [loves/hates] me"). A student with a fixed mindset avoids challenges, gives up easily, sees effort as fruitless or worse, ignores useful negative feedback, and feels threatened by the success of others. Meanwhile, a student with a growth mindset embraces challenge, persists despite setbacks, sees effort as the path to mastery, learns from mistakes and criticisms, and finds lessons and inspiration in the success of others.

People with a growth mindset believe that they can develop their abilities through hard work, persistence, and dedication; brains and talents are merely a starting base (Dweck, 2006). Creating opportunities for success in mathematics is important, but offering students a series of easy tasks can lead to a false sense of self-efficacy and can limit access to challenging mathematics. Ironically, research indicates that students need to experience periodic challenge and even momentary failure to develop higher levels of self-efficacy and task persistence (Middleton and Spanias, 1999). Achieving a balance between opportunities for success and opportunities to solve problems that require considerable individual or group effort requires teachers to design curricular materials and instructional practices carefully (Woodward, 1999).

Dweck's research also shows that the types of praises and validations that teachers offer have influence on the type of mindset fostered for the students. The research identifies teachers that can have a fixed mindset who tend to perceive the struggling students to be not sufficiently smart in math, whereas those that have a growth mindset would see struggling students as learners who need the appropriate guidance and the necessary feedback to improve. In other words, growth mindset teachers see this challenge working with struggling students as an opportunity to learn from their mistakes and misconceptions.

Before we can develop mathematically proficient students, we need to make efforts to develop persistent and flexible problem solvers by looking deeply at our students, the instructional practices, and the mathematical tasks that we present to them. Teaching with a belief that intellectual abilities can be fostered and cultivated through effective pedagogical practices should be integral part of helping students become successful at mathematics. As mentioned from research, we can start by taking the time to establish classroom norms that embrace mistakes as opportunities for learning and validate students multiple strategies and partial understandings so that we can help complete their understanding by connecting and or repairing their mathematical understanding.

Below are reflective prompts that the authors from that chapter developed to foster persistence, flexibility, and clear communication in their mathematics classroom (See Table 2.1). Such questions like "Did someone else solve the problem in a way you had not thought of? Explain what you learned by listening to a classmate?" can help students consider other approaches to problem solving so that they can begin to evaluate strategies based on their clarity, efficiency, and connections to other shared strategies. Setting up a classroom that values clear and respective communication and flexibility and persistence from the beginning of the school year will help students understand that these are the expectations and the norms for the classroom.

In this same way, teachers need a collaborative support network that can provide the time and space for them to inquire about their instructional practice. Professional learning communities and lesson study teams provide that supportive network for teachers to develop as reflective practitioners who persevere through challenges and work with other colleagues to examine a problem of practice from their daily teaching episodes.

Over the years, we have learned a great deal about how students learn mathematics and how teachers develop their teaching practices as they collaborate on lesson study. Lesson study is a model of professional learning that offers situated learning through collaborative planning, teaching, observing, and debriefing that afford opportunities

Table 2.1　Reflection prompts to encourage persistence and flexibility in problem solving

Clear Communication	Respectful Communication	Flexible Thinking	Persistence
What math words could help us share our thinking about this problem? Choose 2 and explain what they mean in your own words.	Did someone else solve the problem in a way you had not thought of? Explain what you learned by listening to a classmate.	What other problems or math topics does this remind you of? Explain your connection.	What did you do if you got stuck or felt frustrated?
What could you use besides words to show how to solve the problem? Explain how this representation would help someone understand.	Did you ask for help or offer to help a classmate? Explain how working together helped solve the problem.	Briefly describe at least 2 ways to solve the problem. Which is easier for you?	What helped you try your best? or What do you need to change so that you can try your best next time?
If you needed to make your work easier for someone else to understand, what would you change?	What helped you share and listen respectfully when we discussed the problem? or What do you need to change so that you can share and listen respectfully next time?	What strategies did you use that you think will be helpful again for future problems?	Do you feel more or less confident about math after trying this problem? Explain why.

Source: Suh, Graham, Ferranone, Kopeinig & Bertholet, 2011.

for teachers to reflect individually and collectively. Teacher educators have embraced lesson study, originating from Japan, because it empowers teachers and provides a collaborative structure for eliciting reflection for critical dialogue about pedagogical content knowledge (PCK) among teachers (Lewis, 2002; Lewis, Perry, & Murata, 2006).

Another effective professional development model is called Instructional Rounds (City, Elmore, Fiarman, & Teitel, 2009), which is a practice adapted to education from the field of medicine where practitioners work together to solve common problems and improve their practice. In medicine, the clinical rounds consist of training how to care for patients, presenting the medical problems and treatment of a particular patient to doctors, residents, and medical students. In education, it is designed to help schools, districts, and state systems support high-quality teaching and learning for all students.

Instructional Rounds help teachers examine closely at what is happening in classrooms in a systematic, purposeful, and focused way. Typically, the first step in an Instructional Rounds process is determining a "problem of practice" followed by collective observation and debrief. The shared experiences designed around targeted Instructional Rounds that focused on the instructional practices such as posing rich meaningful problems, modeling using multiple representations, orchestrating mathematics "talk" and responding to students' questions, and determining how to assess student understanding of mathematical concepts helped teachers focus on important instructional practices. One of the teachers wrote who participated in Instructional Rounds stated in her reflection,

> *Watching the teachers teach a lesson that was open-ended helped me alleviate some of my fears of teaching through problem solving. I am glad that the teacher allowed students to convince each other and justify their thinking. It allowed for students who approach the problem in different ways, understand a different perspective or solution strategy.*

In each of our lesson study and Instructional Rounds, we focus on some of the essential research-based professional development resources that we use as high-leverage practices. These include working with teachers to unpack the mathematics, choose worthwhile tasks through cognitive demand analysis, set goals to enact some of the core teaching practices through research lessons, integrate technology to amplify the mathematics, and use formative assessment to assess their mathematical proficiency.

2.2   UNPACKING THE MATHEMATICS FOR DEEPER CONCEPTUAL LEARNING—CONCEPT MAPPING

In our lesson study planning, we work with our teachers to identify a content standard or topic that presents a problem of practice. Typically, teacher teams select a topic in their curriculum that presents a challenge in their instruction or presents a gap in students understanding as revealed by their pre-assessment or benchmark assessments. Once the team selects the content strand that they want to focus on for their lesson study, the team spends some time delving into the content standard by unpacking the mathematics using a concept map. Similar to Liping Ma's (1999) "knowledge package," the concept map is a way to unpack teachers' understanding about the subject-matter knowledge of the concept.

Knowledge packages for any topic can contain both procedural and conceptual elements, and map out the concepts that are prerequisite and future mathematics concepts that build upon one another. Ma found that teachers with a conceptual understanding of a topic viewed related procedural topics as being essential to student understanding. Before we start a lesson study, we ask teachers to map out the conceptual understanding of a topic. We start with the concept at the center of the concept map then from there, map out and link the big ideas that are foundational skills and prerequisite to the core concept and the related skills, procedures, and strategies that are critical to developing fluency and efficiency.

Next, teachers map out and name the various visual representations that students see in their everyday life or in school such as manipulatives and models. In addition, teachers identify the important mathematics vocabulary, relationships between concepts that is essential in providing access to mathematics, and help in the mathematics discourse (see Figure 2.1). This unpacking process provides opportunities for teachers to engage in discussion about the vertical learning progressions as teachers from different grade levels discuss the learning objectives specific to their grades.

It also provides an opportune time for a math coach or the professional leader to introduce teachers to relevant research-based articles and materials for teachers to consider. This also marks the beginning of the lesson study cycle often referred to the "study" cycle because teachers bring to the table the problem of practice or an area in their curriculum that seems most troublesome to teach and/or learn and gather all their curricular materials and lessons that they have used in the past for close examination.

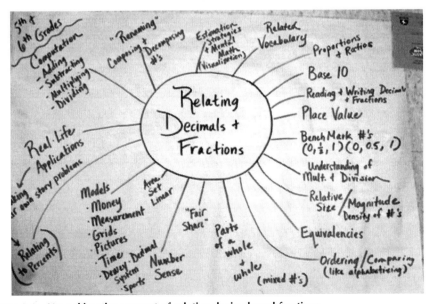

Figure 2.1 Unpacking the concept of relating decimals and fractions.

2.3   CHOOSING WORTHWHILE TASKS THROUGH COGNITIVE DEMAND ANALYSIS

Once teachers have unpacked the mathematics and identified the curricular topic for the lesson study, we engage teachers in problem solving. Selecting a series of rich tasks that "reintroduces" teachers to the big mathematics ideas prepares them for the lesson study and provides them with the experience of being a learner solving the problem. This real experience of going through the process of solving the problem provides them with a better understanding of how to anticipate potential student strategies and potential pitfalls and misconceptions.

Since lesson study is not about reinventing the wheel by creating new problems or lessons, we invite teachers to bring in their curricular materials and resources to present rich problems to consider for the lesson study. Although we have teachers with diverse ranges of experiences, the most challenging part of teaching through problem solving is selecting a rich and worthwhile task. To select a rich task, teachers must focus on the mathematical content, as well as the different ways in which students learn the mathematics. Knowing what their students already know and can do, what they need to work on, and how much they can go beyond their comfort zone is essential in task selection. If tasks are selected well, it also provides the teachers opportunities to learn about their students' understandings, interests, dispositions, and experiences.

To help teachers with this selection process, we introduce our teachers to the Smith and Stein's (2012) article *Selecting and Creating Mathematical Tasks: From Research*

Table 2.2   Focusing on problems that require higher cognitive demand (Smith & Stein, 2012)

Higher-level demands (procedures with connections)	Higher-level demands (doing mathematics)
Focus students' attention on the use of procedures for the purpose of developing deeper levels of understanding of mathematics concepts and ideas.	Require complex and non-algorithmic thinking—a predictable, well-rehearsed approach or pathway is not explicitly suggested by the task, task instructions, or a worked-out example.
Suggest explicitly or implicitly pathways to follow that are broad general procedures that have close connections to underlying conceptual ideas as opposed to narrow algorithms that are opaque with respect to underlying concepts.	Require students to explore and understand the nature of mathematical concepts, processes, or relationships.
Usually are represented in multiple ways, such as visual diagrams, manipulatives, symbols, and problem situations. Making connections among multiple representations helps develop meaning.	Demand self-monitoring or self-regulation of one's own cognitive processes.
Require some degree of cognitive effort. Although general procedures may be followed, they cannot be followed mindlessly. Students need to engage with conceptual ideas that underlie the procedures to complete the task successfully and that develop understanding.	Require students to access relevant knowledge and experiences and make appropriate use of them in working through the task.
	Require students to analyze the task and actively examine task constraints that may limit possible solution strategies and solutions.
	Require considerable cognitive effort and may involve some level of anxiety for the student because of the unpredictable nature of the solution process required.

to Practice on cognitive demand and their task analysis framework. Tasks with high levels of cognitive demand are referred to as "procedures with connections" (when procedures are connected meaningfully to concepts) or as "doing mathematics" (which is an inquiry-based approach with no specific pathway prescribed to solve the problem and is quite open).

The lower-level demands are described as "procedures without connections" (which uses procedures, formulas, or algorithms that are not actively connected meaningfully) or "memorization" (which is simply a reproduction of previously memorized facts). The lower levels of memorization and procedures without connections are excluded from consideration for lesson study. We only allow teachers to choose tasks that fall in the higher levels of cognitive demands such as procedures with connections and doing mathematics (see Table 2.2).

2.4 PROMOTING EFFECTIVE TEACHING PRACTICES TO OPTIMIZE THE LEARNING ENVIRONMENT

When deciding on a research goal for their lesson study, teacher teams decide on a content learning goal as well as select several of the core teaching practices that they want to focus on in their research lesson. This allows the teachers to set a personal teaching goal besides the student learning goal. In the *Principles to Actions*, NCTM (2014) calls for the mathematics education community to focus our attention on the essential core teaching practices that will yield the most effective mathematics teaching and learning for all students (see Text Box 2.1).

Over the years, mathematics education scholars have challenged the profession of teaching to identify a common set of high-leverage practices that yield effective teaching (Ball et al., 2009; Grossman, Hammerness, & McDonald, 2009; Lampert, 2009; McDonald, Kazemi, & Kavanagh, 2013). High-leverage practices have been defined as "those practices at the heart of the work of teaching that are most likely to affect student learning" (Ball & Forzani, 2010, p. 45).

Authors of the *Principles to Actions* responded to this challenge by defining eight core teaching practices (see Text Box 2.1) drawn from research that includes: (1) Establishing Mathematics Goals to Focus Learning (Hiebert et al., 2007); (2) Implementing Tasks That Promote Reasoning and Problem Solving (Stein et al., 2009); (3) Using and Connecting Mathematical Representations (Lesh, Post, & Behr, 1987); (4) Facilitating Meaningful Mathematical Discourse (Hufferd-Ackles, Fuson, & Sherin, 2004); (5) Posing Purposeful Questions (Chapin & O'Connor, 2007); (6) Building Procedural Fluency from Conceptual Understanding (Hiebert & Grouws, 2007); (7) Supporting Productive Struggle in Learning Mathematics (Dweck, 2008); and (8) Eliciting and Using Evidence of Student Thinking (Sherin & van Es, 2003). Because many of these eight practices are related and support one another, teacher teams often would state several of these practices as the focus of their professional learning goals. In the following chapters, we highlight several lesson vignettes that showcase how teachers implemented some of these eight Mathematics Teaching Practices outlined in the *Principles to Action*s during our lesson study.

Text Box 2.1   Core Teaching Practices from the Principles to Action, NCTM (2014)

Implement tasks that promote reasoning and problem solving. Effective teaching of mathematics engages students in solving and discussing tasks that promote mathematical reasoning and problem solving and allow multiple entry points and varied solution strategies.

Support productive struggle in learning mathematics. Effective teaching of mathematics consistently provides students, individually and collectively, with opportunities and supports to engage in productive struggle as they grapple with mathematical ideas and relationships.

Build procedural fluency from conceptual understanding. Effective teaching of mathematics builds fluency with procedures on a foundation of conceptual understanding so that students, over time, become skillful in using procedures flexibly as they solve contextual and mathematical problems.

Establish mathematics goals to focus learning. Effective teaching of mathematics establishes clear goals for the mathematics that students are learning, situates goals within learning progressions, and uses the goals to guide instructional decisions.

Use and connect mathematical representations. Effective teaching of mathematics engages students in making connections among mathematical representations to deepen understanding of mathematics concepts and procedures and as tools for problem solving.

Facilitate meaningful mathematical discourse. Effective teaching of mathematics facilitates discourse among students to build shared understanding of mathematical ideas by analyzing and comparing student approaches and arguments.

Pose purposeful questions. Effective teaching of mathematics uses purposeful questions to assess and advance students' reasoning and sense making about important mathematical ideas and relationships.

Elicit and use evidence of student thinking. Effective teaching of mathematics uses evidence of student thinking to assess progress toward mathematical understanding and to adjust instruction continually in ways that support and extend learning.

We have used the Japanese Lesson Study Professional Development model (Lewis, 2002; Lewis, Perry, & Hurd, 2004) where we immersed teachers in vertical teams, collaboratively planned, taught the first cycle, observed, debriefed, and taught the second cycle to come to reflect both individually and collectively. In doing so, we reveal the importance of *establishing mathematics goals to focus learning*, which we referred to as the math agenda during our research lessons. We call it the math agenda because it evokes a sense of immediacy as the word a*genda* literally means "the things that must be done" in Latin, and it communicates its importance in the planning process.

With that math agenda at the forefront, teachers determine what task can be *Implemented so that we promote reasoning and problem solving*. Through the use of skillful posing of purposeful questions, we can facilitate meaningful mathematical discourse where students are actively using and connecting mathematical representations as the teacher elicits and uses these representations and strategies as evidence of student thinking to move the math agenda forward. All eight practices are critical when enacting an exemplar problem-based lesson. Depending on the lesson, certain teaching moves may be more accentuated in some lessons than others; however, all eight of these practices ensure a rich math lesson and one should strive for employing all of these practices when planning math lessons.

In one of our past research lessons, the multi-grade team of teachers selected rich tasks to teach at multiple grade levels. The team met to plan their lesson objectives and anticipated student responses. While planning, teachers were asked to focus on these four assessment questions:

1. What does a student at your grade level need to know or be able to do to access this problem?
2. What specific lessons and strategies that you have used in the past will build on this problem?
3. What might be problematic to the students that would require scaffolding in order for them to understand this topic?
4. Develop an assessment task that would be appropriate to your grade level.

As part of the lesson study, teachers studied the mathematics content related to the research lesson, planned the lesson, taught the lesson in different grade levels, and debriefed after each cycle. In the following lesson study case, teachers decided to start the lesson study cycle (see Figure 2.2) in a third-grade classroom to see how younger

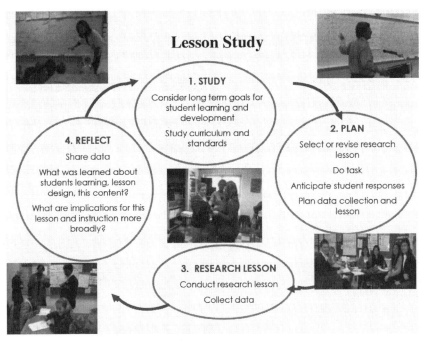

Lesson Study

1. STUDY
Consider long term goals for student learning and development

Study curriculum and standards

2. PLAN
Select or revise research lesson

Do task

Anticipate student responses

Plan data collection and lesson

3. RESEARCH LESSON
Conduct research lesson

Collect data

4. REFLECT
Share data

What was learned about students learning, lesson design, this content?

What are implications for this lesson and instruction more broadly?

Figure 2.2   The Lesson Study Cycle (Lewis, 2002).

students approached the task. They observed as the third-grade host teacher taught the lesson and debriefed the lesson outcome in terms of the teaching moves and the student learning.

They collaboratively revised the lesson and geared it up for a sixth-grade class and an eighth-grade class. They decided to break up into two teams, observe the lesson, and then come together as a whole group. Teachers then met again for the second cycle of the teaching in the upper-grade classrooms and debriefed the lesson for the final cycle together as a group. Finally, they combined their learning from the research lessons from multiple grades to present at the final conference.

Our typical model for professional develop begins with a summer institute followed by Lesson Study during the academic semesters. There were a number of goals for these follow-up sessions: to provide teachers with continued support in learning and implementing algebraic content; to supply materials and strategies to the participants; to provide opportunities for vertical articulation between and among grades levels to share ideas/resources; and to analyze student learning and work samples.

2.5 INTEGRATION TECHNOLOGY TO MOTIVATE AND DIFFERENTIATE LEARNING

To develop our teachers teaching mathematics in the digital age, we took careful attention to integrate technology into our professional development. The Technology Principle in the Principles and Standards of School Mathematics (NCTM, 2000) state that, "Technology is essential in teaching and learning mathematics; it influences the mathematics that is taught and enhances student learning" (p. 24). The phrase "influences the mathematics that is taught" is what determines the ambitious teaching goals in the mathematics classroom.

The word "enhances" is what characterizes technology as a tool with high-leveraging power because technology has specific affordances that can enrich learning tasks (Suh, 2010). Niess and Walker claim that (2010) "many digital technologies have proved useful for students learning mathematics: graphing calculators, applets or virtual manipulatives, spreadsheets, computer algebra systems, and dynamic geometry tools. Each of these technologies provides visual representations that enable students to explore mathematical ideas in more dynamic ways."

However, just by having technology in the classroom does not guarantee that technology is effectively implemented in the teaching and learning of mathematics. The complexity of teaching with technology stems from the notion that teaching in itself is a complex endeavor. Shulman (1986, 1987), coined the term Pedagogical Content Knowledge (PCK) to describe the specific knowledge needed to teach effectively that includes content knowledge, knowledge of students' thinking, and knowledge of mathematics education and pedagogy.

In mathematics education, PCK has been expanded to include Mathematics Knowledge for Teaching (MKT), which is the "knowledge necessary to carry out the work of teaching mathematics" (Hill, Rowan, & Ball, 2005). MKT includes specific high-leverage practices such as use of mathematical explanations and representations, interpretations of student responses, and the ability to avoid math errors and imprecision.

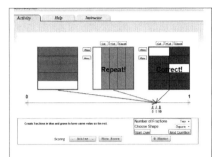 Equivalent Fractions Finder http://www.shodor.org/interactivate/activities/EquivFractionFinder/	I selected this tool because my student struggled with fractional parts and because this tool allows the whole to be broken into fractional parts in several different ways. Students can manipulate the tool to create equivalent fractions in several different ways. I encouraged the student to create images as I have done below in the screenshot. Based upon my assessment, it seems the student is used to seeing fractional parts as the same size and shape. It's important that he understand the concept of fair shares. By creating images that are not what we normally see as fractional parts, it will deepen his understanding of this fraction concept. The student can save time by not having to color blocks repeatedly. Because the tool is online, students can divide the units in several different ways and they can do it multiple times.
Fraction Bars http://www.mathplayground.com/Fraction_bars.html	My student seemed to have a great understanding of equivalent fractions. I chose this tool to challenge him and to move on from fraction concepts to adding and subtracting fractions with like and unlike denominators. Using this tool, students must add and subtract fractions with like and unlike denominators. So, it addresses the content well. Students must think critically about making the best choice for their move based upon their knowledge of equivalent fractions and the ability to move all tracks to one in the least amount of moves. I would use this tool to expose the student's understandings of equivalent fractions by also having him keep a journal of why he chose to make each move.
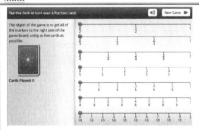 Fraction Tracks http://illuminations.nctm.org/Activity.aspx?id=4148	My student seemed to have a great understanding of equivalent fractions. I chose this tool to challenge him and to move on from fraction concepts to adding and subtracting fractions with like and unlike denominators. Using this tool, students must add and subtract fractions with like and unlike denominators. So, it addresses the content well. Students must think critically about making the best choice for their move based upon their knowledge of equivalent fractions and the ability to move all tracks to one in the least amount of moves. I would use this tool to expose the students understanding of equivalent fractions by also having him keep a journal of why he chose to make each move. The online fraction tracks game has an advantage over the paper version of the game because it can correct your move in real time. The program will not allow a student to make an incorrect move.

Figure 2.3   Sequencing technology applets to reflect on the mathematics learning progressions.
Source: (Suh, 2016).

Teaching with technology adds another layer of complexity to the PCK framework. Understanding how to teach with technology referred to as Technological Pedagogical and Content Knowledge, TPACK, (Mishra & Koehler, 2006) integrates a third component into teachers' specialized knowledge for teaching—integration of technology into instruction.

TPACK includes understanding how technology can be used to represent concepts, knowledge of pedagogical techniques that use technology to effectively teach content, familiarity with ways that technology can help students understand particularly difficult topics, and knowing how technology can be used to build on existing knowledge. Virtual manipulatives have been described as "interactive, web-based visual representations of a dynamic object that presents opportunities for constructing mathematical knowledge" (Moyer, Bolyard, & Spikell, 2002, p. 373).

In our work with teachers, we ask teachers to evaluate technology applets to see how it "amplifies" the mathematics. We used the word "amplify" to mean the way in which technology offers affordances that would not be available in a physical manipulative and how the connections to the mathematics concepts are brought to clarity.

One of the practice-based activities that help teachers think deeply about the learning progressions for a specific concept is called *Mathematics Tech-knowledgy across the Learning Progression*, where one selects three related applets that could be used to teach and learn that concept. This helps teachers plan and teach a lesson using technology and assess a student's understanding about a concept using a variety of representations. Figure 2.3 is a sampler of three related fraction applets that a teacher chose to use during her unit on fraction. On the right description, the teacher explains how the applet will be used to "amplify" the mathematics for a student that she was working with one-on-one.

2.6 ASSESSING STUDENTS UNDERSTANDING THROUGH A PROBLEM-BASED TASK

Finally, assessment is what guides our instruction. There are many formative and summative assessment strategies that teachers employ in their mathematics classroom. We used the five strands of mathematics proficiency to assess student understanding. In the condensed version of *Adding it Up* (NRC, 2001), the authors used Understanding, Computing, Applying, Reasoning, and Engaging (UCARE) as an acronym to stand for the five strands.

1. **Understanding: (Conceptual Understanding)** Comprehending mathematical concepts, operations, and relations—knowing what mathematical symbols, diagrams, and procedures mean.
2. **Computing: (Procedural Fluency)** Carrying out mathematical procedures, such as adding, subtracting, multiplying, and dividing numbers flexibly, accurately, efficiently, and appropriately.
3. **Applying: (Strategic Competence)** Being able to formulate problems mathematically and to devise strategies for solving them using concepts and procedures appropriately.

4. **Reasoning: (Adaptive Reasoning)** Using logic to explain and justify a solution to a problem or to extend from something known to something not yet known.
5. **Engaging: (Productive Disposition)** Seeing mathematics as sensible, useful, and doable—*if* you work at it—and being willing to do the work (NRC, 2001, p. 9).

We used the five strands as assessment criteria in our rubric for assessing students' mathematics proficiency. In this UCARE Rubric, we provided a place for comments because we believe that this assessment is more important as a way to gauge how the students are showing these strands of proficiency and rating scale would not be accurate. The comments can help gauge the areas that a teacher may want to focus on for the development of the child's mathematical proficiency (see MMI Toolkit 2).

In one of the research lessons, we presented the students with the problem below called Measuring Cups (see Text Box 2.2). It was a problem that was rich in doing mathematics and provided opportunities for teachers to assess the different dimensions on the UCARE Rubric.

Text Box 2.2   A Math Happening 2: Measuring Cups

Lucy has measuring cups of cups of sizes 1 cup, ½ cup, 1/3 cup, and ¼ cup. She is trying to measure out 1/6 of a cup of water and says, "if I fill up the ½ cup and then pour that into the 1/3 cup until it is full, there will be 1/6 cup of water left."

1. Is Lucy's method to measure 1/6 of a cup of water correct? Explain
2. Lucy wonders what other amounts she can measure. Is it possible for her to measure out 1/12 of a cup? Explain.
3. What other amounts of water can Lucy measure?

—Problem from the Illustrative Math Website

One of the students excitedly worked on this problem at the problem center. He demonstrated all aspects of the UCARE criteria. He showed engagement with the task using the measuring cups experimenting and making conjectures. Soon he and his partner were explaining to each other, and he used what he knew to reason through Lucy's method. He applied what he knew about fraction equivalence to demonstrate

Figure 2.4   Student engaged in mathematizing the problem. *Source*: Authors.

that he could formulate and carry out a plan and solve the problem using appropriate math strategies by drawing a picture and connecting it to the procedure of renaming the fraction to equivalent fractions. In this way, he demonstrated mathematical proficiency in terms of understanding, computation, application, reasoning, and engagement.

Think about it!

How can you use the UCARE rubric to assess your students' mathematics proficiency? What are some other ways you are able to assess these important strands of Conceptual Understanding, Procedural Fluency, Strategic Competence, Adaptive Reasoning and Productive Disposition?

Chapter 3

Engaging in Mathematical Modeling in the Elementary and Middle Grades

Text Box 3.1   A Math Happening 3a: Planning for the Table Tennis Championship

Next week, there will be a table tennis championship. Plan how to organize the league, so that the tournament will take the shortest possible time. Put all the information on a poster so that the players can easily understand what to do.

—Problem from the PRIMAS Website

3.1   MATHEMATICAL MODELING IN THE ELEMENTARY AND MIDDLE GRADES: WHAT ARE THE BUILDING BLOCKS?

Mathematics educators have examined models and modeling in relation to problem solving with a body of evidence that suggests modeling activities are quite successful for most students (Lesh & Doerr, 2003; Lesh & Zawojewski, 2007; Schorr & Koellner-Clark, 2003; Schorr & Lesh, 2003; Zawojewski & Lesh, 2003). In *Second Handbook of Research on Mathematics Teaching and Learning*, Lesh and Zawojewski (2007) described that learning mathematics takes place through modeling, "Students begin their learning experience by developing conceptual systems (i.e., models) for making sense real-life situations where it is necessary to create, revise, or adapt a mathematical way of thinking using a mathematical model" (p. 783).

Traditionally, in many classrooms, applied problem-solving experiences do not come until the end of the unit when all skills are introduced and mastered. Lesh and Zawojewski (2007) with their research on model eliciting activities suggest the opposite, so that the "mathematical modeling drive the learning in the conventional curriculum and traditional story problems become a subset of the applied problems through which students learn mathematics" (p. 783). In their description see Figure 3.1, when modeling is the approach to teaching mathematics concepts, "mathematical ideas and problem solving capabilities are co-developed during the problem-solving process." The constructs' processes and abilities are needed to solve "real-life problems (i.e., applied problems are assumed to be at intermediate stages of development, rather than 'mastered' prior to engaging in problem solving) (p. 783)."

Models-and-Modeling Perspective on Problem Solving
Traditional problem solving is treated as a subset of applied problem solving (i.e., model-eliciting activity).

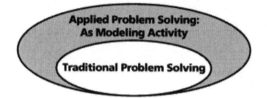

Solving applied problems involves making mathematical sense of the problem (by paraphrasing, drawing diagrams, and so on) in concert with the development of a sensible solution. Understanding is not thought of as being an all-or-nothing situation, and mathematical ideas and problem-solving capabilities co-develop during the problem-solving process. The constructs, processes, and abilities that are needed to solve "real life" problems (i.e., applied problems) are assumed to be at intermediate stages of development, rather than "mastered" prior to engaging in problem solving.

Figure 3.1   Diagram from Lesh and Doerr (2003) work as appeared in Lesh and Zawojewski (2007).

Mathematical modeling may be thought of as an *unstructured implicit problem-solving process.* A typical mathematical modeling process entails introducing a problem with context, which promotes problem solving and requires a qualitative rather than quantitative analysis. Explicit problem solving often involves the gathering of information, determining what needs to be solved, and using well-known direct problem-solving methods (such as those that can either be seen as routine problems for a particular concept) to come to a solution. However, when the problem is unstructured (i.e., mathematical modeling), one is often required to employ implicit problem-solving methods (such as a creative nonroutine approach).

Mathematical modeling has a very distinct meaning and involves teachers and students mathematizing authentic situations, and requires the application of mathematics to unstructured real-life problem situations. Mathematical modeling has been encouraged and is often used in secondary mathematics courses where real-world applications are emphasized. However, we will introduce creative ways to engage teachers and students in the elementary and middle grades to use mathematical modeling and problem solving to promote twenty-first-century skills such as collaboration, communication, critical thinking and creativity. The ways we have decided to use the terms models and modeling are in no means exclusive or all inclusive to the ways mathematics educators and researchers have used them. Instead, the ways we incorporate and integrate these ideas and practices are ways we have found to be important places for mathematics teaching and learning as seen through our research lessons from our part lesson studies.

We discuss mathematical modeling as a process of connecting mathematics with real-world situations. As stated in the Common Core Standards for Mathematical

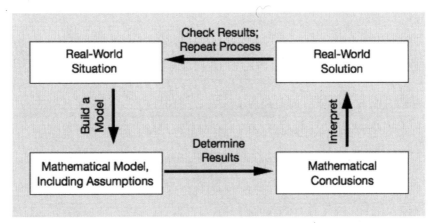

Figure 3.2   Four-step modeling cycle used to organize reasoning about mathematical modeling.
Source: (from Reasoning and Sense Making [NCTM, 2009]).

Modeling, "Real-world situations are not organized and labeled for analysis; formulating tractable models, representing such models, and analyzing them are appropriately a creative process." These real-world problems tend to be messy and require multiple math concepts, a creative approach to math, and involves a cyclical process of revising and analyzing the model.

The figure above (Figure 3.2) outlines a cycle often used to organize reasoning in mathematical modeling (from Reasoning and Sense Making, NCTM, 2009). The steps identified in this four-step modeling cycle illustrates how a real-world problem can be translated to a mathematical model under specific assumptions, which can then be solved using appropriate mathematical tools. The solutions can then be interpreted in terms of the real world and in turn helps validate the predictive capability of the model proposed.

An important way to align our standards and teaching practices is to think about and unpack the ways we teach and learn mathematics across the learning progression. So let's consider a high-school standard called mathematical modeling. As you read the description from the CCSSM document, think about ways this topic applies to elementary and middle grades? What would be the precursor to mathematical modeling in the earlier grades?

In our work with teachers, we used mathematical modeling process (see Figure 3.3) that we modified from the steps defined by the Society for Industrial and Applied Mathematics SIAM—Moody's Mega Math Challenge—which is a national mathematical modeling contest for high-school students sponsored by The Moody's Foundation (see http://m3challenge.siam.org/resources/modeling-handbook).

1. **Pose the Problem Statement:** Pose questions. Is it real world and does it require math modeling? What mathematical questions come to mind?
2. **Make Assumptions, Define, and Simplify:** What assumptions do you make? What are the constraints that help you define and simplify the problem?
3. **Consider the Variables:** What variables will you consider? What data/information is necessary to answer your question?

4. **Build Solutions:** Generate solutions.

5. **Analyze and Validate Conclusions:** Does your solutions make sense? Now, take your solution and apply it to the real-world scenario. How does it fit? What do you want to revise?

6. **Present and Justify the Reasoning for Your Solution**. (Modified from the SIAM—Moody's Mega Math Challenge website)

One of the teachers from our mathematical modeling project was so inspired by the professional development workshop that he decided to engage students in the beginning of the year with mathematical modeling. He began by creating a mathematical modeling bulletin board to reinforce his commitment to incorporating mathematical modeling as part of his instructional routine in his mathematics classroom.

Above his math tool shelf, his bulletin board displayed the six steps: P = Pose the Problem; A = Make Assumptions; V = Define the Variables; S = Get a Solution; A = Analyze the Model; R = Report the Results. He launched his school year with a mathematical modeling unit called *Proposal for a Sport Stadium*. His fourth-grade class was starting the year with place value to the millions and estimation and computation (Relates to CCSSM fourth grade: Students generalize their understanding of place value to 1,000,000, understanding the relative sizes of numbers in each place. Depending on the numbers and the context, they select and accurately apply appropriate methods to estimate or mentally calculate products).

Fourth-grade standard 4.1. The student will (a) identify orally and in writing the place value for each digit in a whole number expressed through millions; (b) compare two whole numbers expressed through millions, using symbols (>, <, or =); and (c) round whole numbers expressed through millions to the nearest thousands, ten thousands, and hundred thousand.

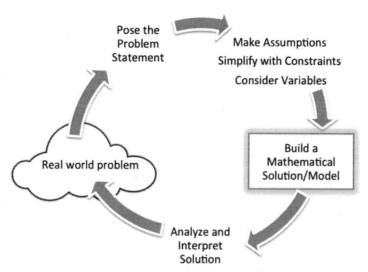

Figure 3.3   Math modeling process. Planning resources created based on math modeling process as described by Bliss, Fowler, and Galluzzo (2014).

Fourth-grade standard 4.2. The student will (a) read, write, represent, and identify decimals expressed through thousandths; (b) round decimals to the nearest whole number, tenth, and hundredth; (c) compare and order decimals; and (d) given a model, write the decimal, and fraction equivalents.

He posed the problem statement:

Text Box 3.2   A Math Happening 3b: Proposal for a Sport Stadium

The governor of your state wants to build a new sports stadium in one of the five big cities in your state. Propose a plan for the new sports stadium.

This problem tied in not only with the mathematics standards but with their social studies standards related to learning about their state. They also worked in their teams while enhancing their technology and research skills and their communication arts using Google map, Excel spreadsheet, and other Internet resources. In terms of mathematics, the teacher noted that mathematical modeling allowed for students to work with large numbers when researching about the capacity of stadiums and researching the top populated cities within their state and had no difficult making sense of the place value.

The numbers they were reading (6–9 digits) made sense to them, and they could understand the magnitude of numbers because they could relate it to the capacity of a sports stadium. In addition, he was ecstatic that students came up with related mathematical ideas through this mathematical modeling task that would help him build meaning to other mathematics standards that he would teach throughout this year. In our debrief with the teacher, he listed many of the mathematics connections that this mathematical modeling task offered for now and for later in the year. For example, in discussing the cost of the stadium, materials used in construction, size, and cost per seat, students were working with decimal place value and computation with decimals. In financing a large project, students talked about loans, investments, wages, and running costs, which exposed them to percent and economics and financial literacy.

In terms of geometry and measurement, students were brainstorming shape, size, and considering scale as they planned for where they would build their stadium within the open land they found on Google map. In thinking about seating plans to maximize capacity, they thought about prime and composite numbers and realized composite numbers give you the most flexibility in arranging rows and columns. In considering the use of the stadium, they were researching and estimating the entry cost versus running costs, profitability, sale of food, and merchandise. Finally, for statistics, students analyzed the stadium use by age, gender, and nationality. Another related mathematical modeling task for the future would be to investigate and model the emergency evacuation time for the stadium. The teacher noted that the time investment in the stadium project was worthwhile and could be leveraged throughout the year to bring meaningful connections to this real-world scenario.

In addition, as we worked with teacher co-designers on lessons focused on mathematical modeling, we identified five critical norms (see Figure 3.4) needed in the classroom to ensure success. Teachers recognized that they needed to (a) choose a context that provided an authentic problem in which students can engage in the mathematics;

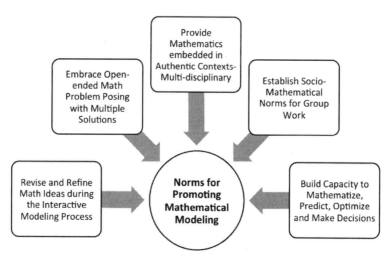

Figure 3.4   Norms for promoting mathematical modeling. *Source*: Authors.

(b) provide appropriate scaffold to help students revise and refine their mathematical ideas during mathematical modeling; (c) build in opportunities and capacity to mathematize, predict, optimize, and or make decisions for the mathematical modeling process to be worthwhile; (d) both teacher and students needed to embrace the open-ended nature of the mathematical modeling task that had multiple solutions depending on the assumptions made; and finally, (e) both teacher and students needed to establish agreed upon socio-mathematical norms such as persevering through complexity and productive struggle.

Think about it!

What mathematical modeling tasks could you incorporate into your curriculum that would elicit many of the mathematics standards you teach for your grade level? Share them with your colleagues.

3.2   MATHEMATICAL MODELING THROUGH UNSTRUCTURED REAL-WORLD PROBLEMS

One of the important ways in which we discussed the modeling of mathematical ideas is the process of connecting mathematical reasoning with real-world situations. These types of problems are open ended and messy and require creativity and persistence.

This inquiry-based problem called *Organizing a Table Tennis Tournament* comes from the PRIMAS website. PRIMAS is an international project with 14 universities from 12 different countries in Europe that have worked together over four years to promote the implementation and use of inquiry-based learning in mathematics and science. PRIMAS believes that in our knowledge-based society, students must develop the ability to attain knowledge and competencies, as well as problem-solving skills.

Knowledge of facts alone is not enough in the twenty-first-century. They believe that students need to develop competencies to apply their knowledge in realistic, problem-solving situations. Students need to also develop competencies for self-directed learning and to explore new knowledge areas. We chose this inquiry-based learning task because it was an appropriate task, that is, elementary and middle-grade students can relate to for an early mathematical modeling experience.

Organizing a table tennis tournament (Unstructured problem from PRIMAS)

You have the job of organizing a table tennis league. Gather the information you need to organize the match. Plan how to organize the league, so that the tournament will take the shortest possible time. Put all the information on a poster so that the players can easily understand what to do.

I. **Pose the Problem Statement:** Pose questions. Is it real world and does it require math modeling? What mathematical questions come to mind?
   1. How many players will take part?
   2. Are these single or double matches?
   3. What is the rule of who plays whom?
   4. How many tables are there?
   5. How long will each game be?
   6. What time will the first match start?
II. **Make Assumptions, Define, and Simplify:** What assumptions do you make? What are the constraints that help you define and simplify the problem?
III. **Consider the Variables:** What variables will you consider? What data/information is necessary to answer your question?

> Seven players will take part. All matches are singles.
> Every player has to play each of the other players once.
> There are four tables at the club. Games will take up to half an hour.
> The first match will start at 1.00 p.m.

IV. **Build Solutions:** Generate solutions.

> *Formulating a model by creating and selecting geometric, graphical, tabular, algebraic, or statistical representations that describe relationships between the variables*

V. **Analyze and Validate Conclusions:** Does your solutions make sense? Now, take your solution and apply it to the real world scenario. How does it fit? What do you want to revise?
VI. **Present and Justify the Reasoning for Your Solution**.

In our professional development for teachers, we gave them the unstructured task above of organizing a table tennis tournament. One of the teachers shared his work stating, "Before starting the table tennis problem, I realized that it was asking for a problem-solving process identical to the one needed for a common issue of mine: creating a sequence/schedule of assigned seats throughout the school year so that all students are able to work with and/or sit next to each of their classmates at least once." It was interesting to see how the teacher was recognizing that he uses mathematical

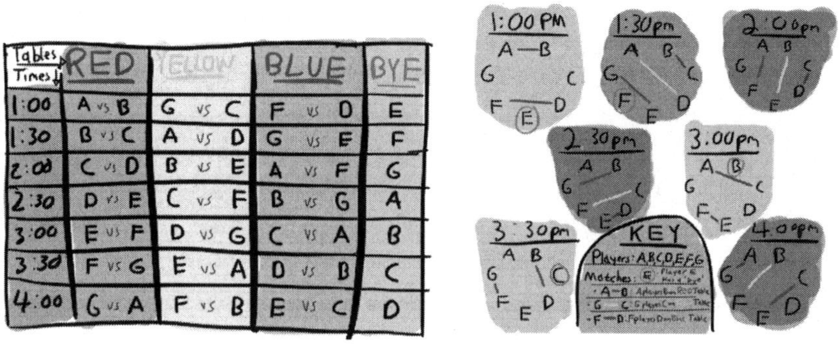

Figure 3.5 Teacher working through an unstructured mathematical modeling task. *Source:* Authors.

modeling in his work as a teacher. The teacher represented his thinking using a diagram and a table (see Figure 3.5).

Another structured way this problem could have been posed is featured below.

You have the job of organizing a table tennis tournament. Seven players will take part. "All matches are singles." Every player has to play each of the other players once. Call the players A, B, C, D, E, F, and G. Complete the list below to show all the matches that need to be played.

A v B, B v C, …, A v C, B v D …

There are four tables at the club, and each game takes half an hour. The first match will start at 1.00 p.m. Copy and complete the poster below to show the order of play, so that the tournament takes the shortest possible time. Remember that a player cannot be in two places at once! You may not need to use every row and column in the table!

Take this same task and consider this setup above to the more unstructured version of this problem presented before. What would be the benefits and challenges of each version of the problem?

Many of the teachers appreciated the nature of the open-ended task stating that it was easier to solve this problem in an unstructured way without being constrained by someone else's approach. They stated that

"I loved that I was not forced to use a specific strategy and that I could model my math thinking the way that works best for me!"; "Multiple approaches adds to everyone's understanding of the concepts."; "If we want our students to become flexible thinkers, we need to allow them opportunities to do this."

As they reflected on solving this problem, teachers saw the value that this type of modeling has allowed students to think flexibly, create their own problem-solving strategies, and become better thinkers.

How does considering these different yet important ways we model math ideas help develop "Strategic Competence" for students and teachers? Strategic competence has been defined as one of the important strands of mathematical proficiency, as the "ability to formulate, represent, and solve mathematical problems" (National Research Council, 2001, p. 116). This strand includes problem solving and problem formulation, which requires students to solve a problem by representing it mathematically: numerically, mentally, symbolically, verbally, or graphically. The key attribute for someone who has strategic competency is flexibility in their problem-solving process and strategies.

Think about it!

Mathematical Modeling is an important content area for High School. What is a developmental appropriate precursor to developing mathematical modeling readiness for elementary and middle school students that are productive and meaningful?

3.3 LESSON STUDY FOCUSED ON MATHEMATICAL MODELING: TRAFFIC-JAM TASK

Text Box 3.3 A Math Happening 3c: The Traffic Jam

There is a 7-mile traffic jam. How many cars and trucks are on the road?

Mathematical Modeling through Unstructured Real-world Problems. This research lesson was focused on mathematical modeling with the process of connecting mathematical reasoning with real-world situations (see Appendix MMI Toolkit 3.2 Planning, Debriefing and 3.3 Evaluating Lesson Study). These types of problems are open ended and messy and require creativity and persistence. When students model such situations, they are applying mathematics in a way similar to how they would visualize this in reality.

Students, therefore, need to make genuine choices about what is essential, decide what specific content to apply, and finally decide if the solution is reasonable or useful. It provides an opportunity to develop and practice their twenty-first-century skills including collaboration, communication, critical thinking, and creativity. After teachers worked on the table tennis task, they wanted to experiment with more open-ended messy problems so they presented the following "traffic-jam problem."

The teachers in this lesson study group felt that this problem met the higher-level demands (Doing Mathematics) in terms of a rich mathematical task (Smith & Stein, 2012). As we examine this one mathematical modeling problem, think about the process one needs to engage in that connects to the Mathematical Modeling Process from the CCSS for High School and SIAM math modeling process. Although this is an elementary task, can you see the parallel in the process a modeler will go through in solving this problem?

The teacher began the lesson showing a photo of a major traffic jam. Then stated the problem statement. There is a 7-mile traffic jam. How many cars and trucks are on the road? To help students make assumptions, define, and simplify the problem, the teacher asked students to think about all the questions that come to mind. Students shared the following open-ended questions:

1. Does a four-lane highway consist of two lanes going in the same direction or four?
2. What types of vehicles are on the highway? Eighteen wheelers, Smart Cars, Motorcycles, etc... .
3. What is the ratio or percent of each type of vehicle?
4. How much, if any, space is between each vehicle?

Text Box 3.4   Mathematical Modeling Phase

Pose the Problem Statement: Pose questions. Is it real world and does it require math modeling? What mathematical questions come to mind?

Make Assumptions, Define, and Simplify: What assumptions do you make? What are the constraints that help you define and simplify the problem?

Consider the Variables: What variables will you consider? What data/information is necessary to answer your question?

(Bliss, Fowler & Galluzzo, 2014)

To answer these preliminary/foundational questions, the students (and teachers) had to find other resources (i.e., videos and traffic definitions). Students took a quick fieldtrip out to the parking lot to measure cars. Having some of this information provided students with a starting point, but quickly students realized that they had to make some assumptions to define and simplify this problem.

For example, they needed to think about the ratio of trucks to automobiles to motorcycles on a given stretch of highway and the average distance between vehicles during a traffic jam. The host teacher mentioned, "I know some questions that all of us have encountered in math class, such as this one, require students to recall and use 'common knowledge' that is not provided (i.e., how many feet are in a mile like knowing 5280 feet in a mile). However, how rare of a problem is it that expects, or requires students to do outside research on 'uncommon knowledge,' (or even better, allows students to set their own parameters or assumptions), before starting the calculations."

Implement tasks that promote reasoning and problem solving. The teacher team chose this particular task and listed the following reasons for why they thought the problem was worthwhile. The task was open ended; modeled a real-life authentic situation, and many students (or most) have had some personal experience that would help them connect with, understand, or at least feel somewhat familiar with the task. Additionally, there was no specific procedure for solving the task; students would have to apply what they know; there was no answer or absolute solution, and students' answers would be as good as their justification of their procedure and rationale.

Ultimately, the teachers chose the task because it met the criteria of being a proportional reasoning problem; higher-order thinking and twenty-first-century skills were required to work through the task; the task required students to present how they reached their answer, there were numerous variations in problem-solving strategies and modeling the original problem (e.g., considering restrictions, car space, ratio of cars to trucks, number of lanes); and the task links to and aligns with many curriculum standards, key skills, and concepts.

Elicit and use evidence of student thinking. The lesson gave an opportunity for the teachers in the lesson study not only to observe student learning but also to help enhance their pedagogical practices. The host teacher commented, "This idea of giving students a 'real-world' math problem was very inspiring. Not only does it reveal and improve students' common sense and/or math sense, but also it provides opportunities for students to apply what they have learned during instruction to these new problems and see the different methods other classmates use to solve the same problems.

I was so impressed by this that I began to implement similar types of problems the last week of school with my fifth-grade students." This collaborative study also gave a chance to analyze student learning through various factors. For instance, the participating teachers reported that most groups forgot to take into consideration space between each vehicle and that there were two lanes of traffic. They also noticed that one of the groups that worked most efficiently and presented very professionally fell into this category. Soon after they realized their mistake by way of another group commenting, they went back to correct part of their answer about the two lanes. They weren't able to change their answer to take into account space in between each car, which would have been more challenging then multiply their answer by two (i.e., % increase, proportions). The work is illustrated in the Figure 3.6.

Supporting productive struggle. The teachers observed that the student group that was most productive and came up with the most accurate and justifiable answer still experienced a significant flaw in their interpretation of their calculations. For the second problem "How long would it take for the cars to clear out of the traffic jam?" the student group correctly found the number of minutes it would take [162 minutes]. However, the teachers noticed that the students in the group used long division to attempt to convert their time to hours. Again, their calculation of the hours was correct [2.7 hours]. The flaw was interpreting this decimal as "two hours and seventy minutes" instead of "two WHOLE hours and seven-TENTHS of an hour" (see Figure 3.7). As a result, they converted their interpretation to "Three hours and ten minutes,"

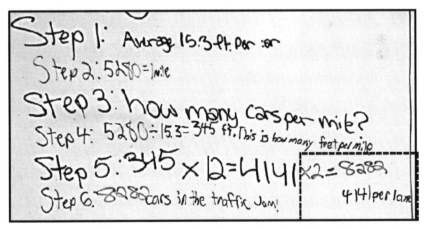

Figure 3.6   **Students making assumptions about the number of cars in a mile.** *Source*: Authors.

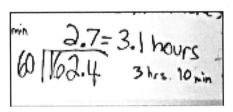

Figure 3.7   **Dividing hours and making sense of decimal.** *Source*: Authors.

which they misrepresented again as 3.1 hours. It was curious why they did not ask, "How many hours are in 162 minutes (two)," and then figure out how many minutes remained (42)?

Teachers also observed that one student group struggled to understand the numbers that they were using throughout the entire class, which was ultimately revealed during their presentation. Although this group, with some help, performed the calculations correctly to determine how many vehicles were in the traffic jam [4022.8571 cars], there was one major problem: It was a decimal ("How can you have 0.8571 of a car?"). During their presentation, the students were asked if they were able to have "part" of a car. No one in the group understood what the teachers were talking about.

Text Box 3.5   Mathematical Modeling Phase

Build Solutions: Generate solutions. *Formulating a model by creating and selecting geometric, graphical, tabular, algebraic, or statistical representations that describe relationships between the variables.*

Analyze and Validate Conclusions: Does your solutions make sense? Now, take your solution and apply it to the real world scenario. How does it fit? What do you want to revise?

Present and Justify the Reasoning for Your Solution.

(Bliss, Fowler & Galluzzo, 2014)

The teachers felt they understood that you could not have 0.8571 of a car driving around the highway; however, the teachers realized that the students in this group were all "lost in the numbers," probably overwhelmed by this "rich task" that they never fully grasped. (This made the host teacher wonder how many of his students were lost in numbers during math class, and/or while working on math assessments or activities.)

The host teacher concluded, "I feel that this last group's answer reveals some areas of neglect in my math instruction: checking your work, estimating precise numbers, asking questions when you do not understand something, and ultimately using common sense. These, skills just mentioned, are what all students need to succeed in the real world (compared with many of the math standards that we are required to teach). I feel these 'rich tasks' coupled with collaborative learning projects and presentations are an effective way to assess and improve students 'essential math knowledge and skills.'"

Through this case study and professional development with teachers, we have seen models and modeling of mathematics expressed and developed in interrelated ways. Each of these approaches was shown to contribute toward developing strategic competence in both students and teachers. Through our professional development model, we were able to expand teachers' understanding of modeling math ideas and provide them with practical means to do so.

The following reflection from the teacher who led the lesson study for the traffic-jam problem captures this. "I find it ironic that these 'higher-level demanding' problems are called 'doing mathematics' because you can't start 'doing the math' until you research and/or agree on some assumptions, tasks that you would 'TYPICALLY' find in science and other subjects. The professional development experiences that I take back are redefining what math problems, math class, and 'doing the math' should encompass: not just plugging numbers into calculators and equations, but exploring and understanding the nature of the tasks, accessing relevant knowledge and experiences and making appropriate use of them while working throughout the task, and applying unpredictable and new approaches that aren't explicitly suggested by the task. All of the descriptions/characteristics of 'higher-level demanding problems (doing mathematics)' have become relevant because I saw and heard for myself this process with my students while implementing the 'traffic-jam' task."

This chapter offers a snapshot of what mathematical modeling for solving real-world problems looks like in an elementary and middle-grade classroom. Launching a unit with a motivating and intriguing mathematical modeling task can help students see how mathematics is an important tool we use to make decisions in our everyday life. Throughout the book, we share several benchmark problems that have been considered at multiple levels to engage students in conceptual learning and enhancing their understanding of the application of mathematics in the real world. Such problems provide rich mathematical and inquiry-based tasks that require the use of twenty-first-century skills, namely communication, collaboration, critical thinking, and creativity.

Think about it!

Describe the role of the teacher and the students engaged during mathematical modeling task. How might that role be similar or different than when engaged in a traditional mathematics classroom?

3.4 PROMOTING THE TWENTY-FIRST-CENTURY SKILLS

The traffic-jam problem clearly gives the students an opportunity to engage in communication, collaboration, critical thinking, and creative problem solving, the four pillars of twenty-first-century skills. The problem allowed the students to begin the work they were assigned without any bias or opinions about what is or is not expected from the task. The misconceptions and misrepresentation that arose in the process helped them to get a better insight. Such student insights often open up new problem-solving strategies or even questions overlooked by the teacher.

The process of mathematical modeling provided students with opportunities to develop their twenty-first-century skills (P21) *Learning and Innovation Skills* which emphasize the 4 Cs: communication, collaboration, creativity, and critical thinking (see Table 3.1).

Mathematical modeling challenges students to use their mathematics communication as they collaborate on a problem. Students also use creative problem solving and critical thinking as they work to identify variables and make assumptions to build a mathematical model. In one of our STEM lesson studies, we had students designing a package that was environmentally friendly (Suh, Seshaiyer, Moore, Green, Jewell, & Rice, 2013).

In the project, *Being an Environmentally Friendly Package Engineer*, students were given objects for which they needed to design a package. They were given a large

Table 3.1   Twenty-first-century skills (Partnership for 21st Century Skills, 2011)

Critical Thinking and Creativity
Reason Effectively/Use Systems Thinking
1. Use various types of reasoning (inductive, deductive, etc.) as appropriate to the situation

Make Judgments and Decisions
1. Effectively analyze and evaluate evidence, arguments, claims, and beliefs
2. Analyze and evaluate major alternative points of view

Solve Problems
1. Solve different kinds of unfamiliar problems in both conventional and innovative ways
2. Identify and ask significant questions that clarify various points of view and lead to better solutions

Work Creatively with Others
1. *Demonstrate* originality and inventiveness in work and understand the real-world limits to adopting new ideas

Collaborate with Others
1. Demonstrate ability to work effectively and respectfully with diverse teams. Assume shared responsibility for collaborative work, and value the individual contributions made by each team member

Communication
1. Articulate thoughts and ideas effectively using oral, written, and nonverbal communication skills in a variety of forms and contexts;
2. Use communication for a range of purposes (e.g., to inform, instruct, motivate, and persuade) (Partnership for 21st Century Skills, 2010)

graph paper to create a prototype. One group created a "4 × 4 × 4" cube and then realized that they had a lot of wasted space. The student decided to redesign the package into a "4 × 4 × 2" rectangular prism in order to use more space, to be cost-efficient, and more eco-friendly (see Figure 3.8). To evaluate their design, students were asked to calculate the volume for their packages and the surface area.

The design phase involved an iterative cycle. Students created their prototype after discussion and then altered and modified the design based on the following factors: efficiency of space, economical, eco-friendly, or appealing design. An evaluation criterion was to decide which packaging design was most efficient. Students had to negotiate as they collaborated on their design. In the 5/6 upper-grade classrooms, we were able to provide the same scenario to explore packages but added more creative designs including cylinders and triangular prisms.

An interesting discussion that the class had was to think about what determines the best packaging container. If you want a package for something without a particular shape of its own, *and* minimize the amount of packaging material used, a sphere is the most efficient because it has the lowest surface-to-volume ratio of any geometric solid. In addition, round containers are generally used for any application requiring great strength. However, if all the packages were spheres like a soccer ball, packing multiple sphere packages would create empty space between containers. So if you are trying to pack something into multiple containers, the sphere is not the most efficient shape. Instead, a rectangular prism or cube might be the most efficient. This was a

Figure 3.8 The packaging iterative design phases.

Table 3.2   Prompts for students to self-assess and peer-assess after a problem-solving task

Assessing your Twenty-first-century Learning Skills in Mathematics				
Prompts to assess your 4 Cs contribution	**Critical Thinking:** How did you solve this problem in new ways linking what you know?	**Creativity:** What new approaches did you consider to solve this problem or did you invent a strategy that was efficient?	**Communication:** Did you share thoughts, questions, and solutions?	**Collaboration:** How did you work together to each a goal, using your knowledge, talents, and skills?
Self-assessment				
Peer group				

great discussion to have about why most real-world packaging is box-shaped rather than spherical.

Assessing student skills and knowledge is essential to guide learning and provide feedback to both students and teachers on how well they are doing in reaching desired twenty-first-century learning goals (Trilling & Fadel, 2009). Some of the ways to assess students' twenty-first-century skills are to use a simple assessment rubric (see Table 3.2). Self-assessing one's own contribution to group projects can help develop students' self-monitoring skills and accountability in group collaboration.

Think about it!

How does the mathematical modeling process prepare our students to be creative problem solvers for the 21st century?

3.5   TECHNOLOGY INTEGRATION IN PROBLEM POSING AND PROBLEM SOLVING

Today in our current digital age, students are described as "digital natives" meaning that they love and embrace technology. In fact, some of them would rather use video chat than use a phone to call their friends! With the advances in technology, there are excellent ways to capture everyday events that present themselves as mathematical

Figure 3.9 The meatball problem from 101qs.com.

moments or math happenings. These math happenings can often be mathematical modeling tasks.

Several blogs offer teachers and students great launching points to develop their problem-posing, problem-translation, and problem-solving skills. One interesting blog is http://www.101qs.com/. This website offers photographs and short video clips that are interesting to students. Students watch the video clip and pose mathematical questions. A fun video clip is from 101 qs and is called *Meatballs* by Dan Meyer. You are presented with a boiling pot with meatballs. In Act One, Dan Meyer asks, Will it overflow?

The follow-up questions include: How many meatballs will it take to overflow? What is a number of meatballs you know is too high? What is a number of meatballs you know is too low? In Act Two, he asks, what information would be useful to know here? Four pieces of data are provided: the height remaining in the pot; the diameter of some sample meatballs; the diameter of the pot; and the number of meatballs. Act Three provides the video and teacher materials. Besides the novelty of the video-based problem approach, the site encourages students to pose problems and solve problems based on the data provided. With exposure to sites like this, students can bring in their own photos and video clips that capture a math happening. In this way, we develop students' awareness of mathematics to their world, math-to-self and math-to-math connections.

3.6   A RELATED RICH PROBLEM TO EXPLORE

1. Sports Stadium
   The governor of your state wants to build a new sports stadium in one of the five big cities in your state. Propose a plan for the new sports stadium.
2. Drafting a Pitcher
   You are the general manager of a major league baseball team, and you have the first pick in the upcoming draft. Who would you pick and how would you decide on the best pitcher? You need to be able to defend your pick using data available about your player.

   You can present any one of the mathematical modeling prompts and use the following mathematical modeling approach (below) to engage your students in creative mathematical modeling.

Math Modeling Task
Drafting a Basketball Player

The Task

You are the general manager of a major league Basketball team, and you have the first pick in the upcoming draft. Who would you pick and how would you decide on the best basketball player? You need to be able to defend your pick using data available about your player.

Teacher's note: You may change it to any sport that students have connections with, like pick the best swimmer, baseball pitcher, soccer player, etc.

Big Ideas
Statistics & Data Analysis

Recognize a statistical question as one that anticipates variability in the data related to the question and accounts for it in the answers

Chapter 4

Understanding Numbers and Operations

There are 100 lockers in one hallway of the Excel School. In preparation for the beginning of school, the janitor closed all of the lockers and put a new coat of paint on the doors, which are numbered from 1 to 100.

When the 100 students returned from summer vacation, they decided to celebrate by working off some energy. The came up with a plan: The first student ran down the row of lockers and opened every door. The second student started with locker #2 and closed every second door. The third student started with locker #3, and changed the state of every third locker door. The fourth student started with locker #4 and change the state of every fourth locker door, the fifth student started with locker #5 and changed the state of every fifth locker door, and so one, until 20 students had passed by the lockers.

Which lockers are still open after the 100th student is finished? Which locker or lockers changed the most?

4.1   LESSON STUDY VIGNETTE: PRIME AND COMPOSITE NUMBERS

This classic locker problem exposes students to considering the important nature of numbers including even and odd numbers, *factors, multiples, prime numbers, composite numbers,* and *perfect squares.*

Suppose you're in a hallway lined with 100 closed lockers. You begin by opening every locker. Then you close every second locker. Then you go to every third locker and open it (if its closed) or close it (if its open). Continue this for every nth locker on pass number n. After 100 passes, where you get to locker #100, how many lockers are open?

Our teachers in the grade band fourth through sixth planned a lesson study around this locker problem. The goal of their lesson was to solve problem and model a mathematical situation that would reveal a relationship between factors and multiples.

The Common Core Math Standard in the fourth grade reinforces the concept of factors and multiples.

Gain Familiarity with factors and multiples.

4. Find all factor pairs for a whole number in the range 1–100. Recognize that a whole number is a multiple of each of its factors. Determine whether a given whole number in the range 1–100 is a multiple of a given one-digit number. Determine whether a given whole number in the range 1–100 is prime or composite. (CCSS-M)

During the launch of this lesson, students warmed up by giving examples of factors and multiples and then determine the greatest common factor for two or more numbers and the least common multiple for two numbers. They were also asked to categorize numbers by looking for prime numbers, composite numbers, perfect squares, and even or odd numbers. The warm-up helped remind students of the difference between factors and multiples and the number of factors for all prime numbers.

The host teacher who delivered the research lesson had a student read the problem out loud and asked another student to restate the problem to be sure everyone understood the problem. The math agenda for her research lesson was to engage the students in problem solving and reasoning as students analyzed the nature of different numbers. Odd 1, 3, 5, 7, 9, 11, ... even 2, 4, 6, 8, 10, ... square 1, 4, 9, 16, 25, 36, ... prime 2, 3, 5, 7, 11, 13, 17, 19, 23, 29, 31, ... composite 4, 6, 8, 9, 10, 12, 14, 15, 16, ... triangular 1, 3, 6, 10, 15, 21 (as seen in the handshake problem), and the interesting Fibonacci numbers 1, 1, 2, 3, 5, 8, 13, 21. Number shapes like the triangular numbers like 1, 3, 6, 10 can be arranged in the shape of a triangle. Just as the square numbers can be arranged in squares.

In the locker problem, students have to look for a pattern between the actions they take opening and closing the lockers and the number of factors each number has. They see that there is a relationship between the factors a locker number has and whether it is open or closed at the end. As students realize that they need to systematically keep track of the actions they are making as they open and close lockers, it affords

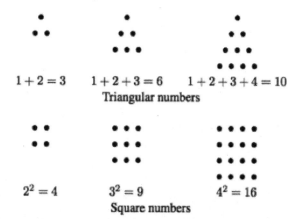

$$1+2=3 \qquad 1+2+3=6 \qquad 1+2+3+4=10$$

Triangular numbers

$$2^2 = 4 \qquad 3^2 = 9 \qquad 4^2 = 16$$

Square numbers

Figure 4.1 Figurate numbers—triangular and square number patterns.

the opportunity to encourage mathematical practices of *looking for and making use of structure* and *looking for and expressing regularity in repeated reasoning* (Standard 7 & 8 of the CCSSM, 2010).

The host teacher noted after the lesson, "I should have defined the phrase, 'changed the state' better for the students' understanding." The phrase "changed the state" links to the number of factors for each locker number. Changing the state of the lockers results in a pattern related to the number of factors of each locker number.

For all the lockers that had an even number of factors, the locker would be closed and the lockers with an odd number of factors would stay open. The only locker numbers with the odd number of factors turn out to be the square numbers since 4 has (1, 2, 4), 9 has (1, 3, 9), etc. The factors 2×2 are counted once, not double counted, so all square numbers will have an odd number of factors. The classic locker problem is a rich benchmark problem that is familiar in the school curriculum and which provides multiple entry points to access a variety of math content in number theory (For more details, see Seshaiyer, Suh & Freeman, 2011).

4.2   VISIBLE THINKING IN MATH: USING MULTIPLE REPRESENTATIONS AS RECORDS OF STUDENTS' STRATEGIC THINKING

Representations can be useful tools to reveal the mathematical thinking that students engage in as they reason through a problem. In one of the research lessons, the teacher had students act out the problem by having the students hold books representing lockers. When the students came to the front of the class to become "lockers," it helped some of the students visually represent the "change in state" for the locker problem.

The use of the manipulatives and "acting it out" provided students' access to the problem, but students quickly realized they needed a systematic way to record what was going on with each change of state. The technology tool shown in Figure 4.4 and the paper number chart were nice ways to use the affordance of keeping count of the changes to each locker. The resulting record showed the number of factors of each locker number and was more efficient to keep track of changes than manipulatives such as chips and cards. The teachers had students present their approaches, helping students to make connections and see patterns between the multiple representations of the problem. This gave them more evidence to verify their conjectures about the numbers and the state of the lockers. The use of a number line and the number chart also helped students record the pattern while solving the problem.

Using this thinking sheet helped students talk about the problem more deeply. They noticed how every number has two factors, 1 and itself. Therefore, every locker is opened on the first pass and shut on the pass where the student number equals the locker number. In addition, all numbers (lockers) *except perfect squares* have factors that occur in pairs, so that every locker except those whose number is a perfect square has its state changed an even number of times: It gets changed and then changed back, or opened and shut again. Only perfect squares have a duplicate factor pair like $3 \times 3 = 9$, so that the state of these lockers is changed an odd number of times or opened and left open.

Figure 4.2   Student uses cards to open and close to act out the locker problem. *Source*: Authors.

As teachers planned for the lesson, every member of the lesson study team was asked to work out the problem for homework. One of the teachers created the Power-Point shown in Figure 4.4 that was used in his research lesson.

The PowerPoint helped to organize and keep track of the information. The tool was used to help the students to see numbers and number sense as a mathematical topic with order and within a built-in system of relationships. These patterns can be used to enhance the conceptual understanding and student thinking about fundamentals of number theory including communicating about the classification of numbers as primes, composites, connecting with the concept of factors and multiples, and

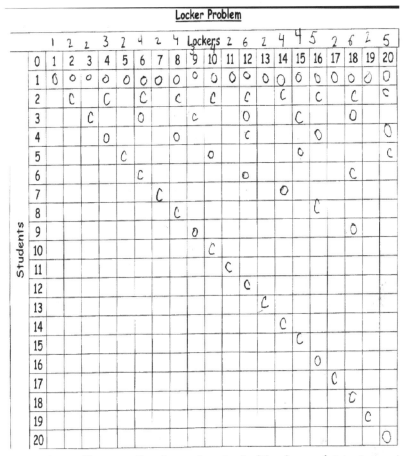

Figure 4.3 Locker problem recording sheet to keep track of the change of state. *Source*: Authors.

Figure 4.4 Locker PowerPoint simulation.

realizing how this understanding of common factors connects to reducing fractions, thus extending the conceptual understanding from patterns of whole numbers to fractions. The lesson was extended in some grades by visiting the Sieve of Eratosthenes; prime and composite numbers in context; arithmetic sequencing; common multiples; figurate numbers, and perfect squares (see Resource List at the end of the chapter) to continue the investigation of patterns in numbers and factors.

Posing purposeful questions. The teachers developed some probing questions that elicited students to think more deeply about number relationships.

1. Given the numbers of several lockers that were touched by:
   a. two students. How are these numbers related or similar? What are they called?
   b. any odd number of students. How are these numbers related or similar?
   c. any even number of students. How are these numbers related or similar?
   d. three students. How are these numbers related?
   e. four students. How are these numbers related?
2. How can you determine how many students have touched a specific locker
3. Given the first locker touched by:
   a. both Student 4 and Student 6? How do you know?
   b. both Student 5 and Student 13? How do you know?
   c. both Student 12 and Student 30? How do you know?
   d. two students of your choice. Show your work.
4. Given two students' numbers, how can you determine which locker will be the first touched by both students? (Select and record two students' numbers and show your thinking.) How can you determine which locker will be the last touched by both students?
5. Given two lockers, how can you determine which students touched both?
6. Which lockers are still open after the twentieth student is finished? Which locker or lockers changed the most?

Think about it!

How does the locker problem provide an opportunity to explore number relationships, particularly the relationship between factors and multiples, prime and composite and square numbers?

4.3 ZOOMING IN ON THE LEARNING PROGRESSION OF NUMBERS AND OPERATIONS

Introducing students to the wonderful patterns in numbers and the structures of multiplication and division through interesting problems can be an engaging way to develop an appreciation for mathematics. There are multiple interpretations and structures for operations, such as addition, subtraction, multiplication, and division, and building these structures in interrelated and deep ways will help build mental models for students as they build on mathematical ideas in later grades. The authors from *Putting Essential Understanding in Practice, Multiplication, and Division* state that,

"The way in which you teach a foundational concept or skill has an impact on the way in which students will interact with and learn later related content. For example, the types of representations that you include in your introduction of multiplication and division are the ones that your students will use to evaluate other representations and ideas in later grades." (Dougherty, Lannin, Chval, & Jones, 2013, p. 5)

A great way to develop meaning for operations is by using mathematical representations to model and interpret practical situations. Posing "math happenings" in class allows students to see how mathematics is all around them. They can develop an understanding of the meanings of multiplication and division of whole numbers through activities and problems involving equal-sized groups, arrays, and area models. In addition, using story problems allows students to be exposed to division contexts that involve partitive and measurement models. The use of area models to represent the distributive property in multiplication and can later be used to multiply fractions using the area model and also when learning algebra and multiplying two binomials using the area model and algebra tiles.

The Principles and Standards of School Mathematics (2000) introduced by the NCTM placed central importance on understanding and sensemaking in learning mathematics; for example, the Learning Principle states, "Students must learn mathematics with understanding, actively building new knowledge from experience and prior knowledge (p. 20)." This calls for traditional basics such as multiplication facts, to be used in conjunction with new basics such as reasoning, learning with understanding, and problem solving. It is important to support the latter by incorporating new basics such as providing pictorial connections in an elementary classroom to help understand the process of multiplication better.

An alternative approach to memorization is an inquiry-based approach, which focuses on understanding and explaining the meaning for operations. To develop fact fluency, memorization and practice taught along with alternative approaches, such as pictorial or graphical or hands-on approaches, help students understand multiplication in a much more efficient fashion. The following sections discuss some ways students can learn facts and procedures with understanding by thinking about facts they already know (derived facts) and applying some useful properties to establish a connection between abstract and concrete multiplication through conceptual understanding. In addition, we can motivate students to learn multiplication through a discovery learning process using pictorial representations and manipulatives.

According to the learning progression document for operations and algebraic reasoning,

"Students will rely on [understanding the meaning and properties of multiplication and division and on finding products of single-digit multiplying and related quotients] for years to come as they learn to multiply and divide with multi-digit whole number and to add, subtract, multiply and divide with fractions and with decimals." (From The Learning Progression documents at http://math.arizona.edu/~ime/progressions/, K, Counting and Cardinality; K–5, Operations and Algebraic Thinking, p. 22)

The important multiplication structures include using (a) equal groups of objects, (b) arrays of objects, and (c) multiplicative comparisons. For the equal group interpretation for multiplication, one of the factors refers to the number of objects in a group and the other is a multiplier that indicates the number of groups. For example, three cookies on a plate (number of objects in one group) and four plates (multiplier that indicates four groups). An array of objects is represented in rows and columns in a rectangular shape, and students are typically used to seeing this in the real world with chairs setup in the theater, displays at the grocery store, or just in organized arrangements of objects. A great literature connection is *One Hundred Hungry Ants*. Hundred is a nice composite number that has many configurations that students can display; 5 by 20 array, 10 by 10 array, 25 by 4 array, and 50 by 2 array and their commutative pairs.

Text Box 4.2   One Hundred Hungry Ants by Elinor J. Pinczes

(Multiplication interpreted as an Array Model)

Ants marched in 4 rows with 25 ants in each row. How many ants were there?

In the book *Remainder of One*, the main character Joe has to solve a problem where he has to think of an array so that he is not left out.

Text Box 4.3   Remainder of One by Elinor J. Pinczes

(Remainder)

Relining the 25 bugs in his squadron from two lines to three lines to four lines, until inspiration and good math thinking result in five lines of five, and Joe fits in at last.

The third interpretation for multiplication, that is called multiplicative comparison, can be somewhat more sophisticated than the two previous structures of equal groups and array of objects because it introduces the notion of proportional reasoning and scale factor. In addition, it is a foundational mathematics concept to understanding a ratio as a multiplicative comparison of quantities.

According to the *Developing Essential Understanding of Multiplication and Division for Teaching Mathematics in Grades 3–5* by Otto, Caldwell, Lubinski, & Hancock (2012), an important interpretation for multiplication is the scalar process.

Essential Understanding 1a

In the multiplicative expression, $A \times B$, A can be defined as a *scaling factor*.

Multiplication is a scalar process involving two quantities, with one quantity—the *multiplier*—serving as a scaling factor and specifying how the operation resizes, or rescales, the other quantity—the *multiplicative unit*. The rescaled result is the *product* of the multiplication.

In the fourth-grade CCSS (CCSSM, 2010) for mathematics, multiplication is introduced as a comparison:

Operations and Algebraic Thinking
4.OA Use the four operations with whole numbers to solve problems.

1. Interpret a multiplication equation as a comparison, for example, interpret $35 = 5 \times 7$ as a statement that 35 is 5 times as many as 7 and 7 times as many as 5. Represent verbal statements of multiplicative comparisons as multiplication equations.
2. Multiply or divide to solve word problems involving multiplicative comparison, for example, using drawings and equations with a symbol for the unknown number to represent the problem, distinguishing multiplicative comparison from additive comparison. (CCSS-M)

A great literature link to discuss the multiplicative comparison is the book called *If you Hopped Like a Frog* by David Schwartz. In this book, Schwartz uses proportional reasoning and amazing pictures to help students see what would happen if they had the same abilities as amazing animals. If you hopped like a frog, he says, you could jump from home plate to first base in a single bound. Since frogs are able to jump 20 times their body length, how far would a human being jump?

Text Box 4.4   *If I Can Hop like a Frog* by David M. Schwartz

(Multiplication interpreted as a Multiplicative Comparison Model)

Frogs are champion jumpers. A 3-inch frog can hop 60 inches. That means the frog is jumping 20 times its body length. If you hopped like a frog, How far could you hop?

Using mathematics literature is also great way to provide a meaningful context to the distinct meanings of partitive and measurement/quotitive division.

Text Box 4.5   *The Doorbell Rang* by Pat Hutchins

(Partitive Division)

Fair Share is a common division structure familiar to even young children. In the case of *The Doorbell Rang*, Mother bakes 12 cookies and first she shares with 2 children, then the doorbell rings and 4, 6, and then 12 children join them having to share the cookies fairly.

For the partitive division interpretation, students are working on making equal groups, or sharing and distributing an amount to known number of groups. In the case of *The Doorbell Rang*, the children are partitioning the amount of cookies (dividend) into the number of children at the house (the number of groups indicated by the divisor) and then needing to find the number of cookies each child can have (items in each of the groups).

The measurement model is also known as the quotitive division interpretation. In a measurement division problem, students know how many should go in each group, and they have to find out how many groups there will be in all. In the case of the scenario in divide and ride, they know the number of children who want to get on rides at the amusement park and are encountered situations with 2-seater, 3-seater, and 4-seater rides.

Text Box 4.6   *Divide and Ride* by Stuart Murphy

(Measurement/Quotitive)

The measurement model is illustrated in the book *Divide and Ride* where 11 Children go to the park and get into 2-seater and 3-seater rides. They need to model measuring off a quantity to find how many groups/sets can sit in the ride.

These two books provide a great springboard to discuss the important distinctions between different interpretations for division: partitive (fair share division) and quotitive (measurement division).

4.4   TEACHING STRATEGIES: USING MATH HAPPENINGS TO SHOWCASE REAL-WORLD MATHEMATICS APPLICATIONS

One of the best ways to illustrate the differences in multiplication and division is to use children's literature or introduce a math happening that occurs in our everyday life. In Suh's article (2007) *Tying It Altogether,* she discusses the important five strands of mathematics proficiency (seen in Figure 1.1 on page 3) and shares a classroom practice called "math happenings." This routine was a way to bring in real-life problems, which students found relevant, that became the centerpiece for their problem-solving activity. Each Monday, the teacher came to school and told the students that she had a *math happening.*

The students were genuinely interested because most students love stories their teachers tell about their lives. She would find an interesting math happening that occurred over the weekend, for example, a measurement conundrum she faced when installing a playground in her backyard when having to abide by the building restrictions, space constraints, and the esthetics of the yard. Students needed to figure out if the configuration would fit in different arrangements in their small, fenced backyard. This math happening became part of their math routines and soon students started bringing in their own math happenings. Having the personal mathematics connections made the process of problem solving and reasoning worthwhile for her students, and they communicated their solutions in a convincing manner so that they could help their teacher or friend solve a math happening.

Using a math happening or literature connection where one poses different contexts for remainders can help students make sense of division. Here are a few different scenarios to consider: How does each different context make one think differently about the remainders?

1. I had 20 balloons. I wanted to give them to my 3 children so that each child would have the same number of balloons. How many balloons did each get?

2. A pet storeowner has 14 birds and some cages. She will put 3 birds in each cage. How many cages will she need?
3. A father has 17 cookies. He wants to give them to his 3 children so that each child has the same number of cookies. How many cookies will each child get?
(Problems from Otto, Caldwell, Lubinski & Hancock (2012) *Putting Essential Understanding to Practice Grades 3–5*)

What would you do with the remainders in these three scenarios? The three different contexts allow for one to consider different ways to "treat" the remainder. In the case of the balloons, there are 2 remaining balloons that you cannot really share equally among 3 kids. In the case of the pet store, you can fill 4 full cages but 2 birds will be without a cage. The reality is that you cannot just keep the birds loose so you may want to get an extra cage. Finally, the last example with the cookies, one would be left with 2 extra cookies and if one wanted to share them by dividing them into fraction, that would solve that problem.

There is much to talk about with remainders. Take another example,

Mom had $25 and wanted to give her 4 kids money to spend at the carnival. How much could she give each child?

Each child can get $6 each, but mom would have $1 remaining. This problem begs the student to consider taking the remainder and changing it to a decimal $0.25 so that each child can get $6.25.

Think about it!

How does providing a variety of contexts for multiplication, division and scenarios with remainders deepen students' understanding of the operations? Create your own scenarios with different interpretations for multiplication and division.

4.5 CONNECTING PROCEDURAL FLUENCY AND CONCEPTUAL UNDERSTANDING

With computation, traditionally, and in today's mathematics classrooms, there seems to be a lot of dependence on *memorization* that has short-circuited the learning of fundamental arithmetic operations and the development of analytical skills and the use of properties. Facility in multiplication involves both an understanding of the concepts and memorization of the facts. While some experts agree that students must quickly retrieve multiplication products from memory, current research draws varied conclusions concerning the effectiveness of various approaches to helping students memorize multiplication facts.

It is important and helpful for students to learn the basic mathematical facts including multiplication, but they should also understand the meaning of the basic operations involved in the process before being expected to have fact fluency (Van de Walle, Karp, & Bay-Williams, 2014). NCTM affirms that developing number sense, gaining fact fluency and understanding arithmetic operations through conceptual understanding is a critical aspect of the elementary mathematics curriculum.

Here are a few examples:

"The curriculum should focus on the development of understanding, not on the rote memorization of formula."

"The 9–12 standards call for a shift in emphasis from a curriculum dominated by memorization of isolated facts and procedures and by proficiency with paper-and-pencil skills to one that emphasizes conceptual understandings, multiple representations and connections, mathematical modeling, and mathematical problem solving."

"Classroom observations should gather information about whether mathematics is portrayed as an integrated body of logically related topics as opposed to a collection of arbitrary rules that students must memorize."

Employing such alternate ways to teach multiplication in the elementary grades can help reinforce conceptual understanding. For example, one may employ pictorial representations to review, demonstrate, and teach multiplication in elementary classrooms. This can help facilitate discussions about strategies for finding an answer prior to asking them to memorize. Such an approach can not only help to strengthen the skills of weaker students who often struggle to do multiplication through memorization but also help the students who often just memorize to visualize and verify their answer.

Representations that illustrate multiplication and division. A representation that has generality is one that has a lot of general use (has versatility) to represent different mathematics contexts. A number line is a representation that allows one to use it for counting and cardinality, to represent addition and subtraction, and for many other purposes.

In multiplication, we can illustrate the interpretation that multiplication is repeated addition.

This number line representation can help illustrate the commutative property with jumps as shown in the figure: Four jumps of 3 is 12, and three jumps of 4 is also 12 (see Figure 4.5).

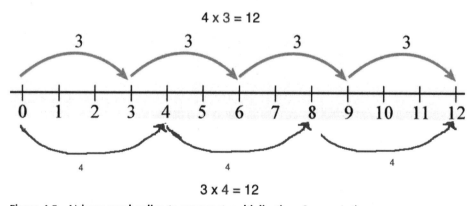

Figure 4.5   Using a number line to represent multiplication. *Source*: Authors.

Multiplication-Area Model. The array and area model can be a great way to teach multiplication and has great connections to measurement and geometry concepts of considering the length and width of rectangular shapes. Using the area model students can look for patterns in multiplication and the commutative property. Using a giant multiplication chart, students can build the arrays for the facts and look for patterns in numbers.

Think about it!

What opportunities for Sense-Making and Pattern Seeking are afforded with this visual below?

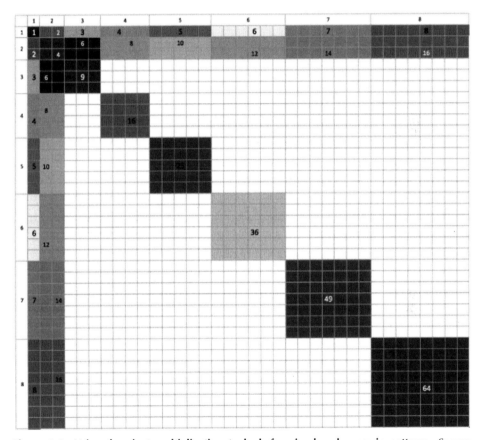

Figure 4.6 Using the giant multiplication to look for visual and numeric patterns. *Source:* Authors.

One of the activities that many teachers engage in is creating a giant multiplication chart to actually show students that they do not have to memorize all 100 facts (up to 10) or 144 facts (up to 12). In fact, the zero property and the identity property can easily knock out many. Then, we start with familiar facts like times 2 and times 5. The clock is a friendly reminder to count by 5s and students love the singsong nature of skip counting by 5s. Times 3 is often thought of "times 2 plus 1 more set" for example 3×6 is $2 \times 6 = 12$ plus 6 more to get 18. Rehearsal may be necessary for students to build up quick recall and develop automaticity.

Times 4 is often thought of as "double doubles" so if I know double 7 is 14 which is 2×7 then I can double that and get 4×7 is 28. That same idea can be used for times 6, double my times 3, and I know my times 6. Times 9 is always popular because students take pride in learning what they believe are the toughest facts, and they seem to be very proud when they learn $9 \times 9 = 81$. But times 9 has lots of wonderful patterns like the digital sums for all the products being always equal to 9, like 18 is $1 + 8 = 9$ and 27 is $2 + 7 = 9$ and so on. But more importantly 9 is 1 set away from 10 so they can use the multiples of 10 to get to a familiar fact they know, for example, I know 8×10 is 80 and 8×9 is just one set of 8 less than that so it will be $80 - 8 = 72$. For some abstract thinkers, they may think $(n \times 10) - n = n \times 9$

Text Box 4.7   Understand Properties of Multiplication and the Relationship between Multiplication and Division

CCSS.Math.Content.3.OA.B.5

Apply properties of operations as strategies to multiply and divide. *Examples: If $6 \times 4 = 24$ is known, then $4 \times 6 = 24$ is also known. (Commutative property of multiplication.) $3 \times 5 \times 2$ can be found by $3 \times 5 = 15$, then $15 \times 2 = 30$, or by $5 \times 2 = 10$, then $3 \times 10 = 30$. (Associative property of multiplication.) Knowing that $8 \times 5 = 40$ and $8 \times 2 = 16$, one can find 8×7 as $8 \times (5 + 2) = (8 \times 5) + (8 \times 2) = 40 + 16 = 56$. (Distributive property.)*

CCSS.Math.Content.3.OA.B.6

Understand division as an unknown-factor problem. *For example, find $32 \div 8$ by finding the number that makes 32 when multiplied by 8.*

The giant multiplication chart above can show how the commutative property allows for the beautiful symmetry of facts. Knowing that 3×8 is the same as 8×3 can help students feeling overwhelmed at first learning all the facts by cutting the number of facts in half. These compositions and decompositions may help students use facts that they know to find easier ways to learn the facts. In addition, it provides students an opportunity to be pattern seekers and discover patterns and strategies; they can use to make sense of the facts they are learning. For example, using this visual, one can see the square facts prominently appearing diagonally across the chart. One might also notice prime numbers only have long boring rectangles going along the edges $\times 1$. This is a perfect connection to prime and composite numbers and discussion about factors. In addition, keen pattern seekers might love to analyze the pattern of what happens when one multiplies even times even, even times odd, and odd times odd.

Properties can help students build a deeper understanding of operations and provide support for learning mathematics facts. One of the ways to build students' mental mathematics flexibility is to use the associative property or the distributive property to compose and decompose facts. Using the area model, students can use the *distributive property* to used derived facts to learn trickier facts (see Figure 4.7).

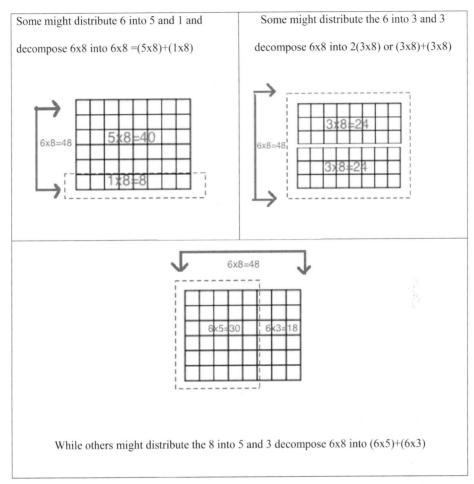

Figure 4.7 Using distributive property to decompose multiplication facts. *Source*: Authors.

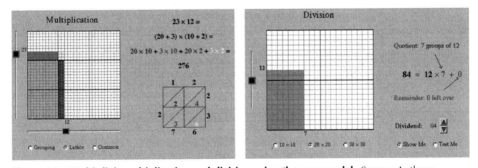

Figure 4.8 Multi-digit multiplication and division using the area model. *Source*: Authors.

The area model is a representational model that has generality because this visual can be used in later grades to represent multi-digit multiplication along with multi-digit division (see figure 4.8).

The idea of distributive property comes into play as we consider the partial products and other methods of multiplication below.

Multiple Representations for Multi-digit Multiplication

Let us now consider multiplying **23 × 12**. The traditional method is as follows:

$$
\begin{array}{r}
23 \\
\times 12 \\
\hline
46 \\
230 \\
\hline
276
\end{array}
$$

We can now look at multiple pictorial representations of the same problem that are each motivated by several important mathematical concepts. First, the distributive property allows us to consider the following representation:

	20	**3**
12	240	36

$$23 \times 12 = (20 + 3) \times 12 = 240 + 36 = 276$$

One can alternatively consider:

	10	**2**
23	230	46

$$23 \times 12 = (20 + 3) \times 12 = 240 + 36 = 276$$

If we were to use expand both 23 and 12 using respective landmark numbers 20 and 10 we can again use a representation that yields the famous FOIL (First-Outside-Inside-Last) which is connected to the partial products and can be seen as the areas of the respective rectangles in the figure.

	10	2
20	200	40
3	30	6

$$23 \times 12 = (20 + 3)(10 + 2) = 276$$

Other pictorial representations, with a historic perspective, include the application of the *vertically and crosswise multiplication* introduced in several cultures (including Indian and Chinese) as well as other procedures such as the Jalousie multiplication (also referred to as Lattice multiplication) introduced by the Persian mathematician al-Karaji in his book *Kafi fil Hisab*. While the latter technique is not intuitively obvious, the former technique brings out the importance of place value. These are demonstrated next (see Figure 4.9).

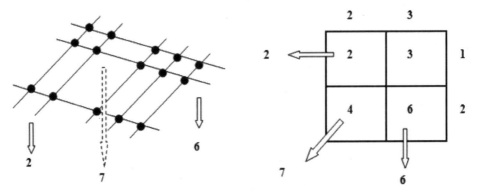

Figure 4.9   Other pictorial models for multiplication.

The above figures show vertically and crosswise multiplication on the left and Jalousie multiplication on the right. Supplementing current teaching methods with such pictorial models help the students to visualize the answer and make sense of the traditional algorithm.

Think about it!

How does providing multiple visuals and approaches help students detect patterns in multiplication and properties of multiplication and become efficient in learning the facts and building conceptual understanding and procedural knowledge?

4.6   TECHNOLOGY INTEGRATION IN PROBLEM SOLVING

There are many technology tools that support multiplication and division tasks. One such tool is the GCP/LCM Tool, shown below. This tool allows students to enter two numbers, which are then factored. These factors are displayed in several ways to model various techniques for representing factorization. The Venn diagram, in particular, gives students a very concrete view of the shared factors, which lead to the GCF, and total factors leading to the LCM.

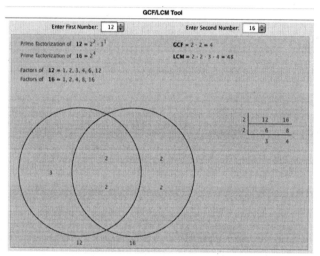

Figure 4.10   Technology applet to visualize factors, greatest common factors and least common multiples.

Chapter Resources & References
The famous locker problem:
https://www.illustrativemathematics.org/content-standards/tasks/938
Locker problem applet
http://connectedmath.msu.edu/CD/Grade6/Locker/index.html
http://www.math.msu.edu/~nathsinc/java/Lockers/
Prime numbers (**Sieve of Eratosthenes**)
http://en.wikipedia.org/wiki/Sieve_of_Eratosthenes
http://www.hbmeyer.de/eratclass.htm

4.7   MORE RELATED RICH PROBLEMS TO EXPLORE

1.   Consider the following pictorial representations. Write the related mathematical statement.

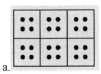
a.

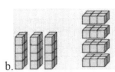
b.

2.   Find the missing number: $25 + 250 = 25 \times$ _____.

3.   Simplify the following expression:

   1. $\dfrac{1 + 2 + 3 + 4 + 5}{2 + 4 + 6 + 8 + 10}$

   2. $56 \times 71 + 56 \times 29$

   3. $.997 \times 24$

4.   What is the area of a rectangle (in inches) whose length is 12 inches and width 2 feet long?

5.   A copy machine can make 8 copies in 12 seconds. How many copies can this same machine make in 2 minutes?

6.   The sum of two prime numbers is 21. What is the product of these two prime numbers?

7.   (AMC8 2006) In the   multiplication problem below A, B, C, D and are different digits.

$$\begin{array}{r} A\ B\ A \\ \times \quad\ C\ D \\ \hline C\ D\ C\ D \end{array}$$

What is A+B?

   (A) 1   (B) 2   (C) 3   (D) 4   (E) 9

Chapter 5

Modeling Math Ideas with Patterns and Algebraic Reasoning

We are building a staircase.

Draw the blocks in the diagram to make the fourth step.

How many blocks in all are needed to make a staircase with five steps?

How many blocks does it take to build just the tenth step?

A staircase has 105 blocks. How many stairs does it have?

5.1   LESSON STUDY VIGNETTE—GROWING STAIRCASE PROBLEM

In this third-grade research lesson, students were shown a three-step staircase composed of squares and their task was to determine the number of squares that make up each step and the total needed to build a staircase for a deck. The mathematical topics that underlie this problem are extending patterns, creating generalizations, and justifying solutions. Students used manipulatives, pictures, numbers, and words to extend the pattern of the staircase. Many of them grabbed the cubes to build the staircase pattern, while some preferred to create the pattern on the graph paper. They immediately saw this as a growing pattern with each stage growing by one more cube (see Figure 5.1).

Supporting productive struggle in learning mathematics. The sample student work, Figure 5.2 is from a fifth-grade intervention classroom. The teachers reflected on their students' work and shared that these students identified as low Tier II and Tier III and had previously failed their grade-level Math Standards of learning test. She states,

One of my most interesting observations was that one of my student's that has an IEP and always states how hard everything is actually worked through the task quite easily

Figure 5.1   Building with Lego manipulatives.

which was very surprising to me. He drew his picture on the back of his paper and then worked. Students saw that they were able to use various ways to solve a problem and still arrive at the same answer. They gained confidence, because they stated that they normally struggle with these types of problems. They were able to justify their answers verbally and in words. Many realized that once they discovered what they were adding they didn't have to build and count. They were able to take the number of steps previously and add 11, then 12, then 13 and then 14 to arrive at 105 blocks. Not all of my students finished the task, but they worked the whole class period. They all demonstrated perseverance in their work. I felt that this lesson was a valuable learning experience for my students. (Missy 5th grade Math Interventionist)

Selecting a task that is accessible to all is an important part of the teaching practices. All students can access the staircase problem. Students began to draw out the staircase and add up all the blocks it took to create the total number of steps they have to figure out (see Figure 5.2). We loved that students were able to engage in the sensemaking with manipulatives (unifix cubes, legos), but quickly realized that they could be more efficient with graph paper and numbers.

One of the teachers who revised the host lesson stated in her reflection that students started out building their staircase because "it seemed like the logical thing to do," according to one member of this group. Once they reached eleven stair steps, they stopped because, "it was a waste of time. It works better with numbers." Another student created a table to figure out the total number of blocks to find how many blocks created each step. This idea of efficiency in strategy will eventually lead the students into understanding that algebraic thinking will allow one to come to a general rule from the computation of all the strings of numbers.

Driscoll (1999) describes this as one of the habits of mind, which he calls "abstracting from computation." This research lesson's goal was not necessarily for students to come to a general rule, but rather, explore the growing pattern in the staircase using

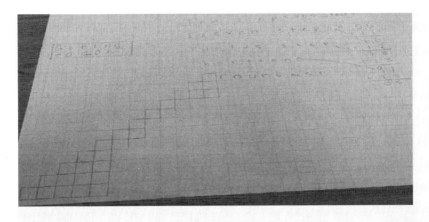

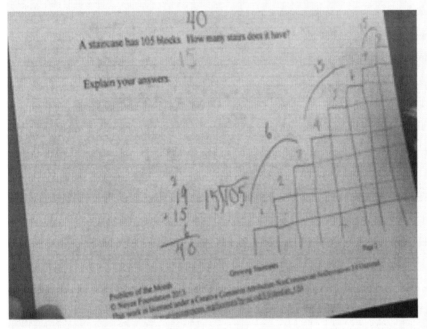

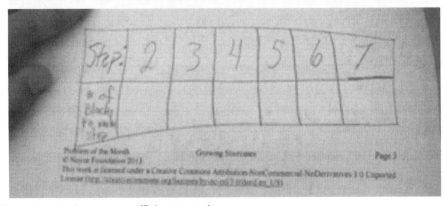

Figure 5.2 Moving to more efficient strategies.

concrete, numbers, tables, and explanations to notice the efficiency in creating a table and how one can organize information. The graphical approach would be readily available after creating a table with x (stage) and y (the number of cubes) values.

Establishing a Math Goal to Focus the Learning. Another related research lesson called the Growing Tower had a different mathematical goal. The host teacher stated that she was inspired to teach this lesson because, "I had an aha moment during the class that helped me have a full understanding of how a constant and a coefficient of a function relate to the graph as well as a concrete model of a function. I decided then to create a lesson to help my sixth-grade math students to see the same relationships." The purpose of this lesson geared to grades 5–7 was for students to create algebraic equations to represent arithmetic and geometric patterns and determine the nth value. In addition, the lesson study team wanted to connect the rule that they come up with important mathematical vocabulary such as constant, coefficient, and the function table.

Students completed a Modeling Math Mat (see Figure 5.4) to demonstrate their thinking as they worked through the problem. The teachers urged students to show their mathematical proficiency with this pattern problem by using various representations to highlight their process of coming to a solution, these included the use of pictures, tables, graphs, explanations in words, and algebraic symbols. Math agenda for the lesson was for students to analyze the patterns in multiple ways and demonstrate these process standards.

1. Communication: Students will explain and communicate their thinking using a variety of formats including words, expressions, equations, and verbal discussion to represent their ideas.
2. Connections: Students will relate sequences and functions to concrete patterns.

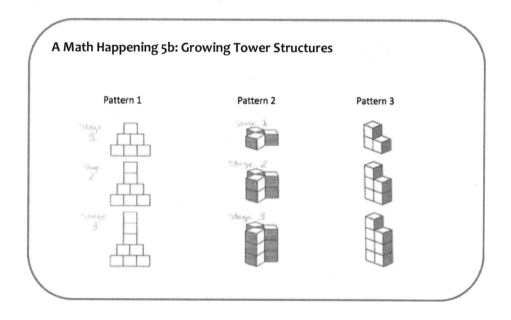

A Math Happening 5b: Growing Tower Structures

Pattern 1   Pattern 2   Pattern 3

3. Problem Solving: Students will recognize patterns from illustrations and will apply a variety of strategies to solve problems.
4. Reasoning: Students will use inductive and deductive reasoning to recognize patterns and apply rules for patterns.
5. Representation: Students will show their thinking via diagrams, tables, and/or words.

Pose purposeful questions. The host teacher incorporated the use of vocabulary throughout the lesson and made sure to connect students' background knowledge and previous grade-level content (y-intercept, constants, coefficients, slope, rate of change, parallel lines, input/output, function table, table of values, verbal expression) into this lesson of extending patterns. The lesson study team also anticipated and prepared questions to pose to students to help students communicate and explain their thinking.

> Do you notice a pattern? Can you use a picture or number sentence to help you extend the pattern? Determine what the next pattern will be? How can you organize the information you're given? How do you relate the shapes to the next pattern?

Posing questions was especially important when checking a student's general rule to their table of values for the staircase. For example, the host teacher asked students, "Does adding three (which works for y-values) work for going across from the x-values to the y-values?" They wanted to make sure that students could differentiate between the recursive rule and the function rule. They were asked to pay attention to visual cues that can be organized and translated to numeric sequences as they explored and interpreted the pattern task and generalized function rules.

To help assess students' mathematical understanding, teacher observers were asked to look for evidence to the following questions:

1. How do students use words or diagrams to support their answer?
2. Do students see how the pattern is being extended?
3. Do the students see how to relate the stage number to the output of the function?
4. Do the students know how to build the formula for the arithmetic sequence?
5. Do more students look at the pattern horizontally or vertically or just numerically, (counting the blocks) is it decreasing, increasing, and how?
6. Should students start by talking through their reasoning/thinking before they connect numbers to the pattern? Should they write down their thinking verbally before translating it numerically?
7. Do students know how to use a table to help organize their thinking (functional thinking)?
8. What stays the same? What changes?

Think about it!

Examine the patterns for the growing towers below. What mathematical learning opportunities do the different patterns offer?

5.2   VISIBLE THINKING IN MATH: USING A MODELING MATH MAT

To encourage the connections among multiple representations, the teachers asked students to map out their thinking using the Modeling Math Mat (see Figure 5.3).

The Modeling Math Mat allowed them to construct their understanding of the picture model in four ways:

1. visually with a drawing,
2. verbally with words,
3. using a function table, and
4. expressing as a rule and an equation

all of which promote algebraic thinking. After making connections among representations, we had the students transfer the pattern on to a coordinate graph to see the relationship to previous patterns.

In the first growing tower, students could quickly identify that the towers grew by 1 more block each time. The verbal explanation came very naturally for students. The difference between a novice and an advanced level (see Figure 5.5) according to the teacher was how the advanced student was able to describe in words the pattern using examples and specific vocabulary, "Stage 1 has six blocks and to get from 1 to 6 you add 5. So each stage is the stage number plus 5, for example, stage 100 equals 105."

Modeling Math Mat- Patterns and Algebra

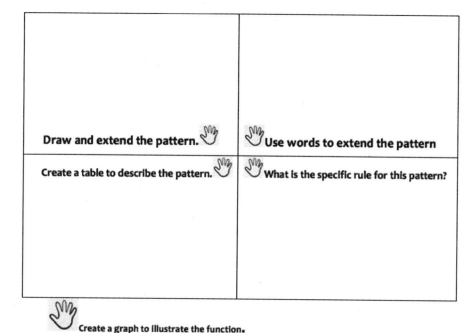

Figure 5.3   Modeling Math Mat to connect the five representations for math thinking. *Source*: Authors.

One can tell in this response how the students are looking for the function rule by looking horizontally in the table from the input number to the output number instead of relying only on the recursive pattern as the novice does. For example, the novice response was, "You add a block to the top of the block to go step by step." In addition, the novice uses numbers as a way to show the computation, while the advanced student is able to abstract from computation arriving at the general rule for the pattern in multiple versions, "*x* plus 5=*y*; add 5 to the stage #; *x* plus 5 equals *y*; the sum of *x* and five equals *y*."

The next two patterns had multiplication in the equation. Since the students were so confused by the move from addition to multiplication in equation, one teacher noted that may be at the beginning of such lessons the host teacher should show students that there are four different possibilities for writing equations—four different operations.

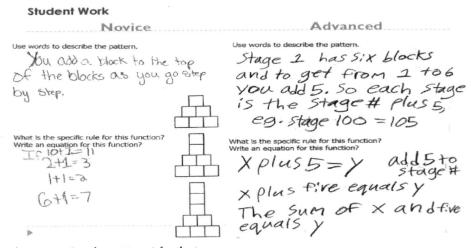

Figure 5.4   Growing pattern 1 for the tower.

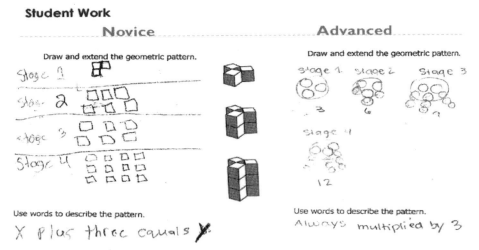

Figure 5.5   Growing pattern 2 for the tower.

It is not always addition, but it can also be subtraction, multiplication, or division so students would not get stuck on the patterns like pattern #2 (see Figure 5.5) and pattern #3 (see Figure 5.6) as some of them did when they did not see a pattern by considering only addition and got frustrated because of that. This helps teachers to also realize that additive thinking is a linear process, but multiplicative thinking is far more complex for students that can involve multiple processes.

Pattern #3 not only expects the students recognize that there is a fixed number that does not change (*y*-intercept) and then added to this fixed part is a multiplicative pattern which is two times the height of the chair (where the 2 refers to the slope). As illustrated in figure 5.6, creating a table to understand the pattern can help in the students' understanding as well. While the table presented does not show this, it may be noted that there is a constant difference of 2 in the number of cubes from one stage to the next. Also note that the table starts at a height of the chair being 2 which is a reasonable point to start but if the pattern was continued backward then the number of cubes corresponding to height of the chair being zero would be −1 which is the *y*-intercept.

The teacher's reflection below noted how she would use these pattern cards throughout the unit.

Thinking about how I may implement this lesson differently next year, I would want to try one pattern once a week throughout the unit. We would start the first pattern at the beginning of the unit so I would be able to identify students' background knowledge, and as the weeks progress, I would relate each part of the unit to the task. After the first pattern, we'd go into our review of graphing and I would connect the need for graphing to representing the pattern on a coordinate plane. I would also use the task to identify that graphing points doesn't always make a picture (like many seem to think from graphing activities in elementary school). Each week, we'd explore a new pattern and make connections that are the most relevant at the time. Perhaps one week the focus will be on how the function tables relate to the graph, another week on the difference between arithmetic and geometric sequences, another week may be identifying the coefficient vs the constant. As the unit progresses, the patterns will get more difficult and the connections will (hopefully) become more deeply ingrained in student thinking and understanding. Perhaps students will even get to the point where I can give them a table and they can create a pattern

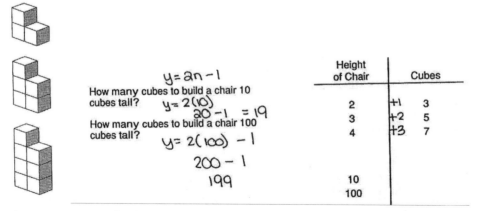

Figure 5.6   Pattern 3 for the tower with a coefficient.

in addition to the other representations. This could be a wonderful example of unique student work where each student is given the same table and they create a poster of the model including their own patterns.

 Thinking Prompt: How does the Modeling Math Mat allow a teacher to assess students' representational fluency?

5.3   PATTERNS AND ALGEBRA: ZOOMING IN ON THE LEARNING PROGRESSIONS

In this section, we share a lesson study around patterns and algebra. The learning progressions that are addressed span across the fourth- through eighth-grade band where students generate numerical patterns using given rules, record them in a table, and graph the corresponding values of the patterns as ordered pairs on the coordinate plane. They extend the table by describing how the *x*-values and the *y*-values change simultaneously. This concept of *covariation* is used to describe the relationship between the two patterns. Describing a rule relating values in the first column to values in the corresponding second column is called a *correspondence* description of the relationship between the two patterns.

> 4.OA.5 Generate a number or shape pattern that follows a given rule. Identify apparent features of the pattern that were not explicit in the rule itself.

Across grades 4–8, a focus of learning progression is on reasoning about number or shape patterns, connecting a rule for a given pattern with its sequence of numbers or figures. For example, given the rule "Add 3" and the starting number 0, and given the rule "Add 6" and the starting number 0, generate terms in the resulting sequences, and observe that the terms in one sequence are twice the corresponding terms in the other sequence. Explain informally why this is so.

> 4.OA.5 Generate a number or shape pattern that follows a given rule. Identify apparent features of the pattern that were not explicit in the rule itself.
>
> 5.OA.3 Generate two numerical patterns using two given rules. Identify apparent relationships between corresponding terms. Form ordered pairs consisting of corresponding terms from the two patterns, and graph the ordered pairs on a coordinate plane.

Developing algebraic reasoning in early elementary mathematics (NCTM, 2000) means that algebraic reasoning includes the following components: (1) understanding patterns, relations, and functions; (2) representing and analyzing mathematical situations and structures using algebraic symbols; and (3) analyzing change in various contexts (p. 37).

According to Carpenter, Franke, and Levi (2003), the artificial separation of arithmetic and algebra deprives students of powerful ways of thinking about mathematics, especially since the fundamental properties that children use in calculating are the basis for most of the symbolic manipulation in algebra. Greenes and Findell (1999) suggest that students develop algebraic reasoning when they are able to interpret algebraic problems by using pictorial, graphic, and verbal description, tables, and numeric representations.

As students evolve through their learning progression, it is important to help them start with an initial numerical understanding of iterative computing (e.g., "add 3") within a single sequence of positive whole numbers. For example, having students extend the pattern

$$2, 5, 8, 11, \underline{\quad}, \underline{\quad}$$

Once they are able to achieve this, the students must be exposed to spatial understanding that may involve representing, for example, the relative sizes of quantities (such as bars on a graph for a yearly census figures) and describe qualitative changes in the amount.

As the learning progression evolves from numerical to spatial then it is essential to elaborate on each of these understandings. An elaboration of the numerical understanding involves not only applying iteratively within a single sequence but also be able to related a sequence of numbers to generate a second sequence of numbers. For example,

1	3
2	6
3	9
4	12

The next step is often to help the students think about an algebraic expression ($y = 3\ x$) or rule associated with this repeated operation. An elaboration of the special understanding involves using continuous quantities along the horizontal axis and recognizes emerging properties such as increasing or linear in the graph connecting different points.

Once students are able to achieve such elaborated understanding numerically and spatially, it is important to integrate them using correspondence relations between differences in the y-values in a table and the size of the step from one point to the next in a related graph. For example, for every 1 step increase in time, a constant 3 degree increase in the y-column of the table and the y-axis in the related graph generates a linear pattern (spatial) with a slope of 3 (numeric) with a corresponding linear relationship $y = 3x$.

5.4   TEACHING STRATEGIES: PROMOTING THE ALGEBRAIC HABITS OF MIND

One way to develop algebraic reasoning and problem solving is to become pattern seekers for mathematical patterns and relationships, describe them using multiple representations, and analyze change. Literature connections are great ways to introduce the idea of becoming a pattern seeker. An investigation with the book, *Two of Everything* by Lily Toy Hong builds on opportunities from previous grades in which students learned about repeating and growing patterns through simple numeric and geometric patterns, repetitive songs, chants, and predictive poems.

Two of Everything by Lily Toy Hong (1993) is a retelling of a Chinese folktale. This picture book introduces the mathematical concepts of doubling and functions. In the story, old farmer Haktak and his wife dig up a large brass pot in their field and discover it has magic doubling powers. However, one day when Mrs. Haktak accidentally falls into the pot, they learn that not everything in life should be doubled. This is a great story to set the stage for exploring number patterns, relationships, and functions. The concept of doubling is critical to teaching addition strategies and is also a prerequisite to understanding multiplication facts for two. A teacher from one of our professional development workshops used this book in her classroom and reflects on her observations.

After reading the book, students explored doubling using a "magic pot" as a conceptual support. The class summarized the story by reenacting the doubling events with a coin purse, a hairpin, and Mr. and Mrs. Haktak. As they retold the story, the teacher had students keep a record of the items that went into the magic pot. By creating a table showing both input and output, the students found a pattern and generated a rule. At the end of the lesson, the class brainstormed what they might put in the magic pot besides the items from the story. The second day, the teacher told the students that the magic pot was doing something different and they had to figure out what was going on. The teacher asked them to write a number on a card and drop the card into the magic pot. For example, when a student dropped in a card with the number 5 written on it, the teacher took the card from the back opening of the magic pot and wrote the number 11 on it.

The class recorded the numbers on another input–output table. With this list of generated numbers, the students looked for the pattern and the relationship between input and output to determine the function. As the list grew, students made and tested their conjectures. If a few students thought they knew the rule before the rest of the class did, they thought of an input number and silently predicted the output number; they could determine whether they knew the function rule without denying other students an opportunity to discover the numeric pattern. The pot was doubling but adding one more. Depending on the students' level of understanding, you can differentiate the challenge by creating a function rule appropriate for the class. Simple addition and subtraction rules are a good place to start, but more complex rules can be created. Starting the school year with this activity encourages students to constantly search for patterns and relationships as they investigate other concepts throughout the year.

5.5 LESSON VIGNETTE: WHAT WOULD YOU CHOOSE? ANALYZING CHANGE IN NUMBER PATTERNS

Functions using an input–output machine like the magic pot can be a great precursor to functional thinking for later grades. Functions can explore the idea of change in a real-life context. Students experience many situations in their everyday lives that represent constant or varying change. Plant growth and temperature change represent varying change, while the cost of an international call can show constant change.

Students analyze the structure of numerical and geometric patterns (how they change or grow) and express the relationship using words, tables, graphs, or a mathematical sentence. The goal is for students to investigate and describe the concept of variable. They practice using a variable expression to represent a given verbal quantitative expression involving one operation, and write an open sentence to represent a given mathematical relationship, using a variable.

> 5.OA.3 Generate two numerical patterns using two given rules. Identify apparent relationships between corresponding terms. Form ordered pairs consisting of corresponding terms from the two patterns, and graph the ordered pairs on a coordinate plane.

In the following research lesson called *Your Dream Job*, lesson objectives focused on students

a. describing, extending, and making generalizations about geometric and numeric patterns and;
b. identifying and describing situations with constant or varying rates of change and comparing them.

Before students began, the teacher asked the students to write their name on an individual Post-It note and "vote" on the option he/she thought would get to $1000 first. The students were told that they could change their answer at any time during the lesson. Students turned to their classmates and turned and talked about the various reasons for choosing either Option 1 or 2. As the students worked on their choices, the teacher asked students to stop and think about their choice after they reached Day 3 and asked if they want to change their original "votes" and why/why not.

Text Box 5.2   A Math Happening 5c: Your Dream Job

> **You just got a dream job and you have two options for your pay.**
>
> Option 1: Your salary will be doubled each day: you will earn $1 the first day, $2 the second day, $4 the third day, $8 the fourth day, and so on.
> Option 2: Your salary will increase $3 each day: you will make $3 the first day, $6 the second day, $9 the third day, $12 the fourth day, and so on.
> Which of the two options will get your salary to $1000 the fastest?

If it is possible, the students can also be asked to represent their results using a graph after Day 3 to help them see any emerging trends spatially. One can anticipate a majority of students will choose Option 2 because on Day 3, the total earnings for Option 2 ($9) is more than the total earning for Option 1 ($4). Having students share their choices independently (or in groups) helps to build a collaborative problem-solving environment in the classroom.

Day	$
1	1
2	2
3	4

Day	$
1	3
2	6
3	9

The teacher repeated this process once again after Day 6, and the students were asked the same question whether they intended to change their votes or not. The teacher used a graph to show the result adding in the new results to the graph after Day 3. Several students noticed that Option 1 ($32) was growing faster than Option 2 ($18), especially after reviewing the graph at Day 6. The iterations for the first four days for each option are plotted on a graph shown. This can generate a lot of discussion in the classroom and can lead to an initial exposure to linear and nonlinear functions or graphs of those functions; terminology such as exponentially increasing helps them understand the concept of steepness in functions or rate of change.

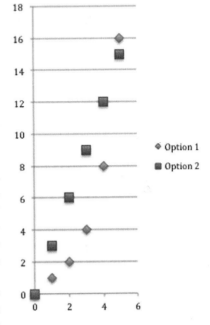

The lesson ended with the teacher reading the book *One Grain of Rice* and then discussing the concept of doubling with students. *One Grain of Rice* by Demi (1997) is about a young village girl who outsmarts a selfish king by asking him to double a portion of *rice* every day for 30 days in order to feed the hungry. Students were amazed at the surprising power of doubling to win more than one billion grains of rice from the king.

Another lesson study team chose to modify an existing related lesson called the MP3 purchase plan. In order to complete this activity, students needed some background knowledge of how to write linear equations, complete a function table, graph on the coordinate plane, and analyze data. The problem was as stated,

> You have decided to use your allowance to buy an mp3 purchase plan. Your friend Alex is a member of i-sound and pays $1 for each download. Another one of your friends, Taylor, belongs to Rhaps and pays $13 a month for an unlimited number of downloads. A third friend, Chris, belongs to e-musical and pays a $4 monthly membership fee and $0.40 a month per download. Each friend is trying to convince you to join their membership plan. Under what circumstances would you choose each of these plans and why?

It is important that students grapple with problem solving and try various solution strategies to find the most efficient one. This process also allows students to explore multiple approaches to problem solving. Some students used number sentences, simple charts, or tables to organize their thinking. After the students worked on the problem individually, they talked to their tablemates and discussed which approach was a better choice. Initially, students will verbalize the mathematical relationship informally; this process is the precursor to translating the verbal description into an algebraic formula.

Once students become comfortable describing patterns and relationships between numbers, using symbols to represent the variables becomes easier. To provide learners access to this problem, teachers developed in advance some questions to ask— for example, "How could you track the money you get each day from choice A?" Organizing information on a table can help students analyze the mathematics in the problem and become efficient problem solvers. Creating a table with the number of days listed from the smallest to the largest number gives students an opportunity to recognize a recursive or iterative pattern. One can also use technology to illustrate the connection between tables and graphs, allowing for a discussion of how each representation shows the rate of change. Relating this problem to banks or allowances can make this mathematics activity realistic and engaging.

Think about it!

How do the lessons shared above help student relate a given situation to writing an equation with variables while developing financial literacy and consumer math?

5.6   TECHNOLOGY INTEGRATION IN PROBLEM SOLVING

Introducing lessons using tools to create sequences and analyzing growing patterns is a powerful way for students to learn about the connections between growing patterns and algebra. Using manipulatives, students can be motivated to model the evolution of the pattern using multiple representations including a table or an algebraic formula or a graph. Having a tool to help them visualize a pattern as they build it is helpful for them to understand the growing nature of the pattern. The following technology tool helps students to not only create any pattern they want but helps them to organize their data in different ways. Consider the following technology tool that includes a dynamic visualization of growing patterns.

The tool allows students to enter any data that they identify from any source such as a textbook or something they have discovered through a hands-on experience. For instance, if the students saw the following pattern (1, 2), (2, 3), (3, 4), (4, 5), etc., then they can enter these numbers into the table provided as

1	2
2	3
3	4
4	5

and when they click "get formula," the tool would give them the following.

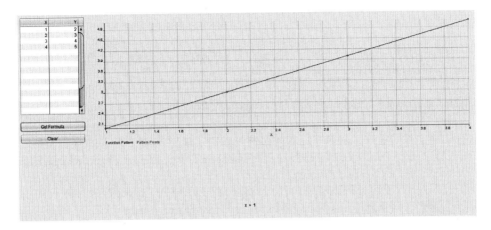

Note that the pattern entered is now described algebraically as $(x + 1)$ as well as the associated graph $y = x + 1$ is shown in the graph. This now helps for the students to make the appropriate connections to the growing pattern being linear.

Another example that can be motivated for example using toothpicks is to have them build a growing pattern using toothpicks with different stages indicating as follows with stage 1 having one square, stage 2 with four, and so on.

A challenging question to ask is to ask them the number of toothpicks required to build stage x. This allows them to formulate a table of growing numbers as (1, 4), (2, 12), (3, 24), and so on. These can then be entered into the technology tool that will yield:

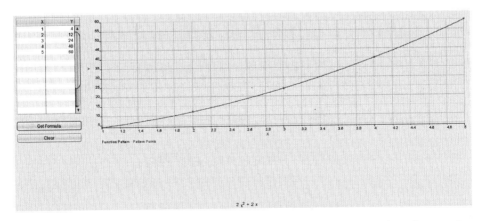

The students are now able to interpret the nonlinearity in the graph and recognize that the function is $y = 2x^2 + 2x$ which may be interpreted many ways. For example, in stage 1, there are two rows of one toothpick and two columns of one tooth yielding $(1 \times 2) + (2 \times 1) = 2 (1 \times 2)$. Similarly for stage 2, there are three rows of two toothpicks and three columns of two toothpicks to give $(2 \times 3) + (3 \times 2) = 2 (2 \times 3)$. Note that the result in each case start to motivate an algebraic pattern given at any stage x but, $(x (x + 1)) + ((x + 1)x) = 2(x (x + 1)) = 2x^2 + 2x$. Such technology-based learning discoveries not only help the students to discover new patterns but also help them to understand these discoveries in a conceptual way being able to make sense of the algebraic formula or the graphical interpretations. Students can try more patterns at: http://completecenter.gmu.edu/java/functionpattern/index.html.

Describe the advantages of using multiple representations, including technology, to develop algebraic thinking.

5.7 MORE RELATED RICH PROBLEMS TO EXPLORE

1.   Identify the next term in the sequence of growing patterns:

    1.1, 3, 5, 7, 9, ____

    2.1, 4, 7, 10, 13, ____

    3.1, 4, 9, 25, 36, ____

    4.5, 10, 20, 40, ____

    5.2, 6, 18, 54, ____

    6.1, 3, 6, 10, 15, ____

    7.1, 1, 2, 3, 5, 8, ____

2.   Consider the following growing pattern:

House #1   House #2   House #3   House #4

    1. How many squares are required to build the house #5?

    2. How many triangles are required to build house #5?

    3. If we use toothpicks for form the houses in each stage, how many toothpicks will be required to build house #10? Explain your thinking?

3.   Consider the following growing pattern of tiles.

4.   How many tiles are there in the next stage? Explain your thinking.

5.   How many squares are in a chessboard?

6. A small conference room has auditorium style seating. The last row has 19 seats and each successive row before it has 2 less seats. If the first row has one seat then what is the total number of seats in the room? (Hint: Try your pattern that you obtain at: http://completecenter.gmu.edu/java/squarenumbers/index.html)

7. Find the number of terms in the sequence: 7, 10, 13... 55.

8. A shopkeeper makes a display of cans in which the top row has one can and each lower row has two more cans than the row above it. If the display contains 100 cans, how many rows does it contain?

9. The first four figures of a pattern are shown.

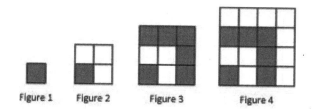

Figure 1   Figure 2   Figure 3   Figure 4

1. If the pattern continues, how many shaded squares will be in the 10th figure?

2. What percent of the 10th figure will be unshaded?

3. Each of the smaller squares has sides of length 3 units. For example, Figure 2 has a total area of $6 \times 6 = 36$ square units. What is the sum of the areas of the shaded regions in the first 10 figures of the pattern?

	Modeling Task
	Patterns in our World

The Task

Look for patterns in the world around us. How can you use math to describe that pattern? (i.e., explore Fibonacci sequence and figurate number patterns)

Big Ideas

Analyze patterns, relationships through arithmetic and algebraic approaches to predict future values of quantities of interest.

Chapter 6

Extending the Mathematical Learning Progressions for Expressions and Equations

Text Box 6.1   A Math Happening 6a: Saving for Mom's Present

Dan and Nick want to buy their mother a birthday present next month. Dan has been saving dimes and Nick has been saving nickels. Dan has saved 18 dimes and Nick has saved 22 nickels. The brothers agree to take a coin out of their wallet each day and put it in a piggy bank for their mother's birthday present. One day, when they looked into each other's wallets, they saw that Nick had more money than Dan. When this happened, how many days had they been saving for their mother's gift?

6.1   LESSON STUDY VIGNETTE: SETTING A MATH LEARNING AGENDA

The following lesson study vignettes explore important algebraic concepts with strategies and tasks for modeling the mathematical ideas and developing algebraic thinking in the early grades. A focus in this chapter is to consider how **establish mathematics goals** can focus the mathematical learning agenda. This lesson was part of a lesson study with a vertical team of third, fifth- and eighth-grade teachers. Originally, this lesson was written and published as an eighth-grade research lesson in Japan.

We were introduced to this problem as the Ichiro problem because it was stated as, "It has been one month since Ichiro's Mother has entered the hospital. He has decided to pray with his younger brother at a local temple every morning so that she will get better soon. There are 18 ten-yen coins in Ichiro's wallet and just 22 five-yen coins in the younger brother's wallet. They have decided to take one coin from each wallet everyday and put them in the offertory box and continue to pray until either wallet becomes empty.

One day, when they looked in to each other's wallets when they were done with their prayer, the younger brother's amount was greater than in Ichiro's. When this happened, how many days had it been since they started their prayers?" The original lesson goal was to have students express the relative size of quantities in inequalities and use inequalities to solve the problems as a procedure: (1) express the less than/greater than relationship of quantities as an inequality. Make them understand the concept of the inequality and its solution; (2) understand the characteristics of the inequality and be able to use them to solve simple linear inequalities. Make them able to apply the use of inequalities to solve word problems.

As we planned for a vertical lesson study, the third-grade teachers set the goal of the problem to develop algebraic thinking as students look for a pattern as the value of the coins continue to decrease. Teachers anticipated students using repeated subtractions as a method of showing the pattern of change. In the sixth-grade lesson, the goal was to see how students organize their information and work through this multi-step problem and observe whether students would use a table or graph to illustrate the change. The eighth-grade teachers had been working with variables so they wanted to see if some groups could come up with an algebraic expression to model the problem (see Table 6.1).

As teachers planned for the research lesson, they were most interested in studying the ways students make sense of algebraic reasoning in the K-8 curriculum by analyzing patterns, and change, solving multistep problems, representing linear relationships, and understanding linear inequalities using multiple representations such tables, graphs, rules, and words. While the third-grade teacher's lesson focused on analyzing a pattern of change, the preplanning session also provided middle-grade teachers an opportunity to share possible student responses. One area that the teachers discussed as a possible student difficulty was with identifying the variables.

Table 6.1 Mapping the learning progression for "Saving for Mom's Present"

Saving for Mom's Present Problem

Dan and Nick want to buy their mother a birthday present next month. Dan has been saving dimes and Nick has been saving nickels in their piggy bank. Dan has saved 18 dimes and Nick has saved 22 nickels. The brothers agree to take a coin out of their wallet each day and put it in a piggy bank for their mother's birthday present. One day, when they looked into each other's wallets, they saw that Nick had more money than Dan. When this happened, how many days had they been saving for their mother's gift?

Learning Progressions

Grades 3–4	*Grades 5–6*	*Grades 7–8*
Grades 3–4: Math Agenda	Grades 5–6: Math Agenda	Grades 7–8: Math Agenda
The student will recognize and describe a variety of patterns formed using numbers, tables, and pictures, and extend the patterns, using the same or different forms.	The student will describe the relationship found in a number pattern and express the relationship using tables, graphs, number sentences, and symbols.	Students will use problem-solving methods of inequalities by comparing and applying the characteristics of solving a simple linear equation.
The student will solve single-step and multi-step problems involving the sum or difference.	Students will solve multistep practical problems involving linear equations.	Students will represent linear relationships with tables, graphs, rules, and words and make connections between any two representations (tables, graphs, words, and rules) of a given relationship.

Table 6.2   Related Task to the Ichiro Problem, also known as "Saving for a Present" task

Related Task— Buying MP3s

You have decided to use your allowance to buy an MP3 purchase plan. Your friend Alex is a member of i-sound and pays $1 for each download. Another one of your friends, Taylor, belongs to Rhaps and pays $13 a month for an unlimited number of downloads. A third friend, Chris, belongs to e-musical and pays a $4 monthly membership fee and $0.40 a month per download. Each friend is trying to convince you to join their membership plan. Under what circumstances would you choose each of these plans and why?

Related Task—Carlos' Cell Phone

Carlos is thinking of changing cell phone plans so he is comparing several different plans.

Plan 1) Pay as you go plan $0.99 per minute

Plan 2) $30 monthly fee plus $0.45 per minute

Plan 3) $40 monthly fee plus $0.35 per minute

Plan 4) $60 monthly fee plus $0.20 per minute

Plan 5) $100 monthly fee for unlimited minutes

What will Carlos need to consider to make his decision? How can Carlos figure out which plan is best for him?

For example, how will students make sense of the difference between the number of coins versus the amount and value of the coins and the number of days. By having teachers from multiple grade levels plan the lesson, teachers unpacked the standards that aligned to the problem and discussed in detail the prior learning building blocks and the connections to related concepts, which helped them see the pattern in the development of ideas. Table 6.1 presents a mapping of the learning progression for a problem related to the original Ichiro problem that was used in the vertically articulated lesson study.

Inspired by this vertical lesson study, our instructional team decided that having a collection of related tasks with vertical connection was important for both teachers as a resource tool but more importantly to expose students to similar and related tasks for deeper learning. This inspiration led us to creating a collection of tasks that we call the "Family of Problems" (see Appendix MMI Toolkit 7). The rationale for the "Family of Problems" was to create a collection of related tasks that were bound by a similar big idea. The following related task all had a conceptual connection to the big idea of relationships and patterns, including (see Table 6.2):

1. Solving linear equations (or inequalities) both algebraically and graphically
2. Slope as a rate of change and *y*-intercept as an initial amount
3. Writing equations of lines in slope-intercept form

6.2   ZOOMING IN ON THE LEARNING PROGRESSIONS FOR ALGEBRA

According to the CCSS, third-grade students "solve two-step word problems using the four operations. Represent these problems using equations with a letter standing for the unknown quantity. Assess the reasonableness of answers using mental computation and estimation strategies."

In the fourth grade, students "represent these problems using equations with a letter standing for the unknown quantity" (NGACBP & CCSSO, 2010). As they move along the learning progression, students learn to "write, read, and evaluate expressions in which letters stand for numbers" in the fifth grade and "write expressions that record operations with numbers and with letters standing for numbers. For example, express the calculation "subtract y from 5" as "$5 - y$" in the sixth CCSSM. In the seventh grade, students "solve real-life and mathematical problems using numerical and algebraic expressions and equations." And in the eighth grade, students "analyze and solve pairs of simultaneous linear equations."

By having the students see both algebraic equations and inequalities as a kind of mathematical statement that represents the conditions of an unknown number or the variable x, students can see how algebraic equations and inequalities as related. In this way, the students' understanding of algebraic equations and inequalities are taken to an even deeper level. The solution to an inequality usually has countless solutions, except in the case when a variable has special limits. The solution therefore can be expressed as a set of numbers in a fixed range, and this is a point where an inequality differs from a simple linear algebraic equation.

Through the collaborative planning and consideration of the multigrade learning goals, teachers were better able to discuss the meaningful distinctions, definitions, and multiple models, while laying out the pattern in the development of mathematical ideas as a concept becomes more complex allowing teachers to bridge the standards. While anticipating student-generated representations, they were able to engage in rich discussion of common misconceptions. Teachers with mathematical knowledge for teaching must have an extensive and complex set of knowledge and skills that facilitates student learning across the learning progressions so that they can respond to students' responses and move the mathematical agenda forward.

As the students evolve through the learning progression in understanding algebraic equations or inequalities in one variable, it is essential to help them to develop the essential knowledge to model situations that can lead to equations in two or more variables to represent relationship between quantities and solve them in a variety of approaches. While it is important for teachers to expose students to solving such systems of equations at appropriate grade levels using formal approaches, it is very helpful for them to provide opportunities for students in elementary grades to try informal ways of solving such problems. Consider the following problem:

Text Box 6.2   A Math Happening 6b: Bikes and Trikes

John's bike shop sells bicycles and tricycles. One day, they had a display outside. There were 12 total vehicles and 29 total wheels. How many bicycles and tricycles are on the display?

One way to model this could be to start solving this problem by splitting the number 12 into 6 bicycles and 6 tricycles as it is often a quick approach. But this would give a total of 30 wheels, which is not the same as that mentioned in the question. This may then prompt students to manipulate the numbers as they go through this "trial and error" approach. For example, they may consider 7 tricycles and 5 bicycles and quickly realize that this would lead to 31 wheels, which is more than the 29 wheels in the problem.

However, this gives them a clue to guess 5 tricycles and 7 bicycles and realize that the number of wheels match as given in the problem. While the approach is an informal trial and error approach, it does give an opportunity for students to reason up and down to solve the problem without having to formulate or solve system of equations formally. Another powerful approach in this problem is to employ the strategy of assuming all 12 vehicles were bicycles, then there would be 24 wheels that leave 5 wheels short. But these wheels can become the third wheel in the list of 12 bicycles which immediately yields 5 tricycles and 7 bicycles as the solution.

Teaching such powerful proportional reasoning strategies not only helps them to get ready for what is to come when they are exposed to system of equations but also helps them to become efficient problem solvers as they evolve through their learning progression. A video demonstration of this can be found at: http://www.pbslearning-media.org/resource/mgbh.math.ee.bikes/mike-and-padhu-bikes-and-trikes/.

6.3 VISIBLE THINKING IN MATH: NAMING, SEQUENCING, AND CONNECTING MATH STRATEGIES

One "Visible Thinking" strategy in mathematics that we encouraged among the lessons was the idea of eliciting multiple representations, naming strategies, and evaluating efficient uses of representations to develop conceptual understanding, and make connections among representations (see Figure 6.1). In the third-grade lesson, preplanning discussions focused on how teachers might expose students to multiple strategies (use of concrete manipulatives: coins, pictures, table, graph) to solve the problem while giving students choice.

Evidence from the jointly planned research lessons indicated that teachers were interested in having students compare their strategies and used questioning as a way to elicit students to look for patterns. One useful tool that teachers used was our problem-solving strategy cards. Teachers laminated the cards and attached magnets and placed them for students to pull down when sharing strategies. This allowed for students to name their strategies. When there was a strategy that students could not name within the strategy cards, they would pull down the student's strategy card and name it with the student's name.

This allowed that student with a unique yet worthwhile strategy to have his name to fame and allow for others to refer to his/her strategy as they connected the strategies shared. The naming process using the strategy cards also helped the class community learn efficient strategies and keep a collective record of the strategies that could be used as a future reference related problems.

Along with the strategy cards, we encouraged teachers to use Stein and Smith's (2011, p. 8) framework called the Five Practices, which breaks down the important process in orchestrating thoughtful mathematical discourse. The Five Practices include: (1) anticipating likely student responses to challenging mathematical tasks; (2) monitoring students' actual responses to the tasks (while students work on the task in pairs or small groups); (3) selecting particular students to present their mathematical work during the whole-class discussion; (4) sequencing the student responses that will be displayed in a specific order; and (5) connecting different students' responses and connecting the responses to key mathematical ideas (see Figure 6.1).

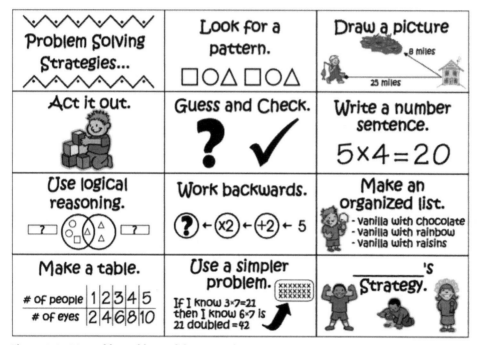

Figure 6.1   Nameable problem-solving strategies.

In their study, Stein, Engle, Smith, and Hughes (2008) stated that when teachers used the Five Practices to anticipate student strategies, they were more adept at identifying multiple strategies during the lesson, and thus better at selecting the student artifacts, and sequencing the order of presentation. This purposeful and thoughtful planning allowed for mathematics discourse to be rich with meaningful mathematics (see Figure 6.2).

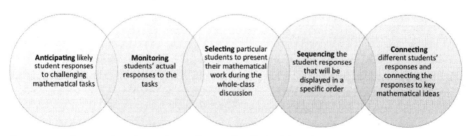

Figure 6.2   Five practices for orchestrating math talk (Smith and Stein, 2011, 8).

Through these intentional teaching moves, the lesson study team for the "Saving for the Present" focused on how students demonstrated their understanding using different strategies and representations. The teachers did not have a prescribed method for the students; instead, students were given the choice of using an approach that made most sense to them. This also allowed for teachers to analyze the most common approaches among students and how they interacted with the mathematics. The following is an excerpt from the third-grade teacher's reflection that described students' interaction with the problem and their problem-solving strategies,

> I had two boys come up to the front of the room and pretend they were the brothers who were saving their money to buy their mom a birthday present. My students were very interested to watch their peers "act it out." One of my students, a very articulate little girl, created her own table. Her table was very close to what I was hoping to find so I had her present it to our class. Working off of her table, I had my class look for patterns on the white board where she was using subtraction. Together we established that the amount of money in Nick and Dan's piggy banks were decreasing. When we "discovered the pattern" I observed that several light bulbs were steadily going off in my students' heads.

Having students work with the "five representations" allowed the class to name the different strategies: using numbers and symbols, manipulatives, words, graphs, and tables. The teacher and the observers shared their *noticings* that students had access to the problem with the physical manipulatives of the coins but when they started putting the coins in their "piggy bank," it was apparent that they had difficulty keeping track. They counted the coins that went in the bank but could not keep track of the amount each of the characters had put in without the help of a recording sheet or a table, which a girl in the class started generating. By working in collaborative groups, others in the group observed and started to mimic her method.

> The students in these groups instinctively wanted to draw a picture or create a table, which a lot of them did, but then they could not translate that into words or a number sentence. We also felt that the use of dry erase boards presented a problem because students would erase their work and start over rather than build on their previous mistakes. — Teacher collaborator and observer at the third-grade research lesson.

The idea of accessibility through multiple representations came up in the sixth-grade and the eighth-grade lessons. The sixth-grade teacher noted how the students took the problem and acted it out while one student kept track of the mathematics:

> Another group of students used a concrete model along with a table and tally marks to record their thinking. The three boys each took on a designated role in the problem. Shequeem was Aleah's brother and Raul played Aleah while Daniel was in charge of keeping track of how much money had been spent with tally marks. This team of boys really worked together to both understand and solve the problem by using many representations — verbal, concrete, and with a table. — Sixth-grade teacher.

Focusing on multiple approaches allowed students greater access to the problem and in turn, more success with the problem. Additionally, teachers promoted the idea of organizing information and keeping track of the changes as an important part of solving the algebraic problems and analyzing the recursive pattern.

The lesson study team intentionally planned for the students to solve the problem in their most natural way, and then to give them opportunities to sit side-by-side with

Nameable strategies

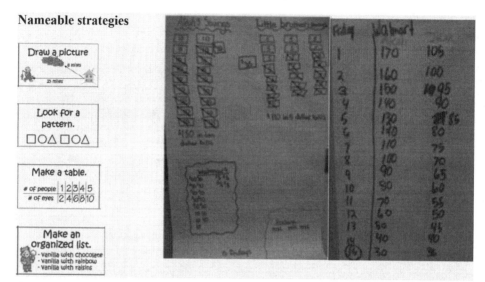

Figure 6.3 Two six-grade students worked individually then compared strategies. *Source:* Authors.

a partner with a Venn diagram to compare their approaches. This built-in activity allowed for rich discussion of comparison and connection between the representations. For example, in figure 6.3, one student compared the quantities by crossing off the same number of coins for each of the brothers, while another student kept track of the remaining balance using a table.

> *One of the focal points of our lesson was to have students look at different strategies to solve the problem and also think about the similarities and differences among their solution paths. We had students use many of the multiple representations that we focused on in our class this summer—concrete, verbal, pictorial, graphically, and symbolic. ——Fifth-grade teacher special educator.*

In order to connect the strategies, the teacher posed important questions for students.

> *Pivotal questions for students: What are some similarities and differences among our strategies? How can you describe your strategy in one sentence? What is happening each day? How will you organize your coins? How will you keep track of how much money Nick and Dan have? What tool could you use to help you solve the problem?—Excerpt from 3rd grade research lesson.*

As teachers co-designed, observed, and revised their lessons, they discussed the vertical algebraic connections stating where in the continuum they would find most of their students in their algebraic reasoning with this particular problem. For example, teachers observed how most of the students in the earliest stages of the learning progression represented their thinking through a *repeated subtraction* method or using a *comparing quantity approach* to show the decreasing values. They also had difficulty fully understanding the word problem and setting up mathematical statements for the relationship that was being expressed.

The lesson study team discussed how the majority of students used the most common two methods we had seen in younger classes—a chart and a drawing. This idea became a critical discussion point. Can students become so fixated by a pictorial or concrete representation that it prevents them from looking for more efficient strategies? Or do most learners need entry into a problem using a concrete, pictorial, or tabular approach to make sense of the problem before advancing to an algebraic equation? What is the teachers' role and how do teachers use questioning to advance students' thinking when they are "stuck"? How can we use classroom discourse and representations as a means of moving student from inefficient to sophisticated strategies? The host teacher also made some "horizontal connections" as she related this problem to other algebraic problems with linear equations called the *cell phone plan problem* where students find the best plan using similar strategies as this problem.

6.4 TEACHING STRATEGIES: USING MISCONCEPTIONS TO REPAIR UNDERSTANDING AND LOOKING FOR EFFICIENCY

An interesting theme that emerged from the collective debrief was the analysis of sophistication of strategies. This multi-grade makeup of grades 3–8 teachers pushed the teams to think across the learning progression and the algebraic vertical connections. In the planning of the lesson, teachers anticipated that students would most likely generate concrete, pictorial, numeric, and tabular approaches which were considered to be more accessible for early grades and graphical, verbal, and algebraic approaches to be more sophisticated. The team also considered presenting a graphical approach if it was not generated by the students, so that students would see the rate of change and be encouraged to interpret the graph based on the context of the problem.

In the sixth-grade lesson called *Aleah's Spending*, the teachers wanted to focus on the multi-representational aspect of algebra. The research lesson was taught in a low-performing mathematics class and the teacher who led the lesson thought that many of her students needed concrete manipulatives. They decided that they would have $10 and $5 bills available for manipulation. The sixth-grade teacher did not anticipate any of the students creating a graph but did decide to have graph paper available just in case. During the observation of the lesson, the other teachers–observers noted how students negotiated meaning among team members and how they worked together to make sense of the problem. As indicated by the host teacher's reflection, which she shared during the debrief, many responses and strategies surprised her. She stated,

> Timeia originally started working with a group that used concrete models to solve the problem, but she quickly moved off to work on her own and began recording repeated subtraction from both Aleah's bank account and her brother's. This was one of the strategies we thought that students may use in our lesson plan; unfortunately Timeia did not get to finish showing her work for this strategy, but it is clear that she sees a repeated pattern occurring in the problem. (see Figure 6.4)

The essential understanding also included how the repeated subtraction that was used is related to the constant slope that was illustrated using a graphical approach.

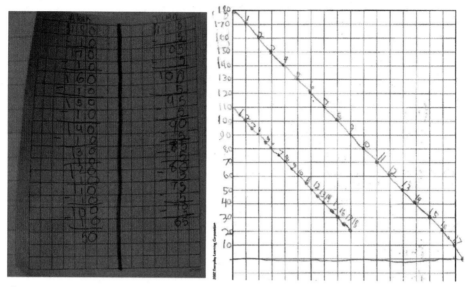

Figure 6.4 Repeated subtraction method and the graphical approach with error but showing initial ideas about the pattern of change.

While there is an error in the calculation, the notion of "decreasing" or "negative slope" starts to evolve as they start to formalize their observation using algebraic reasoning.

Supporting productive struggle in learning mathematics. One exciting mathematical happening was that one of the students that the host teacher anticipated having the most trouble with the problem actually gravitated toward graphing, which the team of teachers perceived as a more sophisticated and unfamiliar approach. She stated her surprise in her reflection:

> Lastly, one of my students who I anticipated having trouble with the task surprised me when he immediately went to graphing the two situations (see Figure 6.4)—Aleah's money and her brother's money. While it took most of his time to set up the scale and the data points did not match up to the days, Thomas could quickly see a pattern of the decreasing values of money in their bank accounts. Seeing Thomas gravitate toward creating a graph was a topic of our conversation during our debriefing session. One of my colleagues even suggested having him graph his multiplication facts; something that he normally struggles with. May be a graph is just more sophisticated to him and something new that he will grasp on to.

Elicit and use evidence of student thinking to build procedural fluency from conceptual understanding. Examine the following students' artifacts and look for efficiency in their problem-solving approach and what the different approaches offers meaning to the solution. One of the important ways to bring meaningful mathematics discourse in the classroom is to ask students to look for the connection from different solution strategies. The ability to analyze among different representations deepens one's understanding.

The following examples were offered for students to compare the tabular approach, algebraic expressions, and the graphical representations created by his students (see Figure 6.5). Andrew approached the problem using a double-sided table, which showed the decrease in money for both of the brothers. He kept subtracting until he found that David had more money and then counted how many days it had been. Andrew found an efficient way to create the table, and instead of listing all the amount decreased each day, Andrew decided to use a number sentence to skip down 10 days using $(18 - 10) \times 10 = 80$ and $(22 - 10) \times 5 = 60$ and used the notation … to show that the pattern continued.

Brian used the days and created $180 - 10y$ for Brian and $105 - 5y$ for David, which eventually led to the discussion of solving for $180 - 10d = 110 - 5d$. When Andrew finished quickly, the teacher encouraged him to solve the problem in a different way to verify his work. Andrew decided that he would graph the values on the table and found the point of intersection was the day at which they had the same amount of money and that the 15th day David had more. Andrew was able to formally show his algebraic thinking through both his table and his graph, however, had some difficulty verbalizing his findings. But overall, he shows that he is developing skills to think in abstract ways.

Brian's strategy in Figure 6.5 also shows how he made sense of the problem by starting with a tabular approach but instead of counting down to the amount each day, he decided to abstract from computation and make a general rule using symbols. This is an important skill that Driscoll (1999) identifies as one of the important algebraic habits of mind. Abstracting from computation allows for one to make a generalized rule for a pattern of change. Brian realized that the amount left in the wallet of the brothers was going to be the $180 - 10$ times the number of days for Dan and $110 - 5$ times the number of days for Nick. The students at this level were not ready to set up an inequality statement from what they had but were at the cusp of this new understanding.

This teacher shared the evidence of the depth in which he examined his student's solution strategies, use of representations, sophistication of ideas, and justification. The teacher had solved this rich task during the summer institute and had collaborated with other teachers to anticipate multiple strategies and sophistication of methods, which provided the specialized mathematical knowledge to perform this analysis. As a result, the teacher was prepared to analyze students' work and marked the learning progression displayed in his classroom and determined where he might go with his students to push their mathematical thinking forward.

In particular, the benchmark problem used across grade levels not only developed the discussion among teachers about the vertical progression of algebraic thinking but also the need for multiple representations and how such representations evolves across grade levels. At the final research lesson presentation, the lesson study team presented their collective learning. The third-grade teacher explained how her students observed patterns in the tables the students had created (such as in Figure 6.4), the sixth- and eighth-grade teachers shared their students' work with the table, equations, and graphs (see Figures 6.5, 6.6) and started discussing the notion of rate of change which led to the discussion of "slope."

Following this, they talked about "steepness" which helped the third-grade teachers connect the tabular approach to the graphical approach. The eighth-grade teacher also

Nameable strategies

Make a table.

Write a number sentence.
5×4=20

Make a graph.

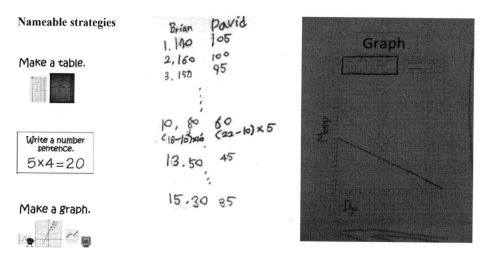

Figure 6.5   Andrew's efficient strategies and graph.

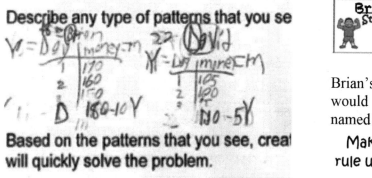

Brian's Strategy would eventually be named as

Make a general rule using symbols.

Figure 6.6   Brian's strategy, short cut.

shared how she could potentially use this activity in her classroom for a stock market game the students were involved in and connect the activity to the topic on linear equations and system of equations that she will teach later in the year.

6.5   TECHNOLOGY INTEGRATION IN PROBLEM SOLVING

One of the essential understandings of the problem involved graphing the situation that was modeled via tabular approach or repeated subtraction method. For those students that are visual learners, a graphical approach is often a great way to engage in a conceptual understanding. The following tool provides an opportunity for students to discover and learn about a variety of important concepts such as slope and *y*-intercept (see Figures 6.7 and 6.8).

The technology allows the students to enhance their learning by manipulating the slope (m) and the *y*-intercept (b) to see when two lines intersect when there is a unique solution and when they are parallel (and not intersect) when there is no solution as illustrated next.

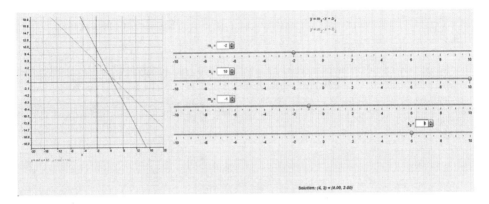

http://completecenter.gmu.edu/java/lineintersection/index.html

Figure 6.7   Learning by manipulating the slope (m) and the y-intercept (b) to see when two lines intersect with unique solution.

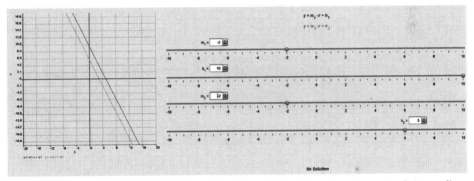

Figure 6.8   Learning by manipulating the slope (m) and the y-intercept (b) to see when two lines are parallel with no solution.

Such technology-enhanced learning helps students to connect to the mathematics in the problem. For example, the problem illustrated in the graphs shown may be thought of as a scenario where two people start with different amounts $10 and $6 as shown. Both lose a constant amount each day. In the first illustration, we assumed this constant amount was different, and hence, we noticed that the lines intersected and the second illustration; the amounts deducted are the same and therefore leading to the same slope for the two lines. Such important connections between algebraic reasoning in the problem make the mathematics more meaningful. Giving the flexibility to the students to manipulate the toolbar to play with values of "m" and "b" helps them to reinforce this discovery learning through technology.

6.6   MORE RELATED RICH PROBLEMS TO EXPLORE

1. Mike's Cycle Shop sells bicycles and tricycles. One day there are a total of 50 wheels in the store. There are the same number of bicycles and tricycles in

the store. How many bicycles are available for sale in Mike's shop that day? Show your thinking in numbers, words, and pictures! How can you convince someone you are correct?

2. On Joe's farm, he raises chickens and cows. One day he counts the number of legs of all the animals on his farm, and he counts 28 feet. Joe goes to bed at 8 o'clock every night. What could Farmer Joe have for animals? Show your thinking in numbers, words, and pictures. How can you convince someone you are correct?

3. John's shop sells bicycles and tricycles. One day there are a total of 176 wheels and 152 pedals in the shop. How many bicycles are available for sale in John's shop that day? Show your thinking in numbers, words, and pictures! How can you convince someone you are correct?

4. Kris spent $131 on shirts. Fancy shirts cost $28 and plain shirts cost $15. If she bought a total of seven then how many of each kind did she buy?

5. Nancy is selling hats and caps. The caps cost $2 and hats cost $3. She needs to make at least $500. Write an inequality to represent the income from the hats and caps sold.

6. Dan and Nick want to buy their mother a birthday present next month. Dan has been saving quarters and Nick has been saving dimes in their piggy bank. Dan has saved 28 quarters and Nick has saved 40 dimes. The brothers agree to take a coin out of their wallet each day and put it in a piggy bank for their mother's birthday present. One day, when they looked into each other's wallets, they saw that Nick had more money than Dan. When this happened, how many days had they been saving for their mother's gift?

Math Modeling Task
Best Cell Phone Plan

The Task

Your friend needs help finding the best cell phone plan based on the family members' needs. Research the cell phone plans and proposes the best plan for your friend's family.

Big Ideas

Solve real-life and mathematical problems using numerical and algebraic expressions and equations.

Chapter 7

Developing Fraction Sense

Text Box 7.1   A Math Happening 7a: Unusual Baker

Miss Baker's Sweetshop likes to cut the cakes differently each day of the week. On the order board, Miss Baker lists the fraction of the piece, and next to that, she has the cost of each piece. This week she is selling whole cakes for $1.0 each. Determine the fractions of each piece of cake and how much each costs if the whole cake is $10.

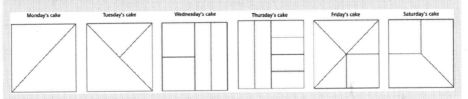

7.1   LESSON STUDY VIGNETTE: THE UNUSUAL BAKER

Our fourth-grade state standard states, "Given a model, the student will write the decimal and fraction equivalents."

Our Math Agenda: The students will

- Understand fractions as parts of a whole.
- Understand the conceptual meaning of the numerator and denominator.
- Understand that the whole must be divided into equal-sized portions or fair shares.
- Use fraction language: whole, halves, and fourths.
- Set models show how subsets of the whole make fractional parts.
- Recognize unit fractions.
- Calculate the price for each piece of the whole.

This lesson was adapted from *Teaching Children Mathematics*, December 2011 and requires students to think about fractional parts of a whole and determine the value of various fractional parts when told that the value of the whole is $10.00. In order to work through the examples, students have options of selecting manipulatives to model the problem, to draw pictures to demonstrate their thinking, or to work abstractly.

Math educators support the notion that "mathematical ideas can be represented in three ways: enactively (concrete representation), iconically (pictorial representation), and symbolically (written symbols)" and that "this idea of multiple representations suggests that children's conceptual development evolves from concrete experiences to more abstract ones" (Cramer & Wyberg, 2009, p. 228). Offering students' choices about how to display their thinking and making connections between various models is an important component of any math lesson that aims to deepen students' mathematical knowledge. As Marshall, Superfine, and Canty (2010) state:

> Translating and moving flexibly between representations is a key aspect of students' mathematical understanding. Presenting students with opportunities to make connections between multiple representations makes math meaningful and can help students see the subject as a web of connected ideas as opposed to a collection of arbitrary, disconnected rules and procedures. Creating a learning environment in which students are encouraged to make connections among different representations has been a central feature of mathematics reform efforts for at least the past decade. (p. 39)

Students who have the opportunity to both create and make sense of multiple problem-solving strategies and solutions develop important foundational understanding. Too often making connection across representations is overlooked, but research has shown it to be a powerful part of the instructional process.

This lesson provides a relatable, real-world context for dividing a whole into fractional parts. Students are given the scenario in which a baker sells whole cakes for $10 and are shown 6 cakes divided in different ways. They must then determine the cost for each of the pieces of cake that are depicted, with each of the 6 cakes being divided into increasingly complex ways. Sharp and Adams (2002) suggest that "teachers who nurture students' construction of fractional knowledge by recognizing and utilizing personal knowledge (such as measuring cups or cake cutting) provide an appropriate foundation for fraction learning" (p. 334).

7.2   VISIBLE THINKING IN MATH: ASSESSING STUDENT LEARNING THROUGH CLASSROOM ARTIFACTS

In terms of misconceptions to be anticipated for this lesson, there are several that the fourth and fifth graders might demonstrate. The students may not understand the following: The value of the slices does not have to be whole numbers (can be decimals); same-sized slices must have the same fractional value and dollar value; half a cake should cost half of the $10 total and one-fourth of a cake should cost one-fourth of the $10 total; and information from the previous day's cake may help in determining the fractions and dollars values for the next day's cake.

Research indicates that there are five levels of progression regarding partitioning:

> We propose that the acquisition of the partitioning process is the culmination of a gradual progression through five levels. Each level is distinguished by certain conceptual characteristics, procedural behaviors, and partitioning capabilities. In particular, the partitioning process is mastered through the successive attainment of five subsets of the unit fractions: the fraction 1/2, fractions whose denominators are powers of 2, fractions with even denominators, fractions with odd denominators, and fractions with composite denominators. (Pothier & Sewada, 1983, p. 316)

If teachers who include this lesson in their instruction keep these levels in mind, it may inform their assessment of student understanding and can guide the follow-up questions they pose to students in both individual and whole-group discussions.

Students who demonstrate misconceptions should be provided multiple opportunities for remediation in order to correct said misconceptions. At the same time, teacher must be cognizant of the role their language and word choice play in student understanding. For example, Siebert and Gaskin (2006) discuss partitioning and iterating. An example of partitioning is when "5/8 is 5 one-eighths, where 1/8 is the amount we get by taking a whole, dividing it into 8 equal parts, and taking 1 of those parts," while an example of iterating is when "5/8 is 5 one-eighths, where 1/8 is the amount such that 8 copies of that amount, put together, make a whole." The authors point out that "these two different ways of conceptualizing 5/8 can lead to a variety of ways of actually creating and justifying the quantity 5/8" (p. 397).

Figure 7.1 illustrates some examples of some of the misconceptions students demonstrated. The first one displayed showed that a student did not think that the triangular fractional part was equal to the square part of the other cake. This misconception is not surprising as students are used to congruent pieces to represent fractions (i.e., fraction circles and fraction bars). This model of having congruent shapes and sizes represent the region model. However, what they see here are two pieces that have the same area. As mentioned before, this is a more complex model related to fraction. The parts must be equal in area but not necessarily congruent.

The next common error displayed by many was when they gave dollar value to each of the fractional pieces. They were able to understand the problem and attack the first day where the baker was dealing with fairly concrete halves. As they moved along, however, they relied heavily on the use of the dollar bills and guess and check. They would divide the dollars evenly into piles based on the number of pieces the

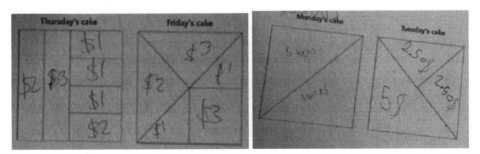

Figure 7.1 **Incorrect and correct responses from Student A and Student B.**

Table 7.1 Mapping out learning progression and ways to differentiate a task across grade bands

Grades 3–4	Grades 5–6	Grades 7–8
VA Math SOL 3.3a: The student will name and write fractions (including mixed numbers) represented by a model.	VA Math SOL 6.2b: The student will identify a given fraction, decimal, or percent from a representation.	VA Math SOL 7.4: The student will solve single-step and multistep practical problems, using proportional reasoning.
For the third grade, the total cost of the cake could be a multiple of 2, 4, and 8 and the fractional pieces could be limited in value. For example, the cake could cost $16 and the only fraction parts shown could be halves, fourths, and eighths. [This is a simplified version of the original task involving.]	For the sixth grade, the baker could start out with more than one cake. For example, the baker has three cakes that cost $10 total. [The whole has changed, therefore the value of the fractions has changed—what looks like one-half of a cake is actually one-sixth of the whole.]	For the seventh grade, the baker could start out with more than one cake and have to provide certain sized portions. For example, the baker starts with four-and-a-half cakes and must provide servings that are one-third of a cake. [This involves fractions divided by fractions.]

baker sliced the cake into. At times, they would divide the dollars with disregard to the fractional amounts.

Meanwhile, some of the students were able to determine the correct cost of each slice of cake for all three days; they were stuck on labeling the fractional parts of each cake.

Teachers used the Exemplar Rubric called the *Thermometer Student Rubric* for their assessment. While this student's work is not complete in the picture, he was able to complete the problem and was determined to be at a "Practitioner" level in all categories. Student B was able to correctly solve the three days' cakes cost per slice as well as the fractional amount. This student's work was assessed as "Practitioner" in understanding and strategies but "Expert" in communication. The student was able to solve all three days and began working on the extension with great enthusiasm. He was able to identify the price per slice of cake as well as define the fractional piece for each cake as well. Table 7.1 above maps out the conversations teachers had about the Fractional Cake problem and the learning progressions in fraction related to this problem. Having a vertical team of teachers also offered opportunities to think about the Fractional Cake problem and consider ways they could differentiate this problem to extend the conceptual understanding of partitioning a whole.

7.3 ZOOMING IN ON THE LEARNING PROGRESSIONS: FRACTIONS

Developing fraction sense is critical to the number sense in middle-grade mathematics. Skip Fennell, mathematics educator and past president of NCTM, stated in the December 2007 *NCTM News Bulletin* entitled *Fractions is Foundational*,

As students develop a sense of fractions, they will also recognize that they must approach the ordering of a set of fractions such as 7/8, 3/8, 5/8, and 9/8 differently from a set such as 3/5, 3/7, 3/4, and 3/8. Such experiences provide students with the background that they need to begin finding common denominators, creating equivalent fractions, and adding and subtracting fractions. Students also need to understand what really happens when they multiply and divide fractions. Far too many students are adept at carrying out these procedures without understanding that products typically get smaller when they multiply fractions and that quotients get larger when they divide them. Experiences with rate and proportion provide middle-grade students with everyday situations that involve fractions as well as contextual links to algebra.

This paragraph elicits important ideas about student learning of fractions and pedagogical implications for teachers. For example, understanding the meaning of fraction and the magnitude of fractions is critical to knowing how to order fractions. As Fennell mentions in his newsletter, ordering of a set of fractions such as 7/8, 3/8, 5/8, and 9/8 is different than a set such as 3/5, 3/7, 3/4, and 3/8 because it requires students to reason through the relative magnitude of these fractions. The first set all have the denominator of eighth so they can think about 1/8 as the unit fraction and see that they can order starting with 3/8 because it is 3 parts the unit fraction 1/8. This corresponds to the Common Core Math Standard:

Develop understanding of fractions as numbers.

CCSS.MATH.CONTENT.3.NF.A.1

Understand a fraction 1/b as the quantity formed by 1 part when a whole is partitioned into b equal parts; understand a fraction a/b as the quantity formed by a parts of size 1/b.

In addition, as students order the rest of the fractions, they can visualize the other fractions being a number line starting with 3/8, 5/8, 7/8, and then 9/8 hopefully also noticing that each fraction is 2/8 away from each other and that 9/8 is a fraction greater than a whole. This relates to the third-grade Common Core Math Standard:

CCSS.MATH.CONTENT.3.NF.A.2

Understand a fraction as a number on the number line; represent fractions on a number line diagram.

The second set of fractions is more complex because they do not have the same partitions or common denominators as the first set did. Yet, the numerators are all the same. Using that piece of information, students who have a strong integrated understanding of fraction will be able to reason through the ordering of the fraction. By examining and visualizing 3/5, 3/7, 3/4, and 3/8, they might think, "If I had to have 3 pieces of a chocolate bar and they were cut into fourth, fifth, seventh, and eighth, which piece would be the largest and the smallest?" They would see visually that ¾ is the largest and 3/8 is the smallest size. Using that reasoning, they can order the fractions from smallest to largest starting from 3/8, 3/7, 3/5, and 3/4. They may be reasoning through benchmark fractions such as ½ to make sense of the relative size. For example, they can use equivalent fractions and benchmark fractions to reason to easily see that 3/8 is less than ½ since 4/8 would be equivalent to ½ and ¾ is greater than ½ because ½ is the same as 2/4 and so ¾ is greater. This relates to the fourth-grade Common Core Math Standard:

CCSS.MATH.CONTENT.4.NF.A.2

Compare two fractions with different numerators and different denominators, e.g., by creating common denominators or numerators, or by comparing to a benchmark fraction such as 1/2. Recognize that comparisons are valid only when the two fractions refer to the same whole. Record the results of comparisons with symbols >, =, or <, and justify the conclusions, e.g., by using a visual fraction model.

One of the most common interpretations for rational numbers is the part to whole relationship (Barnett-Clarke, Fisher, Marks, & Ross, 2011). This interpretation can be visually represented with a continuous region model or a discrete set model. For example, ¼ can be represented as 1 out of 4 parts or can be represented as 1 out 4 discrete objects. In Korean, the fraction ¼ is read "sa boon-eh il" which means "out of 4 parts 1 part" which explicitly states the part to whole relationship. Partitioning a whole into equal parts is an important prerequisite to fractions. In this example, a student shows interesting and creative ways to cut the cake into 1/8. Although the area is not exact, these figures demonstrate an understanding of equal areas.

The second interpretation of a rational number is as a measure and can describe the amount of something (like a distance, an area, a capacity or volume, or a duration in time) in relation to the size of a unit, which is considered equal to 1 (Barnett-Clarke, Fisher, Marks, & Ross, 2011).

A number line is a mathematical model that provides a rich environment for understanding and reasoning about rational numbers (Moss and Case, 1999). The number line is a model that has generality in that it can easily represent the magnitude of numbers and also show the density of fractions. The third interpretation of a rational number is as a quotient and can indicate a division operation: That is, 3/4 can be seen as equivalent to the arithmetic expression $3 \div 4$ (Barnett-Clarke, Fisher, Marks, & Ross, 2011). This interpretation is illustrated in the research lesson highlighted below called the Sharing Brownie task. Two other interpretations include rational number as a ratio and as an operator, which we will focus in the next chapter.

7.4   IMPLEMENTING MATHEMATICAL TASKS THAT PROMOTE REASONING AND PROBLEM SOLVING

Lesson Vignette—Sharing Brownies—Fractions as quotients

In a third-grade lesson study called "Is It Fair," students were exploring the task of sharing 5 brownies with four people.

When presented with the problem, some children made comments such as, "there are not enough children," "there are too many brownies," or "I know it is dividing but I cannot do 5/4." Teachers found that some students had the correct picture, but were not able to label the fraction correctly. Others divided each brownie into fourths and counted the 5/4 but needed a rich meaningful class discussion to connect 5/4 and 1 ¼. Some students needed to be able to see that each person received a whole and 1/4. During the course of the lesson, students, who had no exposure to mixed numbers prior to this lesson, were able to explain basic understanding of 1 ¼ by using words such as 1 whole and ¼ more, a whole and a quarter, or one big piece, and then ¼ of the piece.

Text Box 7.2   A Math Happening 7b: Is it Fair?

There are 4 children who would like to share 5 brownies? How can they share fairly?

When presented with the problem, some children made comments such as, "there are not enough children," "there are too many brownies," or "I know it is dividing but I cannot do 5 ÷ 4." As teachers observed students model this mathematics using tools such as paper brownies, tiles, and drawings, they took memos on ways students communicated their ideas to their tablemates. An interesting dialogue was captured in one of the videoclips where two students had the correct representations, but because it looked different, they were having a great debate and challenge convincing one another about the fair share.

Initially, one student insisted each kid would get 5 pieces and the tablemate insisted it was one whole brownie and a little more.

Nate: I think I have an idea. I think each get a whole and another piece. Like they each have two pieces but one of their brownies is big like the whole and the other is smaller… Ah like one and little more.
Cleo: (with the brownies divided into fourth) May be it's divided equally…what is 4 × 5… (counts on by 5s – 5, 10, 15, 20).

Listening attentively to their discussion, it was clear that the boy who was using color tiles had divided his fraction brownie into fourth and started to count the 4 tiles on each brownie for the 5 brownies and got 20 pieces (see Figure 7.2). The 20 pieces were in the unit of fourth such that what he had was 20/4 twenty-fourth, and when he divided that up among the 4 friends each person received 5/4, however, he continued to refer to it as 5 pieces. Meanwhile, his partner across him had fair shared by partitioning 4 whole brownie among the 4 people leaving him with one whole brownie for each person and one whole brownie left to share among the 4 friends which he later referred to as fourth of a brownie (see Figure 7.2). Because the representations looked different in their own eyes, the two students could not convince each other that they both had the same amount. The boy who used the tile became frustrated and proceeded to cut the brownies into fourth leaving him with 20 fourths. However, the boy kept referring it as 20 pieces and thus 5 pieces for each friend.

The pedagogical dilemma encountered in this lesson study was how to help students connect the different student-generated representations to make sense of the mixed number like 1 ¼ or fraction greater than a whole like 5/4. Teachers found that some students had the correct picture, but were not able to label the fraction correctly.

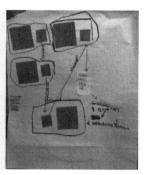

Figure 7.2 Dividing the five brownies into fourth and partitioning brownies to four friends.
Source: Authors.

Others divided each brownie into fourths and counted the 5/4 but needed a rich meaningful class discussion to connect 5/4 and 1 ¼. Some students needed to be able to see that each person received a whole and 1/4. During the course of the lesson, students, who had no exposure to mixed numbers prior to this lesson, were able to explain basic understanding of 1 ¼ using words such as 1 whole and ¼ more, a whole and a quarter, or one big piece, and then ¼ of the piece.

This lesson ended with students sharing their solutions. During the debrief, the host teacher admitted that she had a moment of pedagogical dilemma because some students did not see the connection among the variety of representations. She noted that the concept of working with mixed fractions was a new concept for many and that this productive struggle actually was a great place to start the lesson the following day. Sometimes, the teachable moment can wait another day if the teacher is able to revisit the work from the prior day and take the opportunity to have the class debate and convince one another that the classmate that said, "5 pieces" and the classmate that said "one and a little bit more" could have clarified their mathematical language to say "5 pieces of the fourth or 5/4" and "one and a quarter." The connection needed was to show how 5/4 could be also 1 ¼. Using manipulatives, numbers, and words, students can argue in the mathematics classroom to make sense of the new concepts.

7.5 TEACHING STRATEGIES, USING REPRESENTATIONS, AND OVERCOMING COMMON MISCONCEPTION

The common difficulty lies in the interpretation of the meaning of fractions, which requires explanation through connections with other mathematical knowledge, various representations, and/or real-world contexts. Often students do not realize that they have been exposed to fractions in their everyday activities long before they were formally instructed in school. Such knowledge may be thought of as constructed knowledge, and currently, there is a big gap between this constructed knowledge that students bring to the classroom and the instructed knowledge that the teachers try to deliver. Students, who are mathematically proficient, make the connections between the two bodies of knowledge and students that do not understand may never make the connection. Modeling the mathematics is one way to achieve these connections.

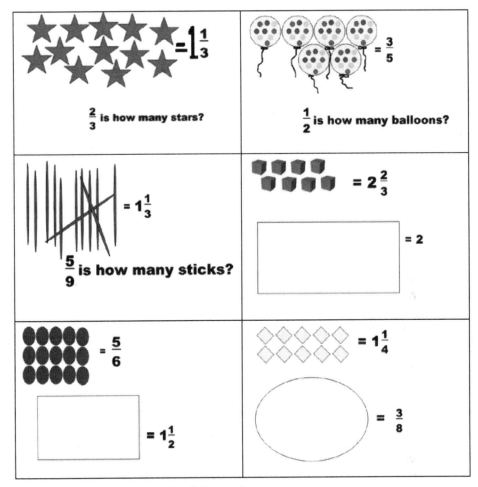

Figure 7.3   What is the whole? Visualizing a unit.

One of the key ideas in fraction is the notion of unitizing (Barnett-Clarke, Fisher, Marks, & Ross, 2011) state, "The concept of Unit is fundamental to the interpretation of rational numbers." (p. 19) Each fraction depends on some unit of measure. One activity that helps students become flexible with their ability to unitize is to use a familiar manipulative like the pattern blocks and change the unit (see Figure 7.3).

According to Lamon, "unitizing is a natural process" (p. 105) that can be thought of "chunking" a specific size of something. For example, 24 eggs can be 2 (dozen) where the dozen is chunked as a unit or it could be 4 (6 packs). One group of teachers wanted to see how students make sense of unitizing fractions. The following fractions were presented to students in grades 5–7.

Students had many different approaches. One question they kept at the forefront of their thinking was finding out "What is the whole?" In the first example, one of the groups changed the fraction 1 1/3 to 4/3 and said if we know that 4/3 = 12 stars and we know 2/3 is half of 12 then we can find out that 2/3 is 6 and one third is 3.9 starts is one

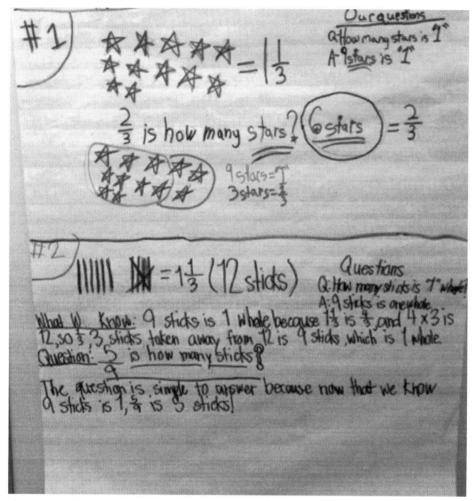

Figure 7.4   Students reasoning through What is a whole? *Source*: Authors.

whole. Students also used the unit fraction to find the whole. For example, students stated that 5/6 = 15 and 15/5 = 3 there for the unit fraction 1/6 = 3 and 6/6 would be 3 × 6 = 18. And 1 ½ would be 18 + 9 = 27 (see Figure 7.4).

7.6   TECHNOLOGY INTEGRATION IN PROBLEM SOLVING

In the following technology applet, students can compare fractions using visuals and converting fractions into decimals. The number line also represents the fraction to show the magnitude of the number. One way to compare and order fraction is to use the relative size or the magnitude to reasonable compare. A second way is to find the decimal form by dividing the numerator by the denominator. Another way is to find common denominators and compare the fractions. In order to find equivalent fractions, students must understand the notion of renaming a fraction. Finding the equivalent fraction by multiplying the numerator and denominator by the same number may not mean much to students except a rule. For example, multiplying

$$\frac{1 \times 3}{2 \times 3} = \frac{3}{6}.$$

But making conceptual connection to that procedure is to connect the idea that multiplying 3/3 is the same as 1.

$$\frac{1 \times 3}{2 \times 3} = \frac{3}{6}$$

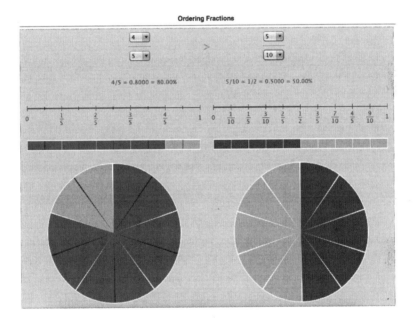

http://completecenter.gmu.edu/java/orderingfractions/index.html

Pattern blocks are great manipulatives to help students build conceptual and procedural understanding of shapes, proportions, equivalence, percentages, and fractions. The six standard pattern blocks include a yellow hexagon, a red trapezoid, a blue rhombus, a green triangle, a tan rhombus, and an orange square as shown below.

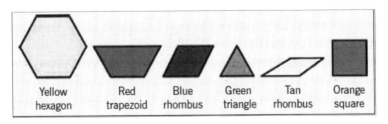

Except for one of the trapezoid bases, all the sides of the shapes are typically of the same length. Also, the areas of the hexagon, trapezoid, rhombus, and triangle are related through their area proportions. While the students can understand these relations by hands-on approaches, it is also helpful to have them discover these relations via technology-enhanced tools. For instance, the following tool provides an opportunity for students to select one of the six shapes in one dropdown box and another one in the other dropdown box and study the relationship between the two. The students have the opportunity to guess their answer before they press the "check answer" tab, which helps them to learn by discovery as follows:

One may also consider asking the relationship to illustrate part of a whole as follows.

To discover the relationships between the other pattern blocks, go to the website: http://completecenter.gmu.edu/java/patternblockactivity/index.html.

7.7   MORE RELATED RICH PROBLEMS TO EXPLORE

1.   Complete the following:

     a.

     b.

2.   Write the statement involving equivalent fractions in the picture below.

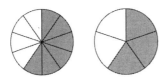

3.   Draw a pictorial justification of the equivalence statement $\dfrac{3}{4} = \dfrac{9}{12}$.

4.   The following illustrations describe the expression $20 \div 5$. Describe the difference
      between the two and your observations.

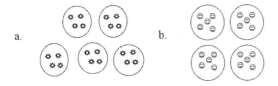

5.   The weight of a rat is 25 grams, and the weight of a small dog is 5 kg. The mass of the
      dog is how times the mass of the rat?

Think about it!

Describe how productive struggle can benefit students?

What classroom norms or routines can you establish in your classroom to nurture perseverance through productive struggle in your classroom?

Math Modeling Task
Paint Color Palette

The Task

You will be creating a new paint color palette for your room. Experiment creating various shades of color using different ratios of 2 different food dyes. Create 5 variations of color, using different amounts of both dyes in 5 different cups. Keep track of your drops in order to document your results and make them reproducible. Name for that color and provide a clear explanation as to why this is the PERFECT name for this shade. Finally make list of 3 different equivalent ratios that would work to recreate this perfect new shade.

S-G-380 Sunny Summer

S-G-390 Lemon Zest

S-G-400 Lime Pop

S-G-410 Green Crush

S-G-420 Limeade

S-G-430 Sparkling Appl

S-G-440 Green Acres

Big Ideas

Analyze ratios and proportional relationships and use them to solve real-world and mathematical problems.

Chapter 8

Modeling Operations with Fractions

Text Box 8.1   A Math Happening 8a: Stuffed with Pizza

Tito and Luis are stuffed with pizza! Tito ate one-fourth of a cheese pizza. Tito ate three-eighths of a pepperoni pizza. Tito ate one-half of a mushroom pizza. Luis ate five-eighths of a cheese pizza. Luis ate the other half of the mushroom pizza. All the pizzas were the same size. Tito says he ate more pizza than Luis. Luis says they each ate the same amount of pizza. Who is correct? Show all your mathematical thinking.

—Problem from the NYC DOE Elementary School
Performance-Based Assessment

8.1   LESSON STUDY VIGNETTE: STUFFED WITH PIZZA—ADDING FRACTIONS

In the lesson study, teachers focused on the relationship between fractions and examined how students would represent each portion of pizza that Tito and Luis ate and compare the two to determine whether someone ate more or they ate the same amount.

This lesson focused on the fourth- and fifth-grade standards where students used visuals to add fractions and compare fractions. Some specific standards that they noted in their math agenda were focusing on the following:

CCSS.Math.Content.5.NF.A.1: Add and subtract fractions with unlike denominators (including mixed numbers) by replacing given fractions with equivalent fractions in such a way as to produce an equivalent sum or difference of fractions with like denominators. For example, $2/3 + 5/4 = 8/12 + 15/12 = 23/12$. (In general, $a/b + c/d = (ad + bc)/bd$.)

CCSS.Math.Content.5.NF.A.2: Solve word problems involving addition and subtraction of fractions referring to the same whole, including cases of unlike denominators, for example, by using visual fraction models or equations to represent the problem. Use benchmark fractions and number sense of fractions to estimate mentally and assess the reasonableness of answers. For example, recognize an incorrect result $2/5 + 1/2 = 3/7$, by observing that $3/7 < 1/2$.

8.2   VISIBLE LEARNING IN MATH—USING TOOLS TO PROVE THEIR THINKING

In one of the classrooms, the teacher wanted all of her students to access the task. She had a large number of English Language Learners and students with specific Math IEPs. The teacher had worked with students on using fraction models and drawing diagrams while naming the fractional pieces. Often times, students will use fraction circles and not remember what each fractional part represents. The teacher was keen on having students name the fractions as they worked through the problem. Many students drew a model with fraction circles and split these into the appropriate segments for each child. Some did not have to convert to equivalents to arrive at an answer, while others used equivalent fractions.

During the class discussion, the teacher made it a goal to give students opportunities to share their representations and especially to link the process of finding equivalent fractions. Student engagement was high partly because of the introduction with a discussion of pizza and their favorite types, and because little background information was needed as all students were familiar with pizza and different-sized slices. Students demonstrated their problem-solving skills through explaining their work with words, numbers, and with pictures. Through this task, students demonstrated their mathematical understanding of fractions, equivalent fractions, and comparing fractions with unlike denominators.

In the first example, Student A (see Figure 8.1) used fraction bars and labeled the type of pizza and displayed the correct portions and Student B used fraction circles and labeled the fraction names. They both were able to show that the amount was the same, but the process was more about finding the correct portion and comparing the two amounts than naming the amount of pizza each boy ate.

In the following example (see Figure 8.2), the student actually combined the fractions by renaming each one to a common denominator of eighth and adding them. She showed her work through her pictures, numbers, and words. This was the last student to share their work after the task.

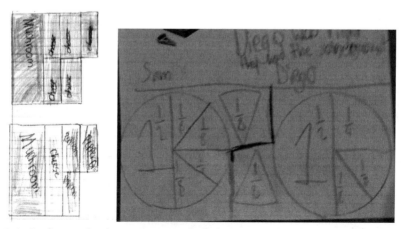

Figure 8.1   Student work using concrete manipulatives.

Another student (see Figure 8.3) used fractions and converted each fraction to a decimal. Decimal units had been taught previously, but no other students chose to work with decimal equivalents.

One of the teachers who retaught this lesson in her own class stated, "The goals of our Stuffed Pizza lesson study task were for students to use mathematical reasoning & language, compose & decompose fraction pieces while renaming fractions, compare fractions, and translate their pictures to numbers and words. When I implemented the lesson with a fifth-grade class, I felt as if all lesson and teaching goals were met.

The task was set up to support students' reasoning skills. Students had to determine which boy was correct in regards to who ate more pizza. Students worked with and

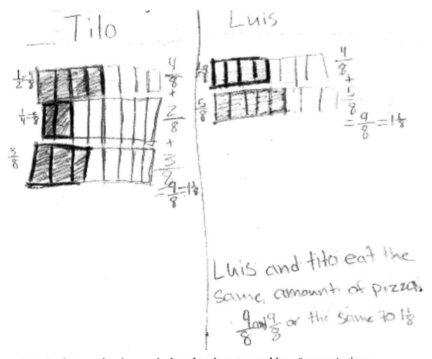

Figure 8.2   Student work using equivalent fractions to combine. *Source*: Authors.

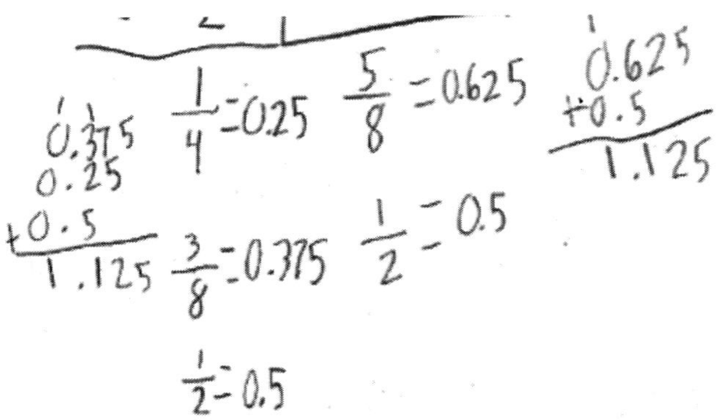

Figure 8.3   Student work using decimals to combine amounts. *Source*: Authors.

manipulated fractions to figure out the total amount that each boy ate. They combined fractional parts of three different pizzas, to find a whole amount for each boy. In order to answer the final question, of who ate more, students had to compare and reason regarding their work."

8.3 LEARNING PROGRESSION IN FRACTION OPERATIONS— ZOOMING IN ON MULTIPLYING AND DIVIDING FRACTIONS

An important upper-grade standard is being able to solve multiplication and division problems in context. Using the area model for multiplication, one can illustrate what happens when one multiplies a fraction by a fraction. Using the area model, one can take ¾ of 2/9 and show how the overlapping area is the product (see Section 8.7). Dividing fractions using the area model one to consider the measurement model in interpretation.

For example, ½ divided by 1/3 can be interpreted, "how many 1/3s can go into ½?" Or "how many 1/3-cup servings can I get from ½ cup?" The first thing one might consider is that the serving size we want is 1/3 cup and then ask how many of that serving size can be found in a ½ cup. If we use the common-denominator method, we would have 3/6 divided by 2/6 and get 3/2 or 1 ½. If we look at it as an area model, what we have is that 1/3 can fit into ½, 1 ½ times (see figure below). This is a measurement division model, where we are measuring off the unit of 1/3 to see how many will fit into ½ (see Figure 8.4).

Apply and extend previous understandings of multiplication and division.

CCSS.Math.Content.5.NF.B.7.c

Solve real-world problems involving division of unit fractions by nonzero whole numbers and division of whole numbers by unit fractions, for example, using visual fraction models and equations to represent the problem. *For example, how much chocolate will each person get if 3 people share 1/2 lb of chocolate equally? How many 1/3-cup servings are in 2 cups of raisins?*

Providing contexts for division of fractions helps students to

interpret and compute quotients of fractions, and solve word problems involving division of fractions by fractions, e.g., by using visual fraction models and equations to represent

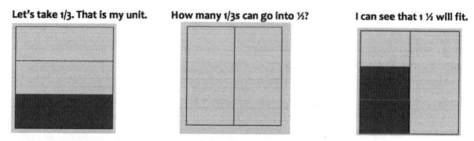

Figure 8.4 Modeling division of fractions using the area model. *Source*: Authors.

the problem. *For example, create a story context for (2/3) ÷ (3/4) and use a visual fraction model to show the quotient; use the relationship between multiplication and division to explain that (2/3) ÷ (3/4) = 8/9 because 3/4 of 8/9 is 2/3. (In general, (a/b) ÷ (c/d) = ad/bc.) How much chocolate will each person get if 3 people share 1/2 lb of chocolate equally? How many 3/4-cup servings are in 2/3 of a cup of yogurt? How wide is a rectangular strip of land with length 3/4 mi and area 1/2 square mi?* (CCSSM 6th grade, p. 42)

In the following lesson study vignette, we zoom in on a lesson on dividing fractions. Through this, we collected evidence of a common challenge with the concept of unitizing fractions.

Mathematics educators have emphasized a constructivist approach to teaching fractions instead of a procedure-focused approach (Bruner, 1986; Glasersfeld, 1990; Schoenfeld, 1985). The latter is based on the invert-and-multiply algorithm that is generally more efficient (Bergen, 1966; Capps, 1962; Krich, 1964) and leads to an algebraic thinking. However, this approach is often confusing for students and results in memorization of the procedure without actual understanding of the concept (Capps, 1962; Elashhab, 1978; McMeen, 1962; Siebert & Gaskin, 2006).

On the other hand, a constructivist approach provides students with an opportunity to build their understanding of the concept as a result of their own learning experience (Bruner, 1986; Glasersfeld, 1990; Schoenfeld, 1985). To reach this goal, students are encouraged to invent their own ways of approaching a problem by working in small groups or individually and discussing their thinking processes with each other (Flores & Priewe, 2013). Afterward, having conceptual knowledge, students are more likely to make sense of procedures when dividing fractions (Carpenter, 1986).

Mathematical ideas can be represented enactively (concrete representations), iconically (pictorial representations), and symbolically (written symbols) (Cramer & Wyberg, 2009). Manipulatives as concrete materials are used to help students build mental representations, which in turn prompts them to think abstractly (Cramer & Wyberg, 2009). Pictures work in similar way (Siebert & Gaskin, 2006). Concrete and pictorial representations are especially useful when teaching division of fractions. Students might use the measurement interpretation of division while solving the problem or repeated subtraction in order to make sense of the concept (Flores & Priewe, 2013).

Research on teaching division of fractions reveals a number of misconceptions students tend to have while learning the concept. The main misconception is a lack of understanding of what the whole is and how the whole as a candy is different from the whole as a serving (Flores & Priewe, 2013). As a result, students are confused about how to interpret the reminder (Flores & Priewe, 2013), which in turn causes inability to communicate when students try to discuss their work.

8.4   LESSON STUDY VIGNETTE: SHARE MY CANDY

Text Box 8.2   A Math Happening 8b: Share My Candy

Jason has 3½ candy bars. He wants to share the candy bars with his friends. He gives as many of his friends as possible ¾ of a candy bar. He keeps the rest for himself.

Part A: How many friends can he give ¾ of a candy bar to?

Part B: How much of the candy bar will Jason keep for himself?

Part C: How does Jason's portion compare with his friend's portion?

Explain your thinking for each part.

The following lesson was delivered in a multi-grade lesson study team of fifth-through seventh-grade teachers. One of the ways, a seventh-grade teacher tried to motivate her students to consider the various interpretations for fractions: she posed the question of what candy they like and then talked about how each could be used to form a fraction (see Figure 8.5).

She then introduced the task called "Share My Candy."

Jason has 3 ½ candy bars. He wants to share the candy bars with his friends. He gives as many of his friends as possible ¾ of a candy bar and keeps the rest for himself.

1. How many friends can he give ¾ of a candy bar to?
2. How much of the candy bar will Jason keep for himself?
3. How does Jason's portion compare with his friends' portion?
4. Use words, pictures and numbers to show your work.

Students were quick to draw or to turn the mixed number and fraction into decimals and use division. The teacher asked if they could use the tiles or construction paper to make manipulatives to solve the problem another way without using division with decimals. Using poster proofs, the teacher asked students to publish their thinking (see Figures 8.6 and 8.7).

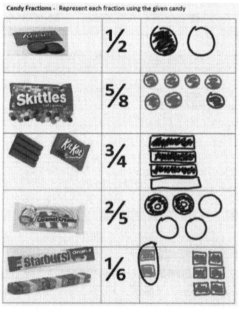

Figure 8.5 Different ways to illustrate fractions.

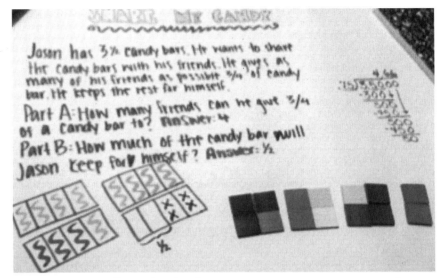

Figure 8.6   Using color tiles as chocolate bars.

Figure 8.7   Student using decimals to make sense of dividing by a fraction. *Source*: Authors.

Again, in the student sample (Figure 8.6), students in this group were quick to convert to decimals and use division. They answered 4 friends after arriving at the answer 4.66. In the candy bar (Figure 8.7), this group chose to split the bars into twelve pieces making the work slightly more challenging, but they successfully split the candy and realized that Jason would have ½ of a candy bar left for himself. The class had a nice discussion about the answer for Jason's portion of ½ of a candy bar. No group ever mentioned ⅔ as a good analysis of Jason's portion in comparison to his friends' portions.

The teacher pointed to one group's drawings of the portions and asked the class, "What fraction of each friend's portion does Jason have for himself?" Asking in that way as students looked at the drawings helped them to see that Jason had ⅔ of the serving size. With that connection, the class revisited the division of decimals and could see the connection to this answer and the 4.66; it's 4 and ⅔ portions!! Using multiple representations (manipulatives, pictures, numbers) allowed for teachers to assess students' level of understanding.

Table 8.1 below maps out the conversations teachers had about Share My Candy problem and the learning progressions in fraction related to this problem. Having a vertical team of teachers also offered opportunities to think about the Share My Candy problem and consider ways they could differentiate this problem to extend the conceptual understanding of operations with fractions.

Table 8.1   Learning progressions across vertical-grade bands for Share My Candy

Learning Progressions across Vertical Grade Bands		
Grades 3-4	Grades 5-6	Grades 7-8
Students are not asked to make the connection between 2/3 of a share and ½ of a candy bar.	Students are prompted to make the connection between 2/3 of a share and ½ of a candy bar, but not expected to make it.	Students were asked to explain/debate: When they drew a picture they got "4 ½" When they "Did the math" Why is there a difference? $1/2$ candy bar vs. $2/3$ serving size
Extensions:		
Ask students to create a similar problem utilizing fractions and any food item. Have students see if they can even out the portions between Jason and his friends. Ask how much each student would get if all children shared the candy bar equally.		

8.5   TEACHING STRATEGIES: STRATEGY MAPPING ON THE BOARD PLAN

Text Box 8.3   A Math Happening 8c: The Turtle Race

Torty the turtle can travel 2/3 of a mile in 1 hour. How long will it take to travel 6 miles?

In a research lesson called the Turtle Race, teachers were asked to anticipate strategies students would use to solve the problem. In Japanese Lesson Study, the board plan from the lesson plan shows how the teachers expect they will select and sequence the sharing of the anticipated strategies. Typically, when teachers plan the sequences of the different strategies, they have specific agenda in mind. For example, they may sequence the strategies based on concrete to abstract such as an algebraic lesson that starts off from strategies that use pictures to numbers, tables and then abstracting from the computation to formulate a rule. Or other times, it could be the very opposite to show how an algebraic approach would be more complicated and perhaps unnecessary because a pictorial approach is more efficient and elegant.

A major goal for this unit was for students to conceptualize ways of thinking about division with fractions. In particular, we wanted students to consider how a common-denominator method for dividing fractions might be embedded within physical models of division situations. In this lesson specifically, students began to explore measurement contexts for dividing a whole number by a fraction. Our goal was for students to develop a way of solving the story problem presented in a way that made sense to them. There were some key ideas that preceded this work:

1. Both sharing and measuring problems can be modeled by division
2. In dealing with "leftovers," we can ask either "what fraction of a group is left" or "what fraction of an item will be in each group"?
3. A divided by B is the same as A/B

On the teachers' plan, the strategy map showed several paths students could take. A popular solution they named the **linear (number line) model** would begin with an open number line marked from 0 to 6 miles. Students would mark off 2/3 mile at a time, and count how many "2/3s" it took to get to the end (9 hours). They hoped that students would keep counting on by 2/3s until they got to 6 or 18/3. Then to know how many hours, students count how many 2/3s they have in 6 (see Figure 8.8).

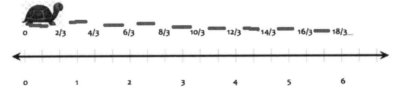

Figure 8.8   Using a number line.

Another model students might use would be 6 discrete circles or rectangles, since some students are accustomed to using fraction manipulatives to think about parts of a whole. These students are likely to use a similar strategy of marking off 2/3 at a time but using a **region model**.

They might mark 2/3 as [|] and see how many units of 2/3 would fit or write in numbers

to keep track of hours.

| 1 | 1 | 2 | | 2 | 3 | 3 | | 4 | 4 | 5 | | 5 | 6 | 6 | | 7 | 7 | 8 | | 8 | 9 | 9 |

Some students may convert 2/3 to approximately 66% since they have recently done work converting fractions into equivalent forms. This method will not be very useful here since the repeating decimal requires some rounding off and may not make the answer as apparent.

Some students may use a 2-column **ratio table** to keep track of both the hours and the miles

Miles	2/3	4/3	6/3 =2	8/3	10/3	12/3=4	14/3	16/3	18/3=6
hours	1	2	3	4	5	6	7	8	9

They considered that some students may use what they called **reasoning up or down** to notice that if 2/3 miles is 1 hour then 1/3 mile = 30 min and think back up to 1 mile = 90 min (or 3/2 hours or 1.5 hours) and multiply 3/2 × 6 miles. This way of thinking most closely resembles the traditional "invert-and-multiply" method.

Students may also use what they know about multiplication of fractions and think 2/3 × (some number of hours) = 6 miles. Students may use a guess and revise strategy to figure out what you could multiply by 2/3 to get 6. They called this is the **missing factor method.**

After drawing models, some students may reflect on their work as 18 thirds divided by 2 thirds = 9 thirds or 18/3 divided by 2/3 = 9.

When asked to write a number sentence to match their work, students may write several equations:

$$2/3 + 2/3 + \ldots = 6$$

$$9 \times 2/3 = 6$$

If someone finds 3/2 in the model, we may choose to ask the class to examine how this 3/2 relates to the 2/3 in the other methods. If symbolic notation seems difficult, we will listen for kids to articulate their answer as 9 groups of 2/3 (9 × 2/3). Again, this gives us an opportunity to relate the different equations and talk about the relationships between them. If someone identifies the problem as a division story, the student will explain how he/she saw the story that made him/her think it was division.

The teachers discussed that they would leave the number sentences using division as it was generated by students. Ultimately, they wanted to see students who could articulate their thinking of the 6 as 18/3 in order to begin to develop the idea that if the pieces are the same, we can divide the numbers as we would normally in whole-number division. The teachers were interested in what informal knowledge students would rely on. Some questions they planned to ask included as follows:

1. What operation would you say you're using to solve this problem?
2. What number sentence can you write that matches your model?
3. How does this problem compare to the cookie problem we worked on yesterday?
4. What makes this a division problem? (or addition, etc., depending on what students say)
5. Where is your answer in your model? In your number sentence?
6. If students use "invert and multiply," where is the 3/2 in your model?

They also wanted their students to demonstrate their current understanding in their problem-solving strategies and related written explanations. For this lesson, the goal was for students to think about the situation and use a method that made sense to them to solve it. Eventually, they would look to generalize methods and for efficiency, but the day's agenda was to begin this process. After this lesson, they would follow up the lesson by investigating whether similar problems can also be solved by converting both numbers to a common denominator, or by examining a reciprocal relationship, and how to deal with problems whose answers don't result in a whole number.

Using this strategy map, teachers embarked on their research lesson and were surprised by their students. They were surprised that more students didn't draw a linear model given the context. They were also surprised that a boy who was typically not a strong student saw 3/2 in the problem. They noticed some students who were accustomed to working only with symbolic forms struggled more than others who were willing to draw a model.

This lesson reinforced the need to choose carefully who will share their work and to be thoughtful about questions we ask to support student thinking and connections. Teachers had many wonderings as they observed their lessons as they shared during the lesson debrief. They wondered, how would students handle "leftovers"? What if he traveled 9 hours and still had a little distance left to go? Which student methods are generalizable and which have specific purposes? What knowledge is necessary before beginning this work and what is gained as we go along?

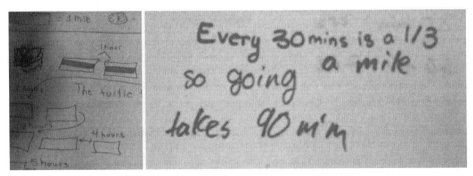

Figure 8.9 Student work showing sensemaking.

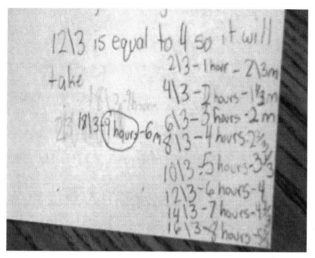

Figure 8.10   Keeping track of the change.

One student modeled discrete thirds and grouped every two together to represent each hour.

The difficult part was keeping track of not only the hours, but also the total miles.

Students in Figure 8.10 found a way to keep track of both the hours and the miles. Teachers felt better prepared to navigate through the classroom discussion because they had participated in the act of anticipating solutions and creating a board plan consisting of their strategy map.

Think about it!

What are all the everyday situations that ratios are used? How can we expose them to our students? Share ideas with your colleagues.

8.6   USE OF STUDENTS' DIVERSITY OF STRATEGIES AS PEDAGOGICAL CONTENT TOOLS

Text Box 8.4   A Math Happening 8d: The Mango Problem

One night, the King couldn't sleep, so he went down into the Royal kitchen, where he found a bowl full of mangoes. Being hungry, he took 1/6 of the mangoes. Later that same night, the Queen was hungry and couldn't sleep. She, too, found the mangoes and took 1/5 of what the King had left. Still later, the Prince awoke, went to the kitchen, and ate 1/4 of the remaining mangoes. Even later, his sister, the Princess, ate 1/3 of what was then left. Finally, the royal dog woke up hungry and ate 1/2 of what was left, leaving only 3 mangoes for the kitchen staff. How many mangoes were originally in the bowl?

One of the research lessons we designed with a group of fourth- through eighth-grade teachers and two math specialists was called the Mango Problem. The problem was rich in that it provided lots of learning opportunity for the students and teachers. *Acting out the problem* was important to be sure the students understood and could visualize the problem. Students were given independent time so that all students could "own" the problem by making sense of the problem first. In addition, we wanted to assess how individuals were making sense or experiencing misconceptions before the group conversation.

Some of the students encountered this problem with the mental model of thinking of fractional parts of the mango as a "region model" and ran into problems when they arrived at the last part of the problem where "*1/2 of what was left, leaving only 3 mangoes.*" This problem requires students to have a more sophisticated understanding of fraction including the "set model" and unitizing.

A seventh-grade teacher who retaught this lesson after the first cycle, reflected on how for an older group of students, the students did not have the same misconceptions as the fourth graders who were beginning to understand the multiple meanings of fractions. This illustrated that the task had an important mathematical agenda embedded in the problem, which was the understanding of unitizing fractions.

I believe many of the 4th graders viewed fractional pieces as 1 whole as opposed to a unitized whole. The 7th and 8th graders had understood the notion of a unitized whole. (Sonny, 7th and 8th grade teacher)

Second, teachers became more intentional about monitoring students' thinking so that they could use student strategies or representations as pedagogical tools for classroom discourse. In the professional development, we focused on how teachers can use tools like student artifacts and representations (diagrams, manipulative models, small group discussions, and numeric notations) to discuss important mathematical ideas. Some nameable strategies included:

Text Box 8.5   Nameable Discourse Moves to Highlight Student Thinking

Discourse Moves:

1. *Connecting*: making connections among representations;
2. *Marking*: marking critical features, which the students should pay attention to;
3. *Directing*: keeping students on task and encouraged to persist;
4. *Extending*: Pressing on for justification;
5. *Clarifying*: clarifying to work through misconceptions/partial understanding
6. *Zooming in and zooming out*: making generalizations.

While planning and anticipating student strategies, teachers noted in their lesson plan that one of the important ideas for *marking* was to look for students making 6 equal groups with 3 mangoes in each group. In addition, teachers would *mark* for students who thought about multiples of 3s or 6s since 3 was the remaining mangos in each group and 6 was the number of groups. *Finally*, they noted that students would need to realize that the amount that was taken was the same portion each time.

The important idea was to see if students were able to unitize by constructing a reference unit.

Teachers noticed that tools can help or hinder the interpretation during the problem-solving process. The tool was only helpful if the learner could attach meaning or match their mental interpretation with the physical manipulatives. From the first cycle, teachers noticed how offering students' access to multiple manipulatives actually hindered their thinking. In the previous excerpt, a student had success with connecting cubes, using it to "chunk" the portion taken by each of the characters. However, there were some students who chose fraction circles and had a difficult time because they could not take their mental picture of 3 remaining mangoes and see they fit into the fraction circles.

They wanted the fraction circles to represent the 3 mangoes remaining in the bowl and the fractional parts that the characters took out of the bowl but did not see how 3 discrete mangos could be represented by a region of the fraction circle. After observing the first research lesson, one of the observers, another fourth-grade teacher decided to experiment by limiting the number of manipulatives to see how students would represent their thinking with the available tools, but wondered whether it would limit some students. Another teacher who taught the lesson to their own classroom decided to allow students to draw their own pictures to represent their own mental images of the problem and found that students were more successful. In their diagrams, teachers noticed how students showed their understanding of unitizing.

One of the observers of the research lesson who retaught the lesson in her own classroom decided to introduce a related problem called the People on the Bus problem, where a fractional portion of the riders got off the bus. This is a classic problem where drawing a picture is more elegant than a formula

> At some stop, 2/5 of the people got off the bus and 3/5 of the original number got on. At the second stop, 1/2 of the people got off and 1/3 of the number that were left on the bus got on. At the last stop ¾ of the people got off, leaving 5 people on the bus. How many people were on the bus before the bus reached the first stop?

Teachers' ability to experiment through multiple research lessons allowed for us to conclude that good problem solvers who have a strong grasp will have versatile mental models to represent the problem whether it is through their own drawings or manipulatives. That is, while some struggled to model the problem with fraction circles, others who had an understanding of unitizing fraction were able to represent each fractional piece as a unit of 3 mangoes and could model their thinking. It wasn't so much the choice of manipulative, rather the types of mental models students had of fractions that allowed them to be effective with manipulatives and other tools for thinking.

One teacher noted that students, who were correct in their thinking and modeling of the mango problem, whether abstractly or concretely, were very confident that they were right. Their models matched, or proved, their thinking. However, students who were incorrect in their solutions were typically dissatisfied with their models as if something was missing that they were unable to explain. And these latter students felt their results were unreasonable or the results lacked adequate proof, so they were confident that they were wrong. However, these students were unable to explain why

First stop: 2/5 gets off

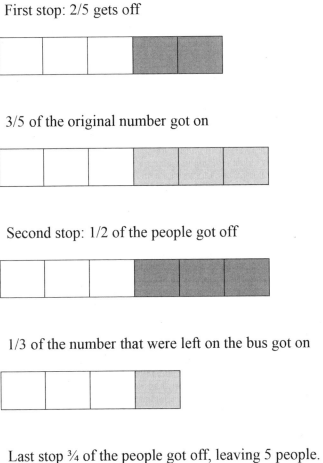

3/5 of the original number got on

Second stop: 1/2 of the people got off

1/3 of the number that were left on the bus got on

Last stop ¾ of the people got off, leaving 5 people.

5

left

So originally,

Figure 8.11 Worked examples of the "People on the Bus" problem.

their solution was wrong. To extend students' thinking, the teacher asked students to share their responses within a group and then each group explained their approach to the problem to the class.

The teacher sequenced their work for display and discussion starting with concrete models, followed by the logical backward design model, then to the guess and check which could be more abstract. The class discussed the connections and differences between each of the three strategies as well as their efficiency and effectiveness. Since the clear and explicit learning goal was to get students to unitize the mangoes so that 1 unit = 3 mangoes, students who engaged in the backward design and the concrete strategy of drawing out models that displayed the unit seemed to arrive at the correct conclusion with greater efficiency and understanding than the guess-and-check method. The effective use of questioning and mathematics discourse in the classroom allowed students' strategic competence to take center stage and moved more students along understanding the efficient and advanced strategies for the problem using multiple models.

8.7   TECHNOLOGY INTEGRATION IN PROBLEM SOLVING

In this section, we see how one can employ technology to enhance the understanding of multiplication of fractions. Consider the multiplication of the fractions 3/4 and 2/9. Each of these fractions may be represented as shown in the tool in Figure 8.12. Note that students can try other fractions using the dropdown box provided. The left square has four partitions three of which are shaded indicating the fraction 3/4 and the square on the right shows two out of nine horizontal sections shaded indicating the fraction 2/9.

Pressing the "multiply" pushbutton then yields an animation of the two boxes indicated move toward each other and form one overlapping square with the respective partitions in the horizontal and vertical directions.

Note that the common overlap consists of six red squares out of a total of 36 which is the result of multiplying the two fractions. Note that the ratio 6/36 simplifies to 1/6 and this can be done by pressing the "change grid" option which yields:

To make the 1/6 more accessible to students, the technology also allows them to move the individual cells, for example, as follows.

For more practice with the technology tool, the students may be encouraged to visit: http://completecenter.gmu.edu/java/multiplication/index.html.

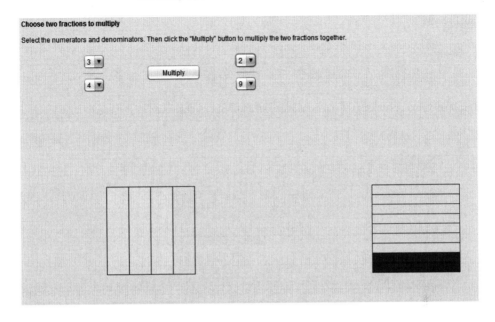

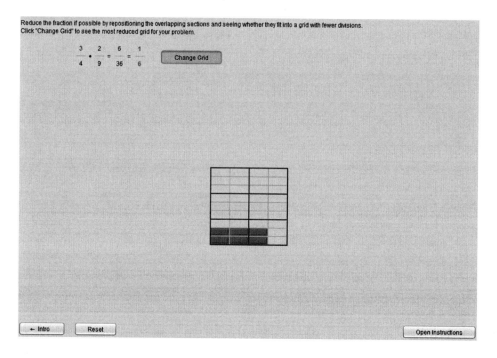

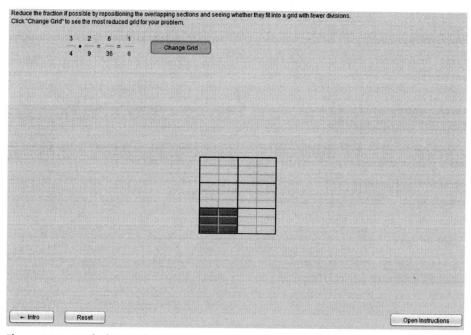

Figure 8.12 Worked example illustrating the steps for multiplying fractions using the area model.

8.8 MORE RELATED RICH PROBLEMS TO EXPLORE

1. There are 4 people sharing 5 cookies. How can you share them so everyone gets a fair share?

2. The PE teacher uses 3/5 of his basketballs in class. Half of the remaining balls are given to students for recess. What fraction of all the basketballs is given to students for recess?

3. Show why $\frac{2}{3} \times \frac{1}{5}$ is the same as $\frac{2}{5} \times \frac{1}{3}$ pictorially.

4. Explain why $3 \div \frac{2}{3}$ is the same as 4 ½ .

5. Kramer spent ½ of his money on rent this month. He spent ¼ of his remaining money on groceries. What fraction of his money did Kramer spend altogether?

6. Nancy made 400 muffins. She sold $\frac{3}{5}$ of them before noon and $\frac{1}{4}$ of the reminder in afternoon. How many muffins did she sell in the afternoon?

7. John wants to order pizza for 18 employees. Each employee should get ¼ of a pizza. How many pizzas should John order? And how much pizza will be left over?

8. One sixth of the paintings Jim has in his gallery are from South America, one third are from Asia and two-fifths of the remainder are from Europe. If he has 12 paintings from Europe, then how many more paintings from Asia than from South American does he have?

9. Kelly has 3/4 yard of ribbon. She wanted to use it to decorate two picture frames. If she uses half the ribbon on each frame, how many feet of ribbon will she use for one frame? Explain your thinking using a suitable model.

10. Jim's height is 2/3 of Libby's height while Libby's height is 3/4 of Laura's height. If Laura is 160 cm tall, then find Jim's height?

Chapter 9

Modeling Math Ideas with Ratio and Proportional Reasoning

Doug's bathtub, when full will drain in 12 minutes. The hot water tap takes 6 minutes to fill the tub and the cold water tap takes 4 minutes to fill the tub. If Doug opens both taps but forget to put in the drain plug, in how many minutes will the tub be filled?

9.1   LESSON STUDY VIGNETTE: THE LEAKY BATHTUB

This rate problem was presented by teachers to their students as part of a lesson study. In their strategies to solve the task, students demonstrated different ways of understanding ratios and a variety of approaches that can be connected to the learning progressions of the CCSSM Standards and to the eight Common Core Standards of Mathematical Practice (MP). This particular task prompted students to think about the relationship of two quantities (the fullness of the bathtub and elapsed time).

The approaches shown in Figure 9.1 began with recognizing and defining the rates involved in this task using rate language 6.RP.1, 6.RP.2, and unit fractions to describe the rates (e.g., 1/6 tub of hot water per minute or 2 gallons of hot water per minute). Recognizing these rates involved looking for structure (MP7), while describing and interpreting the descriptions of the rates involved precise use of language (MP6). The students used the term "per" to state the rates involved in this task reflecting an understanding of the ratios used in this problem. Participants built on this understanding to structure tables and create visual representations to examine the relationships between the quantities in the task (see Figure 9.1).

One of the groups solved the problem by assigning 12 as the total number of gallons that the tub would hold, and used all whole numbers. They created a model using unifix cubes to show that 5 units in (2 units of hot water plus 3 units of cold water), minus 1 unit out is a net of 4 units coming into the tub per minute. Participants tried to make connections between this and 5/12 in, minus 1/12 out are 4/12 in. Another group was able to recognize the proportional relationship between the fullness of the

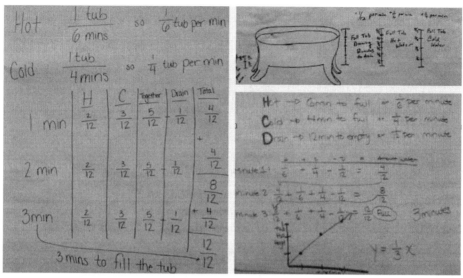

Figure 9.1   Teachers anticipated possible student strategies for the Leaky Bathtub lesson. *Source*: Authors.

bathtub and the elapsed time and represents this relationship with an equation in the form of $y = cx$ where c is the constant of proportionality [7.RP.A.2, 7.RP.A.2.C]. For this task, the equation was $y = 1/3x$, where $c = 1/3$.

This group used the strategy of representing the relationship as a unit ratio [6.RPP.B, 6.RP.A.3.B] and provided multiple representations connecting the structure of the problem with a table, a graph, and an equation. One group, which jumped immediately to using a formula (*rate x time*), struggled to make connections and find a solution for this task. Throughout the process of solving this problem, students demonstrated an ability to use reasoning with rates to solve real-world and mathematical problems. [6.RP.A.3] above are some samples of the anticipated work from the lesson study.

9.2   ZOOMING IN ON THE LEARNING PROGRESSIONS ON PROPORTIONAL REASONING

Among the many topics in the middle-school curriculum, one of the most prominent areas that are conceptually rich and mathematically sophisticated, yet difficult to teach as well as learn is fractions and their counterparts, namely ***ratios and proportions***. The difficulty lies in interpreting the *meaning of rational numbers,* which requires explanations through connections with other mathematical knowledge, various representations, and/or real-world contexts. Often students do not realize that they have been exposed to fractions in their everyday activities long before they were formally instructed in school. An essential understanding of ratios and proportions is the notion that as one quantity in a proportional relationship changes, so does the other quantity—and by the same factor.

"We use *ratio* to mean the comparison of two quantities, and we define *proportion* as an equivalence relationship between two ratios." PEU p. 115

In grades 3–5, students build on their understanding of creating equal groups and partitioning groups into smaller groups of equal size as a foundation for the multiplicative understanding necessary for working with rational numbers and ratios. Students in these grades also investigate situations in which it is appropriate to use partitioning and create equal-sized groups and situations in which it is not. In grades 6–8, students extend this reasoning to contexts that involve a constant rate, such as situations that involve equal rates of speed, the cost of an item per particular unit, and scale models or drawings. Further, students learn to use ratios to convert measurement units and transform units. (p. 117)

Oftentimes, there is a big gap between constructed knowledge that students bring to the classroom and the instructed knowledge that the teachers try to deliver. Students who are mathematically proficient make the connections between the two bodies of knowledge and students that do not understand may never make this connection. Mathematical modeling is one way to achieve these connections.

Teaching proportional reasoning through mathematical modeling and problem solving requires depth of mathematical knowledge for teaching that includes understanding of general content and the domain-specific knowledge of students. Clearly, a solid understanding of proportional reasoning is requisite for moving from elementary grades on to more complex problem solving in the intermediate and higher grades; else, as students' progress from one mathematics course to another, some can get deeply and profoundly lost.

Although it is possible to pick up virtually any chapter in a history book and learn something new, without a strong mathematical foundation of proportional reasoning, an advanced chapter of mathematics could be totally incomprehensible to a student who is unfamiliar with, uncomfortable with, or fearful of the concepts. Because an understanding of proportional reasoning is foundational and the risk of frustration is high, there is a need for mathematics teachers who can ably explain these topics and who themselves have a deep conceptual understanding of them. Noting the difficulties of both learning and teaching mathematics topics that involve multiplicative structures, Lamon (2007) suggests:

> Of all the topics in the school curriculum, fractions, ratios and proportions arguably hold the distinction of being the most protracted in terms of development, the most difficult to teach, the most mathematically complex, the most cognitively challenging, the most essential to success in high mathematics and science, and one of the most compelling research sites.

Our traditional teaching for computational ability, Lamon (2007) contends, has left us pedagogically bankrupt for an age that values connections and meaning, and requires innovative pedagogy. In order for students to make connections, they need to abandon the rote plug-and-play scenario of implementing a formula and rise to levels of comprehension that would enable them to understand why a certain formula or procedure should be used and the inherent relations between multiple representations (see Figure 9.2).

Figure 9.2 Multiple representations in understanding proportional reasoning. *Source*: Authors.

Proportional Reasoning is fundamental to many important mathematical concepts and is often regarded as the pathway to performing well in algebra (Confrey & Smith, 1995; Lobato & Ellis, 2010). This topic is difficult for most students, especially for those who do not understand what is actually meant by a specific proportional situation or why a given solution methodology works (Cramer & Post, 1993). Teachers have also been urged to focus students' attention on the meaning of problems and to help students' value different mathematically correct solutions to a single problem (NCTM, 1989, 1991, 2000). There is still a great need for research in evaluating the effect of solving one proportional situation via multiple solution strategies for example using "unit rate strategy; repeated subtraction strategy; equivalent fractions strategy; size-change strategy; cross-multiplication using equal rates or ratios strategy, relative and absolute thinking strategy and; reasoning up and down strategy" (Lamon, 2007).

Students use proportional reasoning in early math learning, for example, when they think of the number 10 as two fives or five twos rather than thinking of it as one more than nine. This is an essential part of developmental step for students to transition from additive to multiplicative reasoning (Kent, Arnosky & McMonagle, 2002; Sowder et al., 1998). Although additive reasoning can develop intuitively, multiplicative (proportional) reasoning is difficult for students to develop and often requires formal instruction. It requires reasoning about several ideas or quantities simultaneously. It requires thinking about situations in relative rather than absolute terms. For example, if the number of students in a middle school grows from 500 to 800 and

Text Box 9.2   Common Core State Standards for Mathematics for Proportional Reasoning (NGA Center and CCSSO, 2010)

Sixth grade
Understand ratio concepts and use ratio reasoning to solve problems.

CCSS.Math.Content.6.RP.A.1
Understand the concept of a ratio and use ratio language to describe a ratio relationship between two quantities. *For example, "The ratio of wings to beaks in the bird house at the zoo was 2:1, because for every 2 wings there was 1 beak." "For every vote candidate A received, candidate C received nearly three votes."*

CCSS.Math.Content.6.RP.A.2
Understand the concept of a unit rate a/b associated with a ratio a:b with b ≠ 0, and use rate language in the context of a ratio relationship. *For example, "This recipe has a ratio of 3 cups of flour to 4 cups of sugar, so there is 3/4 cup of flour for each cup of sugar." "We paid $75 for 15 hamburgers, which is a rate of $5 per hamburger."*

CCSS.Math.Content.6.RP.A.3
Use ratio and rate reasoning to solve real-world and mathematical problems, for example, by reasoning about tables of equivalent ratios, tape diagrams, double number line diagrams, or equations.

7th grade
Analyze proportional relationships and use them to solve real-world and mathematical problems.

CCSS.Math.Content.7.RP.A.1
Compute unit rates associated with ratios of fractions, including ratios of lengths, areas, and other quantities measured in like or different units. *For example, if a person walks 1/2 mile in each 1/4 hour, compute the unit rate as the complex fraction $^{1/2}/_{1/4}$ miles per hour, equivalently 2 miles per hour.*

CCSS.Math.Content.7.RP.A.2
Recognize and represent proportional relationships between quantities.

CCSS.Math.Content.7.RP.A.3
Use proportional relationships to solve multistep ratio and percent problems. Examples: simple interest, tax, markups and markdowns, gratuities and commissions, fees, percent increase and decrease, percent error.

another middle school grows from 300 to 600, a student thinking in absolute terms (or additively) might answer that both schools had the same amount of increase.

On the other hand, a student that is trained to think in relative terms might argue that the second middle school saw *more* increase since it doubled the number of students unlike the first school who would have needed to be 1000 students to grow by the same relative amount. While both answers seem reasonable, it is the relative multiplicative thinking that is essential for proportional reasoning. This ability to think and reason proportionally is very important in the development of a student's ability to understand and apply mathematics. It is estimated that over 90% of students who enter high school cannot reason well enough to learn mathematics and science with understanding and are unprepared for real applications in statistics, biology, geography, or physics (Lamon, 2001).

While students may be able to solve a proportion problem with a rote algorithm, this does not mean that they can think proportionally. Therefore, it is essential for mathematics teachers to (a) understand how students develop multiplicative (and proportional) reasoning, (b) build on students' prior knowledge of concepts such as multiplication and division of whole numbers to strengthen students' proportional reasoning, and (c) develop learning environments, contexts and experiences for students that encourage multiplicative comparisons to prepare them for higher-level mathematics topics involving proportional reasoning.

The CCSSM (NGA Center % CCSSO, 2010) expects an instructional emphasis on ratio and rate concepts in grades six and seven. CCSSM indicates that grade six students should "understand ratio concepts and use ratio reasoning to solve problems" (p. 42), with a focus on using ratio and rate language in the context of ratio relationships to understand these relationships and conceptualize a unit rate associated with a ratio (see Text Box 9.2).

9.3   VISIBLE THINKING IN MATH: USING REPRESENTATIONAL MODELS FOR PROPORTIONAL REASONING

The CCSSM (NGA Center and CCSSO, 2010) recommend the use of representations to illustrate the concept of ratio and rate reasoning.

> CCSS.Math.Content.6.RP.A.3: Use ratio and rate reasoning to solve real-world and mathematical problems, for example, by reasoning about tables of equivalent ratios, tape diagrams, double number line diagrams, or equations.

Here are some examples of the use of tables of equivalent ratios, tape or bar diagrams, double number line diagrams, or equations.

Back to School Shopping

The cost of 3 notebooks is $2.40. At the same price, how much will 10 notebooks cost?

=$2.40

Students might think that means each notebook is $0.80 since 2.40/3 = .80 and .80 * 10 is $8.00. Or some might consider, 3 * $2.40 = $7.20 which gives me 9 notebooks and I need one more, which is +$0.80 that totals to $8.00.

Sprinting Problem

Mary's best time for running 100 yards is 15 seconds. How long will it take Mary to run 500 yards?

A potential way to approach this is to reason up to go from 100 yards to 500 yards directly and notice the answer is five times the time taken for 15 seconds. It may also be easier to reason up to 1000 yards as students are comfortable multiplying by 10 which yields 150 seconds and then noticing 500 yards is just half of 1000 yards suggest reasoning down or halving 150 seconds.

Track Problem

Sue and Julie were running at the same speed around a track. Sue started first. When she had run 9 laps, Julie had run 3 laps. When Julie completed 15 laps, how many laps had Sue run? (See Table 9.1, Cramer, Post, & Currier, 1993)

Notice the similarity to the last problem. Most students attempt this by writing an equation that is obtained by "cross-multiplication." In reality, noticing that Julie completed 15 laps that is five times should immediately tell us how many laps Sue completed. Of course, there is something implicit in the problem which is not stated directly that is the two runners are running at uniform rates. This is important to solve the problem via proportional reasoning.

In grades 6–8, proportional reasoning problems may be broadly classified into three modeling approaches: (a) Quantitative Proportional Reasoning (QPR); (b) Algebraic Proportional Reasoning (APR) and; (c) Spatial Proportional Reasoning (SPR). Next, we describe the specific mathematics content through benchmark examples developed as a part each of the three modules (QPR, APR, SPR) mentioned earlier.

QPR Module: This module refers to the content knowledge needed to compare and order rational numbers presented in multiple representations including integers, percentages, positive and negative fractions, and decimals. Topics in QPR often focus on fractions and divisions; additions and subtraction of like and unlike fractions; addition and subtraction of mixed numbers; multiplying fractions by whole numbers; fraction of a set; product of fractions; dividing fractions by a whole number; dividing by a fraction. This module also helps to choose and employ appropriate operations to solve real-world applications involving rational numbers. The content developed through QPR can then be applied to concepts in probability to make predictions and decisions. Consider the following benchmark example of Sam and his wife on the next page.

The pictorial technique presented in this example is one of the many ways to become comfortable reasoning and talking about parts of discrete quantities. Note that the problem not only brings out the importance of the concept of "a unit" but they also help guide proportional reasoning. Once this concept is mastered such effective pictorial techniques provide an opportunity to apply them to a variety of related questions which teachers can later supplement in their traditional classroom.

Table 9.1   Number of laps around a track

Sue	Julie
9	3
X	15

Example: *Sam gave* $\frac{2}{5}$ *of his money to his wife and spent* $\frac{1}{2}$ *of the remainder. If he had $300*

left, how much money did he have at first?

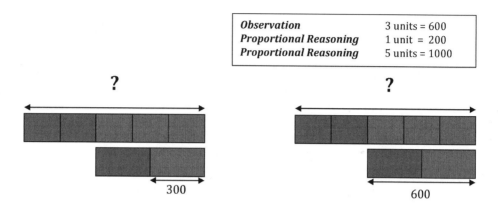

Observation	3 units = 600
Proportional Reasoning	1 unit = 200
Proportional Reasoning	5 units = 1000

For example, consider the following multiple-choice question from a grade 8 classroom:

Apple juice concentrate is mixed with water to make apple juice. Which final mixture has the highest percentage of apple juice concentrate?

F. 400 mL apple juice concentrate mixed with 600 mL water
G. 400 mL apple juice concentrate mixed with 400 mL water
H. 300 mL apple juice concentrate mixed with 600 mL water
I. 300 mL apple juice concentrate mixed with 400 mL water

APR Module: This module involves employing strategies to compare and contrast proportional and nonproportional linear relationships. Topics in APR also estimate and determine solutions to application problems involving percent, decimals, and other proportional relationships such as similarity, ratios, and rates. One important focus, herein, includes making connections among various representations of a numerical relationship such as tabular, graphical, pictorial, verbal, and algebraic equations. In particular, the APR module gives an opportunity to predict and justify solutions to application problems through a variety of strategies including proportional reasoning.

As the algebraic habits of mind evolve, students must be constantly taught to effectively communicate mathematical ideas using language efficient tools, appropriate units, and graphical, numerical, physical or algebraic mathematical models.

John bought a piece of land next to the land he owns. Now John has 25% more land than he did originally. John plans to give 20% of his new, larger amount of land to his daughter. Once John does this, how much land will John have in comparison to the amount he had originally?

This benchmark problem gives an opportunity to help the students to determine the percent increase or decrease for a given situation. This problem is also an example of a

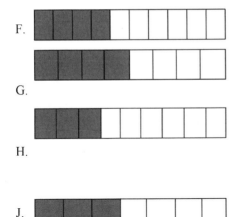

F.

G.

H.

J.

Approach: To answer this, one may be able to illustrate the pictorial approach using "1 unit = 100 ml" in each case as follows clearly illustrating the answer.

common misconception that leads to an incorrect solution. Most students believe that if there is percent increase followed by a percent decrease of the same amount (or vice versa), the answer returns back to the original amount.

To help them understand their misconception, one strategy is to start with 100 units of land as the original piece of land. A 25% increase would be the same as 1.25 (100) = 125 units of land. Now John plans to give 20% of his new piece of land which will leave him with 80% of the new piece of land. This is the same as 0.8 (125) = 100 units of land. One can also see this using the pictorial approach.

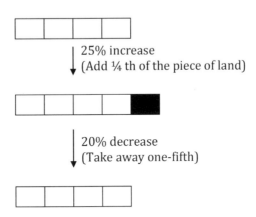

25% increase
(Add ¼ th of the piece of land)

20% decrease
(Take away one-fifth)

SPR Module: Along with QPR and APR, a good proportional reasoning curriculum must also develop a spatial sense through transformational geometry exercises. The proportional reasoning can be built through special exercises that will build students' skills to generate similar figures using graph dilations including enlargements and reductions on a coordinate plane. They will also be trained to use proportional relationships in similar two-dimensional figures or similar 3D figures to determine missing measurements. This module will also provide an opportunity to use proportional reasoning to describe and verbalize how changes in dimensions affect linear, area, and volume measures. Consider the following problem that will allow *students to describe how changing one measured attribute of the figure affects the volume and surface area.*

Example: Given a rectangular prism with a length of 2, a width of 2, and a height of 1:

1. Without changing the length and width, change the height by a factor of n and create a table showing volume for increasing values of n.
2. Write in words the pattern you observe in the volumes.
3. Write an algebraic function for the pattern.
4. Without changing length and height, change the width by a factor of n and create a table showing volume for increasing values of n.

N	Volume
1	
2	
3	
.	
.	
.	

5. Write in words the pattern you observe in the volumes.
6. Write an algebraic function for the pattern.
7. Is the pattern in (iii) the same and why?
8. Without changing the length, change the height and the width by a factor of n and create a table showing volume for increasing values of n.
9. Write in words the pattern you observe in the volumes.
10. Write an algebraic function for the pattern.
11. Write a function to predict the volume if all three dimension change by a factor of n.
12. Repeat all the steps (i)–(xi) for calculating "surface area" instead of "volume."

This exercise can help build spatial reasoning related to change in one dimension versus two dimensions and the effect of varying dimensions on volume and surface area. This activity also helps to explore patterns and discover the relationship between linear ratios, area ratios, and volume ratios.

At a summer institute focused on proportional reasoning, teachers made connections to solving real-world problems [6.RP.A.3]. They were shown packages of 100-calorie snacks, given cereal and asked to show 100 calories of their favorite cereal. Figure 9.3 shows how one teacher illustrated the solution in multiple ways.

Teachers working together helped each other appreciate multiple strategies. One of the teachers commented, "I am so comfortable with mental math and using numbers. I find it hard to think in terms of manipulatives and pictures but seeing how other teachers solved it using these tools really helped me see how my students might approach it. I can truly see the value of hands-on manipulatives for my math students." Other teachers shared, "Today using a ratio table, Karen showed me how to 'pull apart' a ratio so that I could manipulate it more easily." Through the experience of relearning mathematics through multiple models, teachers felt more confident and more "strategically competent" using multiple models and posing rich proportional reasoning problems in class with their students.

The task of the teachers is therefore to help students connect their constructed knowledge to the powerful new ideas that they want to teach them. This, combined

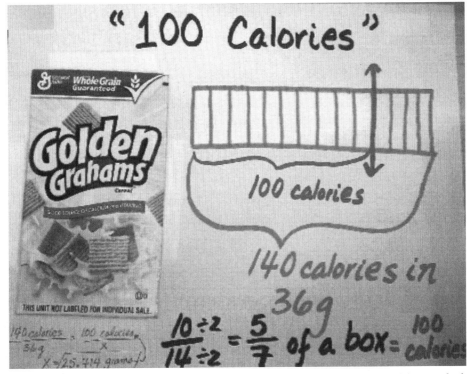

Figure 9.3 100-calorie cereal portions using pictorial approach for the unitizing method. *Source*: Authors.

with the Common Core Standards, creates a great need to enhance teachers' mathematics content and pedagogical knowledge with a special focus on modeling proportional reasoning. It is also essential to understand how these standards translate into classroom practices and assessment strategies. With a growing population of students identified as economically disadvantaged, LEP, and special needs in many school divisions across the nation, teachers need to be proficient in presenting mathematical ideas visually and through multiple representations.

Think about it!

How do these visual representations (ratio tables, double number lines, bar models) help develop a deeper understanding of proportional reasoning?

9.4 LESSON STUDY VIGNETTE: THE CATHEDRAL PROBLEM

For this lesson study, we decided to focus on one specific problem that was provided to the teachers as an opening problem for the day, the cathedral problem that is adapted from Burns, S. (2003):

Text Box 9.3   A Math Happening 9b: The Cathedral Problem

While building a medieval cathedral, it cost 37 guilders to hire 4 artists and 3 stone-masons, or 33 guilders for 3 artists and 4 stonemasons. What would be the expense of just 1 of each worker?

The following sections include the data analysis of teacher thinking that went into solving this problem. Each group was asked to create a poster representing their solution and each teacher was also asked to reflect on how they participated in the problem-solving process and how they would take this problem back to their class-room to present to their students. Photographs of all of the posters created by the teacher groups of the cathedral problem were taken and arranged in order on the day of completion.

Topics included reasoning up and down, direct and inverse thinking, unitizing, and, ratios and proportional thinking. The data from the posters were analyzed for content, connections between concepts, and any possible differences related to the time already spent in the seminar. Data were also analyzed from the teacher reflections for common themes as well as individual perspectives. First, we will present the analysis of the poster artifacts based on what the teachers in the respective groups shared followed by our analysis of the corresponding teacher reflections.

Poster Proofs to Document Visible Thinking

The first group, Figure 9.4 (left), argued that if one artist and one stonemason together made $11, then the total for three of each would be $33. However, they reasoned that because we know that $33 is enough to pay those six workers plus another stonema-son, then one stonemason and one artist must together make less than $11. This group then used the ***guess-and-check method.*** They first assumed that the total for one artist and one stonemason was $8. They tried the combination of $1 for the cost of one art-ist and $7 for the cost of one stonemason ($8 total); however, they discovered that the total for 3 artists and 4 stonemasons was less than the needed $33.

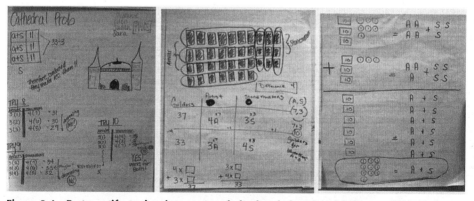

Figure 9.4   Poster artifacts showing guess and check, tabular/pictorial, linear addition. *Source*: Authors.

They tried other combinations but saw that the total cost was decreased; so, they abandoned the idea of an $8 total. They then assumed that the total for one artist and one stonemason was $9. However, their starting guess for the cost of one artist was $2, not $1. They found that the combination of three artists at $3 each and four stonemasons at $6 did total the needed $33. However, when they used these amounts in the second scenario, they found that it did not work: four artists at $3 each and three stonemasons at $6 did not total the needed $37. They then assumed that the total for one artist and one stonemason was $10. Using the same logic, starting at $1 per artist and $9 per stonemason, then $2 per artist and $8 per stonemason, etc., they arrived at a solution of $3 per artist and $7 per stonemason, which they demonstrated would satisfy both requirements.

In all three guess-and-check calculations, they assumed that the artists would earn less than the stonemasons would; so, they arrived at the correct figures for the solutions but had the assignments to the two types of workers backward. They showed that four artists at $3 each and three stonemasons at $7 each would total $33. However, the original question stated that the cost of $33 applied to three artists and four stonemasons. So, although their logic was correct, they made a minor error in the interpretation.

The second group, Figure 9.4 (middle), presented **tabular and pictorial representations** of the two scenarios. There are also several indications that they chose the values of seven and $3 for the costs of the two types of workers, but there is no clear explanation of how they arrived at that conclusion. At the top left of the poster, four rows of seven marks each are made to represent the artists; each group of seven is circled, showing that the cost of each of four artists is $7.

To the right, there are three rows of three marks each, representing that each of three stonemasons earns $3 each. There is no indication that any values other than the correct solution were considered. There is also no indication of exactly how the correct values were calculated. However, at the bottom of the poster, the expressions written seem to indicate that an algebraic solution using two simultaneous equations was employed.

The third group, Figure 9.4 (right), presented a **linear addition solution** using symbols to balance two equations. The top of the poster shows the two scenarios and the bottom of the poster shows the addition of these two. The top left of their poster shows 3 tens (squares) and 7 units (circles) to represent $37. On the right of the equal sign, there are four A's, for artists, and three S's, for stonemasons. Directly below that is a similar configuration to represent a $33 cost for three artists and four stonemasons. The lower left portion of the poster shows 6 tens (squares) and 10 units (circles) to represent $70. This is the addition of the tens (squares) and units (circles) from the two equations on the top of the poster.

On the right side, there are seven A's and seven S's, which are the sum of the A's and S's from the two equations. This group reasoned that they now had a total of seven artists and seven stonemasons and a total of $70. They circled one artist, one stonemason, and the group of ten units (circles) to show that one of each worker would cost $10. This was one of the few groups who answered the question as written. They made no attempt to determine the individual costs for one artist or one stonemason. Members of this group were not unanimous about whether or not they should do so;

however, several members of this group were confident that the question merely asked for the cost for one artist and one stonemason together and that individual costs were not required.

The fourth group (not shown) listed two scenarios and then depicted the artists making $7 each and the stonemasons making $3 each. This seemed to be **working backward**. They reason that $33 and $37 added together equals $70; simultaneously, they reason that three artists and four stonemasons added to four artists and three stonemasons results in seven of each type of worker. If seven artists and seven stonemasons cost $70, the group reasons that one artist and one stonemason cost $10.

An interesting approach to finding the individual cost for each type of workers follows. First, the group realizes that both scenarios have three artists and three stonemasons. One scenario has an extra artist, and the other scenario has an extra stonemason. Based on their conclusion that one artist and one stonemason cost $10, they derive that three artists and three stonemasons cost $30. Using this baseline, they argue that the scenario, which has the extra artist, is $37, which is $7 more than their baseline. Therefore, the artist must cost $7. And, the scenario which has an extra stonemason costs $33, which is $3 more than their baseline. Therefore, the stonemason must cost $3.

While each poster seemed to represent a different thinking behind the solution strategy, teachers were able to make important connections between their respective poster proofs. All five of the possible representation strategies were used by the groups: tables, pictures, graphs, numbers and symbols, and verbal descriptions. A review of the artifacts from the other three groups (B, C, D) revealed a similar variety of approaches. Some groups used a strictly algebraic strategy with the simultaneous equations $4a + 3s = 37$ and $3a + 4s = 33$.

However, there were a variety of other interesting approaches that were employed by the teachers in solving these equations beyond the traditional textbook approaches including substitution, linear addition, or matrix approaches. One group started off with finding ways to arrive at **partitioning** the number 37, including $25 + 12$, $26 + 11$, and $27 + 10$, even though none of these contain one value which is divisible by 7 and another value which is divisible by 3. Their last attempt, though, $28 + 9$, did factor correctly. They then used the same strategy to arrive at partitioning 33, using $19 + 14$, $20 + 13$, and finally arriving at the correct $21 + 12$.

Another group, first wanted to do a **comparison** to determine who made more. They reasoned that the cost with an extra artist was greater than the cost with an extra stonemason, concluding that artists cost more. Using algebra, they found that the cost for one artist was $4 greater than the cost of a stonemason. Their poster used this idea to show that an artist earns $7 and a stonemason earns $3. Another interesting observation involving **parity** was made by one of the groups because the total cost in either scenario was odd and the number of total workers in each scenario was odd, then the individual pay for each type of worker must be odd. If there are four workers of the same type, then their total pay will be an even integer. But, the three remaining workers must have an odd wage or else the total cost would be an even integer. Using the same logic in the second scenario, their poster showed that both types of workers must have an odd value for their daily pay.

As these poster illustrations clearly indicate, the teachers exhibited a wide variation in their thinking. Specifically, the comparison strategy generated a lot of interesting conversation that helped the instructors to bring a nice closure to this problem using proportional reasoning. Since this group demonstrated that one artist must cost $4 more than a stonemason, starting from the first setup of four artists and three stone-masons that costs $37, it became clear to the teachers that adding an artist and taking away a stonemason to this will yield five artists and two stonemasons that costs $41.

Continuing this process, we have six artists and one stonemason that costs $45 and doing this one more time yields seven artists that costs $49 which immediately helps to solve for the cost of an artist which was $7 and from that obtain the cost of a stone-mason which was $3. It was interesting to see such profound thinking from teachers for a problem that most students would normally do using a textbook approach of solving system of linear equations.

9.5 DEEPENING TEACHER KNOWLEDGE AND THEIR STRATEGIC COMPETENCE

Along with in-class activities, the teachers were also given the opportunity to reflect on the problem that they worked on each day. The teacher reflections enabled us to focus on the understanding, reactions, and feelings of the individual teachers. While the posters showed how people in a group approached problem solutions in a variety of ways, the reflections gave us insight into how the individual teachers were feeling about the sessions, about their own competence, and about their classroom practices.

Several themes were observed in the majority of the reflections. These included the value of the struggle, the joy of using conceptual thinking, the importance of clarity, the advantage of building, the benefit of collaboration, and recognizing that there are multiple valid ways in which to approach problem solving, which leads to viewing student work with new eyes.

Teachers appreciated the value of the struggle for several reasons. Being forced to "figure it out" without reliance on rote procedures or "tricks" gave teachers a chance to think about their own thinking. Valuable discussions with their peers ensued. Understanding of concepts was developed. Several teachers reported "Aha" moments concerning ideas about rational numbers which they had formerly accepted but now actually understood, giving them a feeling of liberation. Teachers experienced frus-tration, which made them more sensitive to the same feeling in their students; and, teachers saw the value in developing a thoughtful and defendable approach to problem solution. This is a skill which they want to transfer to their students. A teacher wrote, "I wish more classroom teachers fostered an environment where students can struggle with problems and work together to solve problems. Struggling through and listening to strategies of others has really opened up my thinking."

As the teachers' conceptual knowledge deepened, the teachers began to question their own knowledge and assumptions. Teachers gained such insight and expanded understanding through discussions that they want to incorporate more "talking about it" in their classrooms instead of heading straight for procedural solutions. Class-room discussions of problems and sharing solution strategies are seen as a valuable approach both to clarify problems for our students as well as to develop their concep-tual thinking.

The cathedral problem provided a poignant example of a question which is easy to misinterpret. The question asked, "What would be the expense of just one of each worker?" Whether the answer to the question is "$10" or "$7 for an artist and $3 for a stonemason" may never be resolved. Even after the class discussed the idea that the question did not ask for the individual rates, some teachers were convinced that the question required the rates for both workers. The important point is that the question was, apparently, open to interpretation. Teachers, both in reflections and in verbal commentary, noted that they learned to be very clear when they write questions. One teacher commented to us that she was going to review all of her assessments to ensure that she did not have any "open to interpretation" questions. She showed some angst in saying that she hoped she had not done that to her students in the past.

Teachers reported that the reasoning up and down helped them to break problems into chunks and build on those chunks. They saw how building on known concepts or known quantities gave them a sense of control as opposed to the lost feeling we sometimes experience during the introduction of a completely new idea. The teachers realize that the latter is a source of concern, frustration, and fear in their students. One teacher commented that she never realized how emotional the process could be and that she was gaining a new perspective on her students and how she interacts with them. Another teacher wrote that she would use *reasoning up and down* to help her students focus on what they already know and then guide them in building on that knowledge. Several teachers remarked on the importance of labeling processes so that students have a clear picture of how the concepts tie together; this leads to the development of conceptual understanding and the internalization of concepts and processes for the students.

Teachers appreciated the collaborative nature of the problem-solving process that they engaged in as a part of the institute. No one felt as though they were left to fend for themselves with no help. Struggling through problem solutions with colleagues, analyzing their approaches, questioning their reasoning, and contributing to group efforts were noted by the teachers as being very beneficial to their discoveries during the week. Meetings with colleagues were already planned by several of the teachers to discuss their progress and to choose problems to incorporate the reasoning up and down strategies into their curricula before the start of the school year.

9.6 PROMOTING REASONING TO RICH TASKS

So often an approach to a mathematical problem is formulaic, totally plug and play, and without much attention given to concepts. After all, adding ½ and ½ and getting ¼ does not make any sense if one would only take a few seconds to think about it. The emphasis of thinking, really thinking, about a problem before rushing to get a solution was a major issue for the teachers. For example, another follow-up problem stated that:

Consider the following proportional reasoning problem that the teachers were asked to attempt:

If 1 robot can make 1 car in 10 hours, how long it will take 10 robots to produce 10 cars?

It is far too easy to slip into the mindset that every value in the first scenario has been multiplied by 10. Almost every group had someone do this. However, when that teacher looked at the answer of 10 hours, the realization that the answer made no sense came quickly. One teacher looked at her work, gave a quizzical look, and said, "Now, that just cannot be right. Hmm, why does not that work?" Then, the group thought about the problem and the relationship between the values. The teachers recognized the crucial importance of thinking about the question before crunching numbers.

Mistakes and confusion allowed the teachers to use proportional reasoning and mathematical arguments to do side-by-side comparisons of solutions, or just talk through comparisons of solutions to find where they did not match up. Then, the teachers strategized to determine not only how to proceed but also to determine why one method did not work. For example, "1 robot can make 1 car in 1 hour" does not mean "2 can make 2 cars in 2 hours." Teachers discussed why a simple "multiply through" technique did not work. Teachers benefitted from these discussions in several distinct ways. First, they began to see that real problems involving proportional reasoning are not simply plug-and-play exercises; they are multi-layered challenges which require analysis, sound reasoning, and understanding of the relationships among quantities.

Second, they recognized the profound importance of conceptual understanding as a baseline for strategizing approaches to problem solving. And, third, they gained an acute appreciation for the frustration of their students who apply incorrect procedures and cannot understand why their answers are incorrect. Additionally, as can be seen in the posters, the teachers gained an appreciation for the validity of multiple approaches to problem solution. Several teachers mirrored that idea in their writings.

After having experienced the Robot problem, the teachers planned a lesson study around this topic and presented the following problem to their students:

Text Box 9.4 A Math Happening 9c: The Robot Problem

> If 3 robots make 17 cell phones in 10 minutes, 12 robots can make how many cell phones in 45 minutes?

The various strategies used by students to solve the robot problem can be seen in Figure 9.5. These approaches can be connected to the learning progressions of the CCSSM Standards.

One approach to this task was to set up proportions to solve the problem. This strategy began with the use of ratios in order to describe the relationship between the number of robots and cell phones produced [6.RP.A.1], expressing the given information as 3/17. From this starting place, students showed recognition of the proportional relationships between 3 robots producing 17 cell phones and 12 robots producing x cell phones ($3/17 = 12/x$) [7.RP.A.2.B] and used this to find $\times = 68$ cell phones produced by 12 robots.

Continuing this multistep proportion problem of 10 minutes for 68 cell phones and 45 minutes for x cell phones produced ($10/68 = 45/x$) [7.RP.A.3] giving an answer of 306 cell phones. Another strategy involving recognition and use of proportions computed how many cell phones the initial 3 robots could produce in 45 minutes based on a ratio

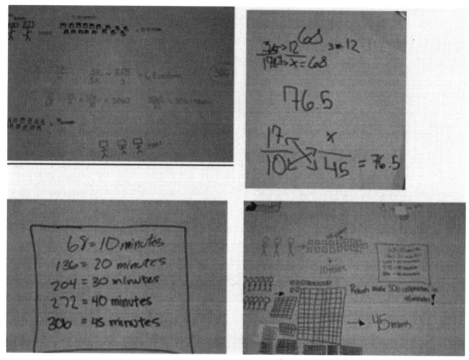

Figure 9.5 Student work showing various strategies for the robot problem. *Source*: Authors.

of 17 cell phones in 10 minutes (17/10 = *x*/45) and then scaled up this number (x = 76.5) by 4 (76.5 *x* 4) because the problem asks about 12 robots instead of the initial [3 6.RP.A.1, 7.RP.A.2.B, 7.RP.A.3]. An additive strategy students used to solve this problem was to visually represent a group of 3 robots producing 17 cell phones in 10 minutes.

This "group" was added together four times to find how many cell phones 12 robots (3 + 3 + 3 + 3) would produce in 10 minutes producing 68 cell phones (17 + 17 + 17 + 17). Students continued by creating a table of values [6.RPP.A] with increments of 10 minutes showing how many cell phones would be produced by 12 robots at 10, 20, 30, and 40 minutes. The additional 5-minute increment was computed by dividing the amount produced in 10 minutes (68) by 2. The last strategy used by students for this problem was finding the unit ratio of how many cell phones 1 robot would produce in 10 minutes [6.RP.A.3B, 7.RP.A.1]. This unit ratio was then used to compute how many units (cell phones) 1 robot would produce in 45 minutes and use this to scale up to the number of units produced by 12 robots.

Our class observations, conversations with participants, review of the team posters, lesson study examinations, and the individual reflections have highlighted several central ideas. Teachers need the opportunity to struggle with problems in order to develop deep understanding of proportional reasoning. While many teachers expressed frustration with the homework problems as well as the in-class problems, they also recognized that their frustration led them to think about proportional reasoning in ways which they had not employed previously.

This led to deeper understanding. Several teachers reported that they now "get" proportional reasoning and are gaining appreciation for the connections between concepts; they attribute this to the experiences of struggling through the investigative problems without the crutch of plug-and-play procedures.

The daily investigations, such as the cathedral problem and the robot problem, led to discussion and exploration of much more than simply trying to find an answer. Teachers questioned each other's thinking and would not allow unsubstantiated assumptions. The focus was on mathematics of the proportional reasoning, not the answer. Teachers were repeatedly heard asking each other, "please explain that again, I don't understand where you are going with this" or "why would that be reasonable way to solve this?" Knowing that numerous approaches to problem solution were both possible and valid freed the teachers to concentrate on the soundness of their approaches, resulting in the teachers being able to develop more profound understanding.

Teachers are learning to think more insightfully and to use proportional reasoning in ways which they have not previously employed. This cannot be expected to occur overnight. The same is undoubtedly true for our students. It takes time and practice before the teachers may see connections between the concepts and techniques which they learned at the summer institute. The rich collaboration and communication experience that the institute provided the teachers with not only helped them to think outside their comfort zone but also helped to impact their beliefs and disposition.

9.7   TECHNOLOGY INTEGRATION IN PROBLEM SOLVING

One problem we have had teachers try is the following rabbit digging burrows problem:

Six rabbits can dig six burrows in 6 minutes. Assuming each rabbit works at the same rate how long will it take eight rabbits to dig eight burrows?

When the teachers were not allowed too much time to think and were asked to tell what they thought the answer was, majority of them admitted that the answer they thought was 8 minutes. It was helpful at that point to employ a technology tool that was developed in-house as a part of this project to clarify their misconception using a pictorial demonstration of reasoning up and reasoning down strategy. First one can illustrate the given input in the problem by the following representation.

Not only is this methodical process helpful to understand the proportional reasoning process but also provides the opportunity for the students to learn conceptually.

9.8   MORE RELATED RICH PROBLEMS TO EXPLORE

1. Solve the following problems:
   a. $10/13 = n/26$
   b. $5/13 = 25/n$
2. A can of fruits cost \$2. How many cans can you buy with \$14?

Note that the students can then use the forward green button step by step to see the following:

The technology tool also prompts the user to say an answer before they proceed to the next step which is a great motivation to try continuing with the process. So the next step yields:

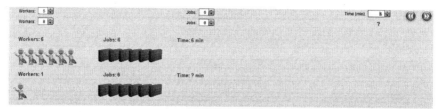

At this point the student can guess the answer or simply go forward which then yields:

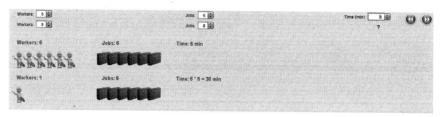

At this step, the teacher can pause and describe the reasoning up process where the number of jobs have been kept fixed by the workers have reduced by a factor of 6 which increases the time by a factor of 6 as well. This is clearly illustrated by the technology. This process continues until the final screen yields:

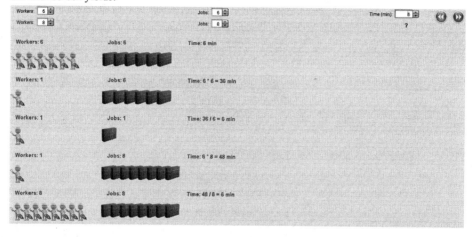

http://completecenter.gmu.edu/java/triplevariation/index.html

3. Five-eighths of a room is now painted. If John did two-fifths of the painting, then how much of the room did he paint?

4. A painting was originally 32 ft tall and 40 ft wide. What is the new height if the painting needs to be reduced to a width of 2.5 ft?

5. Two triangles are similar and the length of their base ratio is 1:2. The smaller triangle has a base that equals 5 and an area that is 110. What is the area of the larger triangle?

6. On a map 7, 72 miles represents 12 centimeters length. How many miles does a 17-centimeter length represent?

7. When I drove up to the gas station, I notice that my gas tank was one-eighth full. I purchased 7.5 gallons of gasoline for $10. With this additional gasoline, my tank now is five-eighths full. How many gallons of gasoline can my tank hold when it is full?

8. A worm climbs a 40-ft tree. Each day he climbs 5 feet, and each night he slides down 2 feet. In how many days will the worm reach the top of the tree?

9. If 2 people can paint 2 rooms in 2 hours then, then how many people can paint 18 rooms in 6 hours?

10. If there are 15 total bicycles and tricycles in a store and there is a total of 37 wheels. How many tricycles are there?

Math Modeling Task
Painting Your Room: Saving Time

The Task

The task is to paint your bedroom, using whatever color you choose but done in the most time and cost effective way. (We only want to spend what we have to in order to get the bedroom fully painted, and we would hope for this project to not take too long)

What do we want to know? What questions should we ask ourselves, to make sure we complete this task in the most time and cost effective way?

How many people will it require to complete the job in half the time?

Chapter 10

Pulling it All Together

Strengthening Strategic Competence through Modeling Mathematics Ideas

10.1 PRACTICE-BASED ACTIVITIES TO FOCUS ON MODELS AND MODELING WITHIN OUR STANDARDS

Through the research lessons from our lesson studies, we have learned a great deal about engaging teachers and students in meaningful and worthwhile problem-solving and mathematical modeling tasks. Working with teachers on understanding the different facets of modeling mathematical ideas revealed that teachers use models and modeling in important and diverse ways in teaching mathematics.

The important but distinct ways teachers used models and modeling were through (a) modeling math with tools—manipulatives, representations, and technology; (b) interpretative models of mathematics concepts (i.e., models for fractions, meanings for operations); (c) modeling math through problem-solving tasks; (d) problem posing; and (e) mathematical modeling through unstructured real-world problems that require problem formulation, real data, and building a model that makes sense in the real world.

Unpacking the different ways models and modeling is used in the curriculum is important for teachers for it serves as means for developing strategic competence and for tailoring optimal teaching sequences that engage students in problem-solving and critical-thinking skills. Through designed professional development activities and lesson studies, we worked with teachers while developing students' and teachers' strategic competence in formulating, representing, and solving mathematical problems.

Research has shown that content-focused professional development leads to improvements in teacher content knowledge when it is focused on student learning goals: highlighting the concepts being addressed, how they are developed over time, difficulties students may encounter, and how to monitor student understanding (Garet et al., 2001; Cohen & Hill, 2001; Desimone, Porter et al., 2002). Sztajn (2011) reports that mathematics professional development is an emerging research field that needs high-quality reports on description of the math professional development and a standard for reporting, including design decisions. As designers and researchers, we were intentional in our design decisions with the goals of developing teachers' specialized knowledge for teaching mathematics.

In designing the professional development, we also considered cognitive demand in the tasks as one of the essential tools that the teachers were introduced to in the summer institute and lesson study. This involved helping teachers understand how to develop open-ended tasks and evaluate the level of cognitive demand the task offered while implementing standards-based mathematics instruction. In particular, the teachers were introduced to the work of Boston & Smith (2009) which helped them to identify the level of the cognitive demand in the tasks they created (low vs. high) and also learnt how to identify the factors related to the decline of the high-level cognitive demand tasks.

Our observations confirmed results presented by Arbaugh & Brown (2005) where teachers showed growth in the ways they considered various proportional reasoning tasks and how this influenced some of them to change their patterns of task choice. This helped us as a measure to evaluate teachers' pedagogical content knowledge. Teachers get frustrated when they do not know what to do, an uncomfortable feeling for the "knowledge authority." Several teachers remarked that "now, I know how my students feel." This same remark was present in numerous reflections as well. Teachers who experience the frustration of struggling will be more acutely aware of it in their students.

Collaboration was not only a great stress reliever but also created a rich learning environment. Several teachers remarked that they would use student groups in their classrooms more frequently because they saw the benefit of such strategies for their own work. We saw many instances of teachers asking others in their group to explain their reasoning. This helped the teachers to understand their colleagues' reasoning and also helped the speaker clarify her/his own thoughts through explanation. Then, the groups at the table discussed whether or not the logic was valid and if they wanted to use that approach. Teachers benefitted from these collaborations in several distinct ways.

First, they began to see that real problems involving proportional reasoning are not simply plug-and-play exercises; they are multi-layered challenges, which require analysis, sound reasoning, and understanding of the relationships among quantities. Second, they recognized the profound importance of conceptual understanding as a baseline for strategizing approaches to problem solving. And, third, they gained an acute appreciation for the frustration of their students who apply incorrect procedures and cannot understand why their answers are incorrect. Several teachers mirrored that idea in their writings. Lastly, another teacher reflected, "I am also starting to think differently about analyzing student work. When problems have the opportunity of yielding a variety of correct answers, it is important to consider what the student is doing and what math they can do and understand."

Lessons Learned from Our Lesson Study and Professional Development Sessions

Through our professional development activities, we learned that developing strategic competence through modeling mathematical ideas encompassed the five important ways we defined modeling mathematical ideas: (1) modeling math with tools, (2) conceptual and interpretative models of math ideas, (3) modeling math through rich problem solving, (4) problem posing, and (5) mathematical modeling of situations through unstructured real-world problems.

We looked at these ways of modeling by immersing teachers in problem-solving and mathematical modeling tasks that then led to the development of their research lesson during lesson study. Throughout these cycles, we examined how both students and teachers made use of models and modeling to understand mathematics.

10.2   MODELING MATH WITH TOOLS AND REPRESENTATIONS TO STRENGTHEN STRATEGIC COMPETENCE

The first way teachers and students modeled mathematics was through the use of tools such as manipulative and representational models. When groups of students were presented with the Sharing Brownie task, they were provided with physical manipulatives and asked to brainstorm the possible tools they could use to tackle this problem. Some students chose to use the physical manipulatives, some chose to draw their work in order to visualize their fractions, and others started by trying to solve the task numerically. One of the teachers, Mary, noted an incident where "I thought a student was playing with the manipulatives, but when I sat down and talked them through it I realized that they had discovered how to break up the whole into pieces."

The variety of approaches evidenced through students' representational models demonstrated the different ways in which they constructed their understandings of the mathematical ideas. The teachers used student models as an opportunity to make sense of their students' thinking and identify future learning opportunities. Alice commented that, "It is clear that this student needs support with naming fractions and labeling" also noting possible extensions such as "a next step might be to show her that 4/4 + ¼ give a total of 5/4." Cindy learned that her students had a hard time seeing that ¼ five times is 5/4 and can also be expressed as 1 ¼. She realized that her students had difficulty expressing themselves precisely. Tina realized that her students needed to learn how to define a numerator and denominator, how wholes can be divided into equal parts (e.g., 4/4) but still be wholes, the importance of labeling, and the many ways to physically divide a whole (vertically, diagonally, horizontally).

10.3   UNDERSTANDING CONCEPTUAL AND INTERPRETATIVE MODELS OF MATH IDEAS TO STRENGTHEN STRATEGIC COMPETENCE

The second way we discussed modeling math was through discussing the different interpretative models (i.e., understanding dividing fractions). For the sharing brownie problem, division was interpreted as a partitive model where it was used to see how many pieces of brownie each of the four children received. As students' examined this task, their interpretive model of the problem was evident. Many of the students started by drawing the five brownies and were able to divide them equally, "fair share" among the four children. However, they struggled with labeling the pieces and writing the fraction.

Other students were able to count to 5/4 but were unable to see that this was the same as one whole and ¼. As students shared their solutions with the class, they noted that the groups had different models of "wholes" resulting in a rich class discussion about how fractions are part of a whole and that "whole" can be divided differently. During the lesson, students who had no exposure to mixed numbers were able to explain their understanding of 1 ¼ using words such as one whole and ¼ more, a whole and a quarter, or one big piece and then ¼ of the piece. This notion of understanding that dividing can be represented as a partitive model is important. Just as it is important that division can also be represented with a measurement or quotitive model, which repeatedly measures off a portion, for example, when interpreting 1 ½ divided by ¼ which can be interpreted as how many ¼ cup servings can I get from 1 ½ cups.

10.4   MODELING MATH THROUGH PROBLEM SOLVING
TO STRENGTHEN STRATEGIC COMPETENCE

The third way we discussed modeling mathematics ideas was through problem solving and task selection. The teachers engaged the challenge and struggle of selecting appropriate tasks. They tried out several problems before settling on the best task for research lessons for their group of students. By selecting a rich task and maintaining its cognitive demand during implementation, teachers provided their students with the opportunity learn more rigorous mathematics (Stein et al., 2007). Students modeled mathematics by wrestling with the selected task and working with their group to find solutions and presented their ideas to the class.

When teachers taught the lesson in their respective classrooms, Alice provided guidance by building on the "dialogue occurring in small groups and students questioning of each other's strategies as well as their own" to help students work together to "develop a final product that made sense to each one of them and had a strong central idea." Giving her students the opportunity to struggle enabled them to be "confident of their final solutions." Tina, another teacher, encouraged her students by letting them know that there was more than one way to solve the problem. Mary maintained a high level of cognitive demand throughout the task saying that she "had the patience and confidence to listen to the students speak and not have my own assumptions."

10.5   POSING TASKS FOR MATHEMATICAL MODELING
THROUGH UNSTRUCTURED REAL-WORLD PROBLEMS
TO STRENGTHEN STRATEGIC COMPETENCE

The last way in which we discussed the modeling of mathematical ideas is the process of problem posing and connecting mathematical reasoning with real-world situations. These mathematical modeling problems are open ended and messy and require creativity and persistence. One of the teachers who incorporated mathematical modeling as one of his regular mathematics routines shared how launching a unit on number sense and place value using the *Sports Stadium Proposal* made the unit more meaningful for students.

Students used multi-digit numbers in context and rounded the large number to estimate and compute the budget. The teacher quickly realized that his students needed to use and learned skills beyond the originally planned standards as the real-world problem required more mathematics to be involved to solve the problem. As Lesh & Fennewald (2013) state "realistic solutions to realistically complex problems usually need to integrate ideas and procedures drawn from more than a single discipline or theory or textbook topic area (p. 6)."

10.6   STRENGTHENING STRATEGIC COMPETENCE FOR MODELING MATHEMATICAL IDEAS

Each of the practices of modeling discussed is connected directly to the Standards for Mathematical Practice. Standard 4 of CCSS-M describes mathematically proficient students who can apply what they know to simplify a complicated situation and can "apply the mathematics ... to solve problems in everyday life." In addition to modeling with mathematics in the four ways presented, the process of selecting and using tools to visualize and explore the task connects with CCSS-M standard 5: use appropriate tools strategically.

Furthermore, as students struggled to make sense of their task by translating within and among multiple representations, they developed an important aspect of strategic competence in mathematics. To help us discuss the important ways that modeling math ideas support teachers' and students' strategic competence, we created this visual to show how all these different modeling activities supports the "ability to formulate, represent, and solve mathematical problems." (NRC, 2001, p. 116).

Through our case study of lesson study and professional development with teachers, we have seen models and modeling of mathematics expressed and strengthened in the different and interrelated ways. In chapter one, we began describing our framework for *Developing Strategic Competence through Modeling Mathematical Ideas* with an analogy of gears that need to work together in tandem. As we conclude our book, we end with this last analogy. Each of the approaches of modeling mathematical ideas was shown to contribute toward strengthening strategic competence in both students and teachers. Through our professional development model, we were able to expand teachers' understanding of modeling mathematical ideas and provide them with practical means to do so.

In addition, we offered several effective teaching practices that have supported teachers' professional practice. First, we planned professional development in vertical team with resource specialists. We have found that having vertical teams allow for a natural dialogue of *vertical articulation among professionals around the important learning progression of concepts and students' developmental readiness*. Collaboration of resource specialists (i.e., math coaches, special educators, English Language Specialists, technology resource teacher, and more) also allow for the diverse expertise to work toward a common goal. It may be hard for one single teacher to attend to all the complexity of the learning environment that makes learning optimal, but with the help of the diverse experts, teacher teams can learn more about how to bring rigor to their lessons, consider cultural relevant teaching approaches while attending to the support needed for diverse learners.

Second, *representational fluency can be one assessment of students' mathematical proficiency*. Having flexibility among the different representations can be a good measure of mathematical understanding. Cramer (2003) discusses the importance of "representational fluency" as she refers to Lesh's translation model and states, "The model suggests that the development of deep understanding of mathematical ideas requires experience in different modes, and experience making connections between and within these modes of representation.

A translation requires a reinterpretation of an idea from one mode of representation to another" (p. 1). One way to think about this is that the more dense the connections between and among the representations, the better the mathematical understanding. This can be thought of being analogous to how the brains synapses become dense as more connections are made and formalize learning makes these connections stronger. This research-based notion not only was supported by two decades of research on the Rational Number Project but also more recently with the visual thinking strategies http://www.visiblethinkingpz.org/. Of course, there are some representations that are more efficient than others; however, we have noticed that teachers and students who can better interpret diverse representations and strategies have a better understanding of the mathematical concepts.

Representational fluency is not easy to gauge; however, for our algebraic lessons, we were able to use the *Modeling Math Mat* to capture students comfort with representing their understanding through five representations: words, numbers, pictures, tables, and graphs. In addition, technology can be leveraged in the way that it affords multiple representations in its media format and the affordances and constraints that can help focus and amplify the essential mathematics.

Third, we feel that it is important to approach the mathematics classroom as a place to develop important *twenty-first-century skills*. Being mathematically proficient will be meaningless unless one can communicate their understanding in a collaborative setting, or apply their knowledge to creative- and critical-thinking situations. In this regards, mathematical modeling tasks that are open ended, real world, and messy can be a great place for students to explore in. The critical component will be for teachers to find mathematical modeling tasks that students care to engage in, find relevant and one that their mathematics background knowledge can provide entry.

Mathematical modeling in the purest sense, as used by industry people and engineers to create predictive models, may be out of reach for elementary students. However, applying the mathematics they know to situations they need to mathematize may be a great precursor for young students. Developing quantitative literacy as students become habitual problem posers and problem solves is an important prerequisite to becoming an efficient mathematical modeler.

Fourth, we spent a lot of time talking about the importance of navigating through students' diverse strategies and being able *to anticipate, monitor, select, sequence, and connect strategies*. We feel that naming strategies in this process of the Five Practices was essential to building collective knowledge in the classroom. Providing students the time and space to make sense of the problem in their own respective ways was important to building and adding to an existing schema.

We have learned that many research lessons revealed common misconceptions that were not just blind error but partial understanding or an overgeneralization of a rule or strategy one learned. Understanding how students reason through a problem is pivotal in engaging students in productive discourse about mathematics. Novice teachers do not have the experience base to rely on when planning for potential and common misconceptions; therefore, working with a team of new and seasoned teachers is critical to teachers' professional learning.

Fifth, analyzing students' work and their justification as the centerpiece of analysis during a research lesson is important to teachers' professional learning. Not only does it offer educators the chance to assume the role of learning scientists who can test out their hypothesis for learning but also a way to examine whether or not a certain intervention turns out to be the instrument or strategy that helps students learn a challenging concept. Effective job-embedded professional development models include structures, where professional learning is directly related to the work of teaching include co-teaching, mentoring, reflecting on actual lessons (Schifter & Fosnot, 1993); group discussions surrounding selected authentic artifacts from practice such as student work or instructional tasks; curriculum materials (Ball & Cohen, 1996; Loucks-Horsley, Hewson, Love, & Stiles, 1998); and Lesson study where teachers collaborative plan, observe, and debrief (Lewis, 2002; Wang-Iverson & Yoshida, 2005).

We enjoyed the collaborative nature of designing professional development with content-focused institutes in the summer and the school-based follow-up lesson study cycles in the school year that encouraged vertical articulation and practical application of the teaching practices and the fine grain analysis of how students learn. During this joint ventures with teachers, we witnessed teachers grow as teachers as scholars and teachers as learning scientists. In fact, the time we spent with teachers grappling with the gaps in instructions or student achievement allowed us to spend more time with teachers for professional learning.

A research brief from Stanford's Center for Opportunity Policy in Education released a research brief entitled, "How high-achieving countries develop great teachers," by Darling-Hammond, Wei, and Andree (2010) that states that "most [professional] planning is done in collegial settings, in the context of subject matter departments, grade level teams, or the large teacher rooms where teachers' desks are located to facilitate collective work. In South Korea—much like Japan and Singapore—only about 35% of teachers' working time is spent teaching pupils. Teachers work in a shared office space during out-of-class time since the students stay in a fixed classroom, while the teachers rotate to teach them different subjects.

The shared office space facilitates sharing of instructional resources and ideas among teachers, which is especially helpful for new teachers (p. 3)." This evolution of teachers who professionally see themselves as learning scientists are given the time and space and the respect for professional expertise to make changes in the system which is what we also learned from the Finnish Lesson (Sahlberg, 2011) where we "increase teacher professionalism and to improve their abilities to solve problems within their school contexts by applying evidence-based solutions, and evaluating the impact of their procedures. Time for joint planning and curriculum development is built into teachers' work week, with one afternoon each week designated for this work (p. 9)."

Strengthening strategic competence in our teachers requires collective inquiry into our instructional practices within a job-embedded professional learning environment. More schools are establishing Professional Learning Communities (PLC) so that teachers can engage in collective inquiry of their practice. With this infrastructure in place at many of the schools sites, we have been able to engage teachers in Lesson Study and Instructional Rounds to investigate and co-design lessons.

Conducting lesson study within our PLC affords many opportunities for our professionals. First, it provides a supportive collegial network, which shares a common vision and goal. Teacher teams allow opportunities for co-planning and peer observation of practice. Second, it provides opportunities for analyzing student work and collect student data. This provides time for teachers to collectively reflect about common misunderstandings and gaps that students have and think about what instructional strategies may work for their students' populations.

Finally, the PLC can sustain the lesson study as a way to engaged in structured dialogue about mathematics instruction and student learning. This formalized group affords opportunities for teachers to become leaders within their schools and provide opportunities for school-based coaches to lead their colleagues. Russo (2004) describes school-based coaching in this way, "School-based coaching generally involves experts in a particular subject area or set of teaching strategies working closely with small groups of teachers to improve classroom practice and, ultimately, student achievement. In some cases, coaches work full-time at an individual school or district; in others, they work with a variety of schools throughout the year. Most are former classroom teachers, and some keep part-time classroom duties while they coach (p. 1)."

A promising initiative that has supporting many school-based professional development models have been led by mathematics coaches and mathematics specialists. In our work with professional development, we intentionally recruit teams of teachers from the same school site with their mathematics coach or specialist so that we can be more impactful with the professional learning. Having school members participate together in professional development with the support of a mathematics coach has been instrumental in helping the professional learning sustain even after the summer institute and fall lesson study ends.

Our prior work (Suh & Seshaiyer, 2012, 2014) indicated that the learning curve for teachers is the greatest at the implementation stage following their participation in a PD as they engage in new pedagogical practices. Through multiple iterations, emphasizing the importance of social support in PD, we have refined our model to include coach-facilitated PD as a critical component not previously included. The coach-facilitated PD enhances our existing model to capitalize on the social support that goes beyond collective participation.

Coach-facilitated PD leverages the role of a coach knowledgeable in both content and instructional practice. The PD content promoted algebraic connections *aligned* to the elementary and middle-school curricula and ensured *coherence* to the standards of learning. We encouraged collective participation by recruiting school teams and sustaining the PD into the fall through *Lesson Study*. The goal of lesson study was to provide teachers with continued support in learning and implementing algebraic content, supply materials and strategies to the participants, as well as provide

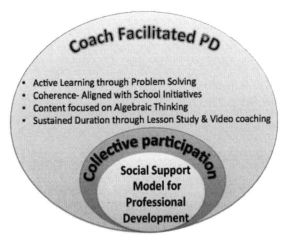

Figure 10.1   Coach-facilitated PD and collective participation providing social support for PD.
Source: Authors.

opportunities for vertical articulation between and among grades levels to share ideas/ resources, analyze student learning and work samples (Suh & Seshaiyer, 2014). The Coach-facilitated PD Model (see Figure 10.1) was a critical piece that ensured the sustainability of the professional learning experiences because the coaches were more aware of specific school/district initiatives and could sustain the professional learning throughout the school year to support teachers' growth.

Through our research, we have identified several affordances of using the coach-facilitated PD model in the school-based PD design. In one of the survey questions, we asked, *How did working in a small school-based team help implement content and new strategies in teaching this lesson? Do you have a teacher or a coach from your own school in this course, if so, how did having a colleague enhance your learning?* Through participants' responses, we found that teachers and specialists had developed different collaborative networks through the coach-facilitated school-based lesson study.

We coded their responses, and there seemed to emerge several collaborative teacher networks that had some distinct connections (see Figure 10.2). The first type of collaborative teacher networks that were evident and obvious was (1) the coach and teacher networks, we had coach facilitation built into the fabric of the PD design. However, we were very pleased to see that there emerged other social networks. The other three were (2) multi-district teacher networks with cross grade "vertical" teacher networks and the same grade "horizontal" teacher networks; (3) school-based PLC teacher networks; and (4) resource specialists networks.

Working with coach from their school or their district, there was immediate trust established in our PD efforts. The coaches working with the university faculty and facilitator showed the collaborative nature of our efforts and teachers saw their coaches endorsing our PD. In addition, we formed lesson study teams as communities of practice where teams of general educators worked with ELL and special needs teachers. In this way, we also saw what we called "collaborative coaching" where different participants shared their different professional expertise.

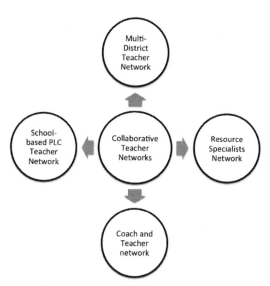

Figure 10.2 Development of collaborative teacher networks. *Source*: Authors.

The special educator and ELL specialists shared their expertise on how the task would need modification to provide equal access for all students and helped generalists anticipate how learners might need extra support to navigate through the problem task. The collaborative ownership in the community of practice allowed teachers to go beyond "your kids" vs. "my kids" and change their belief about who can and cannot do math. With our unique school university partnerships, we have been fortunate to work with multiple districts. Having this multi-district teacher network allowed for knowledge exchange among vertical and grade-level teams of teachers across districts, sharing resources, and strategies.

The work with learning trajectories supported *vertical teaming* by teachers, for it allowed a "chance for teachers to discuss and plan their instruction based on how student learning progresses. An added strength of a learning trajectories approach is that it emphasizes why each teacher, at each grade level along the way, has a critical role to play in each student's mathematical development" (Confrey, 2012, p. 3). An exciting "Carry Over Effect" was noticed among school-based PLC networks who were able to sustained their professional learning beyond the scope of our PD initiative/ The effect of the PD extended beyond even what we could hope. In fact, for novice teachers, this collective experience provided the teachers a jump start and a chance to get to know their support network. This teacher commented on how she was able to build a resource base.

> *Being new to the school and content area, a team helped build a resource base. I started the year knowing people I could go to get help. The coach offers onsite (support) and presents questions to explore other options. Having a team of different teachers provided a variety of strategies. By discussing how they use them, it helped me implement them.*

As we conclude this book, we strive to work with school-based teacher teams with school-based mathematics coaches or mathematics specialists through lesson study.

We hope that the teachers and coaches who use this book will be inspired to be change agents and "pay it forward" by inviting three more teachers and coaches to embrace the Modeling Math Ideas approach. Like in the movie "Pay It Forward," a student, comes up with an idea that he thought could change the world. He decides to do a good deed for three people and then each of the three people would do a good deed for three more people and so on.

Before long, there would be good things happening to billions of people using this model. This movie is a great inspiration for teacher leaders to use this as a "math happening" to impact change in our profession. At stage 1 of the process, we can impact three teachers and coaches. How does the number of teachers we impact grow from stage to stage? How many teachers would be impacted at stage 5? The last challenge that we leave you with in our book is to describe a function that would model the way we can inspire our teachers with the *Pay It Forward* process at *any* stage. In this way, we can sustain teachers' professional learning as they strengthen their strategic competence and have this exponential growth in our professional practice so that we can develop more mathematically proficient students in our classrooms.

Think about it!

What are some creative ways we can "buy" our teachers more time and space for collective inquiry on their teaching practices and enhancing student learning?

Appendix A

Modeling Mathematical Ideas Toolkit*

MMI TOOLKIT 1.0—DEVELOPING STRATEGIC COMPETENCE THROUGH MODELING MATH IDEAS

Developing Strategic Competence through Modeling Mathematical Ideas include the application of mathematics for (1) problem solving; (2) problem posing; (3) mathematical modeling; (4) the flexible use of representational models, tools, technology, and manipulatives to solve problems and communicate mathematical understanding; and (5) the deep understanding of conceptual models critical to understanding a specific mathematics topic.

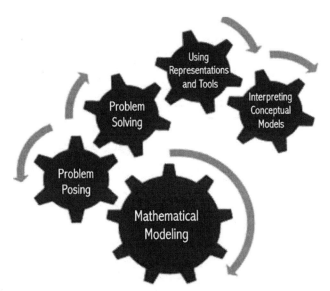

Figure A.1   MMI toolkit 1.0 developing strategic competence through modeling math ideas.

---

*MMI Toolkit Resources will be available on http://completemath.onmason.com/mmi/

MMI TOOLKIT 1.1—PROMOTING MATHEMATICAL PRACTICES

Common Core Mathematical Practices (NGA Center and CCSSO, 2010, p. 6) with Question prompts for encouraging mathematical practices (Suh & Seshaiyer, 2014)

Mathematical Practices	*Questioning prompts*
(MP1) Make sense of problems and persevere in solving them.	Does the problem make sense? What do you need to find out? What information do you have? What strategies are you going to use? Does this problem require you to use your numeric ability, spatial reasoning, and/or logical reasoning? What can you do when you are stuck?
(MP2) Reason abstractly and quantitatively.	What do the numbers in the problem mean? What is the relationship among the numbers in the problem? How can you use number sense to help you check for reasonableness of your solution? What operations or algorithms are involved? Can you generalize the problem using symbols?
(MP3) Construct viable arguments and critique the reasoning of others.	How can you justify or prove your thinking? Do you agree with your classmate's solution? Why or why not? Does anyone have the same answer but a different way to explain it? How are some of your classmates strategies related and are some strategies more efficient than others?
(MP4) Model with mathematics.	How is this math concept used in a real-world context? Where have you seen similar problems happening in everyday life? Can you take a real-world problem and model it using mathematics? What data or information is necessary to solve the problem? How can you formulating a model by selecting geometric, graphical, tabular, algebraic, or statistical representations that describe relationships between the variables?
(MP5) Use appropriate tools strategically.	What tools or technology can you use to solve the problem? Are certain manipulatives or representations more precise, efficient, and clear than others? How could you model this problem situation with pictures, diagrams, numbers, words, graphs, and/or equations? What representations might help you visualize the problem?
(MP6) Attend to precision.	What specific math vocabulary, definitions, and representations can you use in your explanation to be more accurate and precise? What are important math concepts that you need to include in your justification and proof to communicate your ideas clearly?
(MP7) Look for and make use of structure.	What patterns and structures do you notice in the problem? Are there logical steps that you need to take to solve the problem? Is this problem related to a class of problems (i.e., multi-step, work backward, algebraic, etc.)? Can you use a particular algorithmic process to solve this problem?
(MP8) Look for and express regularity In repeated reasoning.	Do you see a repeating pattern? Can you explain the pattern? Is there a pattern that can be generalized to a rule? Can you predict the next one? What about the last one?

MMI TOOLKIT 1.2—PERFORMANCE-BASED ASSESSMENT

Performance based assessment: The Classic Handshake Problem
NCTM: Algebra (Mathematical Problem Solving) Students will apply mathematical concepts and skills and the relationships among them to solve problem situations of varying complexities
1. If everyone at your table shakes hands with everyone else, how many handshakes would there be? 2. If everyone in your class shakes hands with everyone else, how many handshakes would there be?  3. What if there were 100 people in the room? 4. At a birthday party, each guest shakes hands with every guest. If 190 different handshakes take place, how many guests were at the party?

Anticipated Students Response and performance	Tools & Technology
Developing An Algebraic Habit of Mind (Driscoll, 1999) 1. Abstracting from computation 2. Doing and undoing 3. Building a rule from patterns	Manipulatives http://completecenter.gmu.edu/java/handshake/index.html
Signposts for evaluation: Did the student use: ☐ pictures, charts, graphs, or t-tables with supporting explanation ☐ a written explanation with detailed sentences ☐ the equation or number sentence ☐ the answer (Is the answer reasonable? Why or why not?) ☐ the solution to relate to other situations	Teacher Notes: **(1) Understanding-** **(2) Computing-** **(3) Applying-** **(4) Reasoning-** **(5) Engaging-**

Figure A.2   MMI toolkit 1.2 performance-based assessment.

MMI Toolkit 2. UCARE Rubric to assess mathematics proficiency

Student name	Comments (Supporting Evidence)
Understanding (Conceptual Understanding)	
o Understands the problem and task o Makes connection to similar problems o Uses and connects models and multiple representations	
Computing (Procedural Fluency)	
o Proper use of algorithm o Accurate computation o Flexibility in computation	
Applying (Strategic Competence)	
o Formulates and carries out a plan o Can pose similar problems o Can solve problem using appropriate math and strategies	
Reasoning (Adaptive Reasoning)	
o Justifies responses logically o Reflects on and explains procedures o Explains concepts clearly	
Engaging (Productive Disposition)	
o Tackles difficult tasks o Perseveres o Shows confidence in one's ability o Collaborates/Shares ideas	

Overall Assessment:

Figure A.2   *Continued*

MMI TOOLKIT 3.0—SELF-REFLECTION ON TWENTY-FIRST-CENTURY SKILLS (PARTNERSHIP FOR 21st CENTURY SKILLS, 2011)

Critical Thinking and Creativity

Reason Effectively/Use Systems Thinking

- Use various types of reasoning (inductive, deductive, etc.) as appropriate to the situation

Make Judgments and Decisions

- Effectively analyze and evaluate evidence, arguments, claims, and beliefs
- Analyze and evaluate major alternative points of view

Solve Problems

- Solve different kinds of non-familiar problems in both conventional and innovative ways
- Identify and ask significant questions that clarify various points of view and lead to better solutions

Work Creatively with Others

- Demonstrate originality and inventiveness in work and understand the real-world limits to adopting new ideas

Collaborate with Others

- Demonstrate ability to work effectively and respectfully with diverse teams. Assume shared responsibility for collaborative work, and value the individual contributions made by each team member

Communication

- Articulate thoughts and ideas effectively using oral, written, and non-verbal communication skills in a variety of forms and contexts;
- Use communication for a range of purposes (e.g., to inform, instruct, motivate, and persuade (Partnership for 21st Century Skills, 2010)

Prompts for students to self-assess and peer-assess after a problem-solving task

Assessing your Twenty-first-Century Learning Skills in Mathematics

Prompts to assess your 4 Cs contribution	**Critical Thinking:** How did you solve this problem in new ways linking what you know?	**Creativity:** What new approaches did you consider to solve this problem or did you invent a strategy that was efficient?	**Communication:** Did you share thoughts, questions and solutions?	**Collaboration:** How did you work together to each a goal, using your knowledge, talents and skills?
Self-assessment Peer group				

MMI TOOLKIT 3.1—THE MATH MODELING CYCLE*

Mathematical Modeling in the Elementary Grades

Mathematical Modeling involves posing mathematical problems in authentic real life contexts that are relatable to students' personal interests, knowledge and skills.

Mathematical Modeling enables students to use mathematics to help make decisions (i.e., describe, optimize, predict and determine the meaningful solutions to the problem).

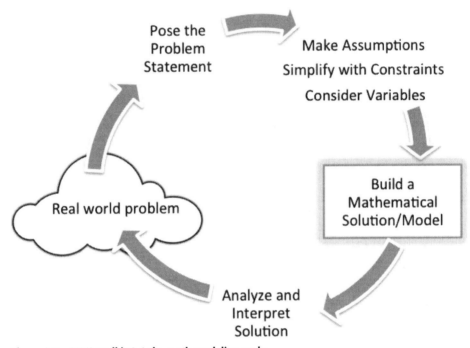

Figure A.3   MMI toolkit 3.1 the math modeling cycle.

*Modified from the SIAM Moody Math Challenge https://m3challenge.siam.org/resources

MMI TOOLKIT 3.2—PLANNING AND DEBRIEFING A MATH MODELING LESSON

To help plan a math modeling lesson, we used six iterative steps that are part of the math modeling process as described by Bliss, K.M., Fowler, K.R., & Galluzzo, B.J. (2014). Math Modeling. Getting Started & Getting Solutions. Society for Industrial and Applied Mathematics (SIAM)

Phases of the Mathematical Modeling Lesson		
Launch	**Explore**	**Summarize**
1. Posing the Problem Statement: Is it real-world and does it require math modeling? What mathematical questions come to mind?	2. Making Assumptions to Define, and Simplify the Real World Problem: What assumptions do you make? What are the constraints that help you define and simplify the problem. 3. Considering the Variables: What variables will you consider? What data/information is necessary to answer your question. 4. Building Solutions: Generate solutions.	5. Analyzing and Validating their Conclusions: Does your solutions make sense? 6. Now, take your solution and apply it to the real world scenario. How does it fit? What do you want to revise?
Iterative process allows students to move back and forth across this process as they revise and refine their thinking.		

Figure A.4   MMI toolkit 3.2 planning for math modeling and debriefing after a lesson study.

Discussions points for Math Modeling Lesson Study

Pre-observation
- What important mathematical ideas and competencies will the task and context afford you as you engage your students in this mathematical modeling process?

Post-observation
- How did students actually engage with mathematical ideas in this lesson? How did mathematical modeling support students use of math ideas, tools and reasoning to answer questions about a contextual situation?

Next Steps
- How will leverage students' mathematical ideas, misconceptions revealed and mathematical opportunities that presented itself in this lesson to build on future lessons?

Source: Authors.

MMI TOOLKIT 3.3—EVALUATING THE MATHEMATICAL MODELING PROCESS

Defining a Problem Statement

- Content: The problem is *posed* in a way that elicits mathematical exploration.
- Process: The problem statement provides opportunities to *describe, predict, optimize, and/or make decisions* on solutions to the problem.
- Context: The problem is *set* in an authentic, real-world situation that is personally meaningful.

Making Assumption and Constraints

- Content: Students *make* reasonable assumptions and identify appropriate constraints.
- Process: Students *discuss and determine* the reasonableness of the assumptions and constraints.
- Context: Students are able to *justify* their assumptions based on information that they gathered in the real-world.

Considering the Variables

- Content: Students *identify* variables that define the mathematical relationships among quantities.
- Process: Students *choose* the appropriate quantifiable variables to identify potential mathematical models.
- Context: Students *collect* real-world data for the variables to establish a mathematical model.

Building a Solution

- Content: Students *apply* relevant mathematical knowledge to build their solution.
- Process: Students *employ* multiple solution strategies to solve the problem efficiently.
- Context: Students *explain* their thinking by using multiple representations with connections to the real-world problem.

Analyzing and Making Conclusions

- Content: Students *validate* their solutions through mathematical reasoning.
- Process: Students *provide* a detailed analysis of their discovery and make conclusions.
- Context: Students *connect* their solutions back to the real-world problem.

Evaluating the Model

- Content: Students can *support* their understanding of the model they created.
- Process: Students *revise/refine* their thinking and critique their peers' solutions.
- Context: Students *interpret* other models to improve their own model to better fit the real-world scenario.

MMI TOOLKIT 4—SHARING MATH HAPPENINGS

Share a Math Happening!

Math happenings occur daily in all of our lives. The math happening lessons serve as a framework for teaching many mathematical concepts within the context of real-life math events. The teacher's role in the math happening lesson is:

- to encourage students to share stories about events that actually happen to them
- to interpret, translate, and represent these stories mathematically, using multiple representations
- to introduce other math concepts for which students are ready.

OBJECTIVE: Model with Math

Share a real-life event (math happening) and pose a question that can be answered using the information given in a math event from everyday life.

MATERIALS: Real world math materials, artifacts, and or manipulatives to engage students.

Figure A.5   MMI toolkit 4 sharing math happenings.

PROCEDURE: Teachers can start with a story that happened to them in their daily life. An example above is about a teacher who wants to stay healthy and likes to buy 100 calorie snacks. She wanted to see if the small one-serving cereals were 100 calories per box. If not, what portion of the box would be 100 calories? After a story has been shared, teachers can share how math is all around us by reading *The Math Curse* by Jon Sciezca and Lane Smith. This is a great read-aloud for students to experience all the math they experience in a given day at school.

- Math happened to me. Let me tell you about it. (Tell the story. Talk outloud what you are trying to find out. What information do I need? Ask the question to help simplify the real world problem.)
- What math happened to you? Tell us about it. Tell me what you did last night, yesterday, or this weekend. (Listen to the event. Probe to gain enough information to make a math story and ask a question.)

Use this organizer to unpack the math!

Math Happening (Tell the story with the problem):	The Math I used:
The Solution:	Connections to other math concepts or real world happenings

MMI TOOLKIT 5 VISIBLE THINKING STRATEGIES

Poster Proofs—This is a visible thinking strategy that requires students to display their work publicly. Similar to publishing writing, we want our mathematicians to publish their work so that others can critique their reasoning.

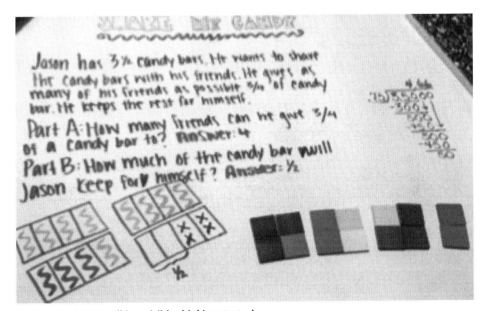

Figure A.6   MMI toolkit 5 visible thinking strategies.

Venn Compare—This visible thinking strategy allows for students to sit side-by-side and compare each other's strategies and discuss similarities and differences in their solution strategies. This encourages students to appreciate multiple representations and evaluate strategies for efficiency and clarity in their representational thinking.

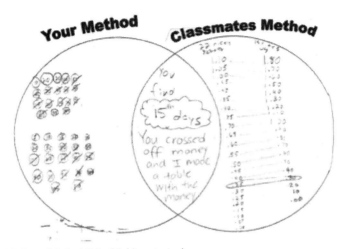

Figure A.7   MMI toolkit 5 visible thinking strategies.

Convince Me—This visible thinking strategy provides opportunities for diverse strategies to be shared in class and evaluate the number of students who also had similar misconceptions and solutions. First the teacher will sort the number of solutions that students came up with on their own. Next, the teacher can ask students with different answers to convince the other group using several different examples.

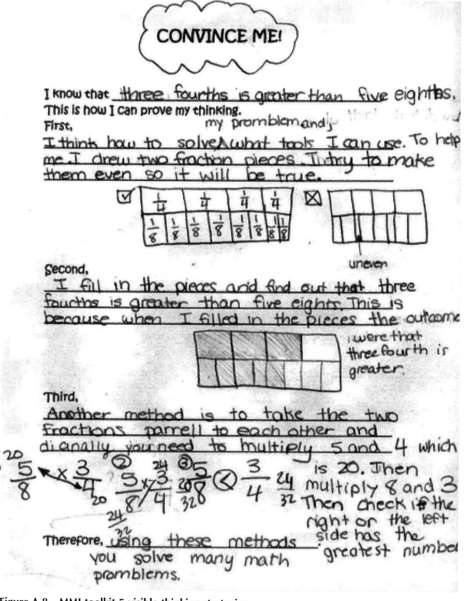

Figure A.8   MMI toolkit 5 visible thinking strategies.

I used to think ... Now I think ... This visible thinking strategy provides an opportunity to share what their pre-conceived ideas were before the lesson and then students are able to share what they think after the lesson. An example of this strategy is asking students to draw all rectangles and after the lesson, some may learn that squares are rectangles as well.

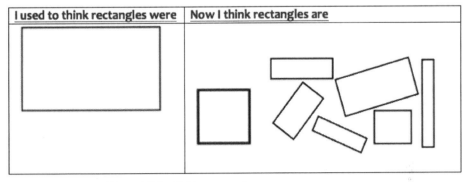

I used to think rectangles were	Now I think rectangles are

Figure A.9   MMI toolkit 5 visible thinking strategies.

MMI TOOLKIT 6 NAMEABLE PROBLEM-SOLVING STRATEGY CARDS

Problem Solving Strategies...	Look for a pattern. ▢○△ ▢○△	Draw a picture. 8 miles / 25 miles
Act it out.	Guess and Check. **?** ✓	Write a number sentence. $5 \times 4 = 20$
Use logical reasoning. [?] ⬭⬭ [?]	Work backwards. ⓪ ← (×2) ← (+2) ← 5	Make an organized list. - vanilla with chocolate - vanilla with rainbow - vanilla with raisins
Make a table. # of people 1 2 3 4 5 # of eyes 2 4 6 8 10	Use a simpler problem. If I know 3×7=21 then I know 6×7 is 21 doubled = 42	_____'s Strategy.

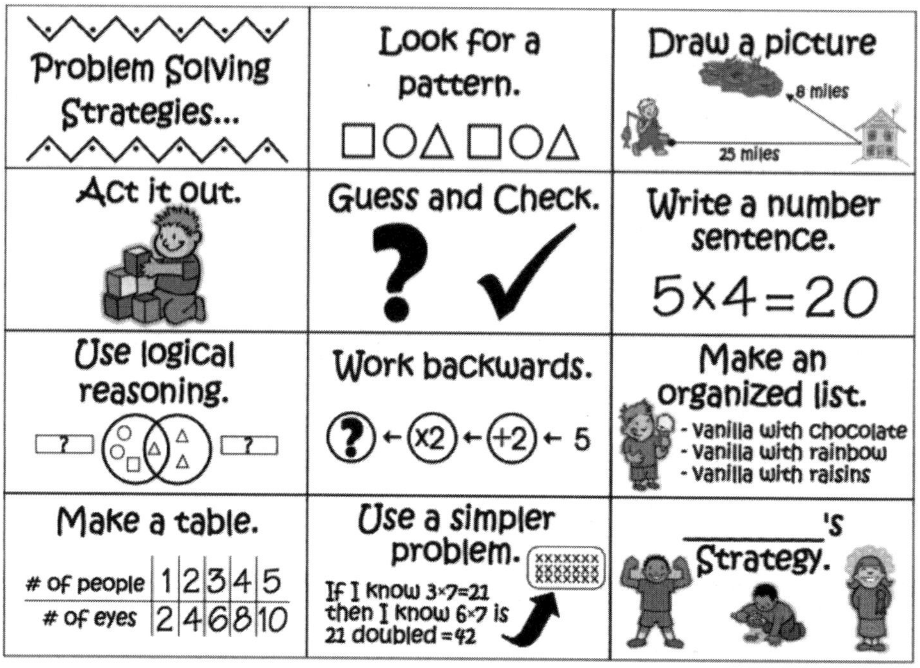

Figure A.10   MMI toolkit 6 nameable problem-solving strategy cards.

MMI TOOLKIT 7 FAMILY OF PROBLEMS

The Ichiro Problem

Adapted from the Lesson Study by:
Linda Gillen, Candice Ives, Steve Klarevas, and Rae Perry
Math 610: Number Systems and Number Theory for K-8 Teachers

The Task

It has been one month since Ichiro's mother has entered the hospital. Ichiro decided to pray with his younger brother at a local temple every morning so that she will get better soon. There are 18 ten-yen coins in Ichiro's wallet and just 22 five-yen coins in the younger brother's wallet. They decided to take one coin from each wallet every day, put them in the offertory box, and continue to pray until either wallet becomes empty. One day when they were done with their prayer, they looked into each other's wallets. The amount of money in the younger brother's wallet was greater than Ichiro's amount of money. When this happened, how many days had it been since they started their prayers?

Big Ideas

- Relationships and patterns
- Solving linear equations (or inequalities) both algebraically and graphically
- Slope as a rate of change and y-intercept as an initial amount
- Writing equations of lines in slope-intercept form

Standards of Learning for Grades 3-4-5	Standards of Learning for Grades 6-7-8
3.19 The student will recognize and describe a variety of patterns formed using numbers, tables, and pictures, and extend the patterns, using the same or different forms.	7.12 The student will represent relationships with tables, graphs, rules, and words.
4.15 The student will recognize, create, and extend numerical and geometric patterns.	7.13a The student will write verbal expressions as algebraic expressions and sentences as equations and vice versa.
4.16a The student will recognize and demonstrate the meaning of equality in an equation.	7.13b The student will evaluate algebraic expressions for given replacement values of the variables.
5.17 The student will describe the relationship found in a number pattern and express the relationship.	8.14 The student will make connections between any two representations (tables, graphs, words, and rules) of a given relationship.
	8.15a The student will solve multistep linear equations in one variable with the variable on one and two sides of the equation.
	8.16 The student will graph a linear equation in two variables.

Figure A.11 The Ichiro problem.

The Ichiro Problem (Continued)

Adapted from the Lesson Study by:
Linda Gillen, Candice Ives, Steve Klarevas, and Rae Perry
Math 610: Number Systems and Number Theory for K-8 Teachers

Standards of Learning for Algebra I

A.4   The student will solve multistep linear equations in two variables, including
  b) justifying steps used in simplifying expressions and solving equations, using field properties and axioms of equality that are valid for the set of real numbers and its subsets;
  d) solving multistep linear equations algebraically and graphically;
  f) solving real-world problems involving equations.
  Graphing calculators will be used both as a primary tool in solving problems and to verify algebraic solutions.

A.5   The student will solve multistep linear inequalities in two variables, including
  a) solving multistep linear inequalities algebraically and graphically;
  b) justifying steps used in solving inequalities, using axioms of inequality and properties of order that are valid for the set of real numbers and its subsets;
  c) solving real-world problems involving inequalities.

A.6   The student will graph linear equations and linear inequalities in two variables, including
  a) Slope will be described as rate of change and will be positive, negative, zero, or undefined;
  b) writing the equation of a line.

A.7   The student will investigate and analyze function (linear and quadratic) families and their characteristics both algebraically and graphically, including
  f) making connections between and among multiple representations of functions including concrete, verbal, numeric, graphic, and algebraic.

Process Goals

* Problem Solving and Reasoning – Students will examine relationships and patterns and use their understanding of slope as a rate of change and y-intercept as an initial amount in the form $y=mx+b$ to determine both algebraically and graphically the relationship between the money in two brothers' wallets.
* Connections and Representations – Students will recognize and use mathematical connections to extend or generalize patterns. Students will use abstract or symbolic representation to record their findings and solve the problem.
* Communication – Students will justify their findings and present their results to the class with precise mathematical language.

Figure A.11   *Continued*

The Ichiro Problem (Continued)

Adapted from the Lesson Study by:
Linda Gillen, Candice Ives, Steve Klarevas, and Rae Perry
Math 610: Number Systems and Number Theory for K-8 Teachers

Related Task – Buying mp3s

You have decided to use your allowance to buy an mp3 purchase plan. Your friend Alex is a member of i-sound and pays $1 for each download. Another one of your friends, Taylor, belongs to Rhaps and pays $13 a month for an unlimited number of downloads. A third friend, Chris, belongs to e-musical and pays a $4 monthly membership fee and $0.40 a month per download. Each friend is trying to convince you to join their membership plan. Under what circumstances would you choose each of these plans and why?

Related Task – Carlos' Cell Phone

Carlos is thinking of changing cell phone plans so he is comparing several different plans.

Plan 1) Pay as you go plan $0.99 per minute
Plan 2) $30 monthly fee plus $0.45 per minute
Plan 3) $40 monthly fee plus $0.35 per minute
Plan 4) $60 monthly fee plus $0.20 per minute
Plan 5) $100 monthly fee for unlimited minutes

What will Carlos need to consider to make his decision? How can Carlos figure out which plan is best for him?

Figure A.11 *Continued*

References

Arbaugh, F., & Brown, C. A. (2005). Analyzing mathematical tasks: A catalyst for change? *Journal of Mathematics Teacher Education, 8*(6), 499–536.

Association of Mathematics Teacher Educators. (2010). *Standards for Elementary Mathematics Specialists: A Reference for Teacher Credentialing and Degree Programs.* San Diego, CA: AMTE.

Ball, D. L. (2003). *What Mathematical Knowledge is Needed for Teaching Mathematics?* Paper presented at the Secretary's Summit on Mathematics. Washington, DC.

Ball, D. L., & Cohen, D. K. (1996). Reform by the book: What is—or might be—the role of curriculum materials in teacher learning and instructional reform? *Educational Researcher, 25*(9), 6–8.

Ball, D. L., & Forzani, F. M. (2010). Teaching skillful teaching. *Educational Leadership, 68*(4), 40–45.

Ball, D. L., Sleep, L., Boerst, T. A., & Bass, H. (2009). Combining the development of practice and the practice of development in teacher education. *The Elementary School Journal, 109*(5), 458–474.

Barnett-Clarke, C., Fisher, W., Marks, R., & Ross, S. (2010). *Developing Essential Understanding of Rational Numbers: Grades 3–5.* Reston, VA: The National Council of Teachers of Mathematics.

Barrett, J. E., & Clements, D. H. (2003). Quantifying path length: Fourth-grade children's developing abstractions for linear measurement. *Cognition and Instruction, 21*(4), 475–520.

Battista, M., Clements, D., Arnoff, J., Battista, K., & Borrow, C. P. (1998). Students' spatial structuring of 2D arrays of squares. *Journal for Research in Mathematics Education, 29*(5), 503–532.

Baturo, A., & Nason, R. (1996). Student teachers' subject matter knowledge within the domain of area measurement. *Educational Studies in Mathematics, 31*(3), 235–268.

Bergen, P. M. (1966). Action research on division of fractions. *The Arithmetic Teacher, 13*(4), 293–295.

Boston, M., Smith, M. (2009). Transforming secondary mathematics teaching: Increasing the cognitive demands of instructional tasks used in teachers' classrooms. *Journal for Research in Mathematics Education, 40*(2), 119–156.

Boston, M. D., & Smith, M. S. (2011). A task-centric approach to professional development: Enhancing and sustaining mathematics teachers' ability to implement cognitively challenging mathematical tasks. *ZDM, 43*(6–7), 965–977.

Bruner, J. (1986). *Actual Minds, Possible Worlds*. Cambridge, MA: Harvard University Press. Retrieved from http://www.hup.harvard.edu/catalog.php?isbn=9780674003668

Bruner, J. (1996). *The Culture of Education*. Cambridge, MA: Harvard University Press.

Burns, S. (Ed.), (2003). September's menu of problems. *Mathematics Teaching in the Middle School, 9*, 32–36.

Carpenter, T. P. (1986). Conceptual knowledge as a foundation for procedural knowledge. In J. Hiebert (Ed.), *Conceptual and Procedural Knowledge: The Case of Mathematics* (pp. 113–132). Hillsdale, NJ: Erlbaum.

Carpenter, T. P., Franke, M. L., & Levi, L. (2003). *Thinking Mathematically: Integrating Arithmetic and Algebra in Elementary School*. Portsmouth, NH: Heinemann. www.heinemann.com

Capps, L. R. (1962). Division of fractions: A study of the common-denominator method and the effect on skill in multiplication of fractions. *The Arithmetic Teacher, 9*(1), 10–16.

Chabe, A. M. (1963). Rationalizing "inverting and multiplying." *The Arithmetic Teacher, 10*(5), 272–273.

Chapin, S. H., & O'Connor, C. (2007). Academically productive talk: Supporting students' learning in mathematics. In W. G. Martin, M. Strutchens, & P. Elliot (Eds.), *The Learning of Mathematics* (pp. 113–139). Reston, VA: NCTM.

Chval, K., Lannin, J., & Jones, D. (2013). *Putting Essential Understanding of Fractions into Practice in Grades 3–5*. Reston, VA: National Council of Teachers of Mathematics.

City, E. A., Elmore, R. F., Fiarman, S., & Teitel, L. (2009). *Instructional Rounds in Education: A Network Approach to Improving Teaching and Learning*. Cambridge, MA: Harvard Education Press.

Clements, D. H., & Sarama, J. (2004). Learning trajectories in mathematics education. *Mathematical Thinking and Learning, 6*, 81–89.

Clements, D. H., & Sarama, J. (2009). *Learning and Teaching Early Math: The Learning Trajectories Approach*. New York: Routledge.

Cohen, D. K., & Hill, H. C. (2001). *Learning Policy: When State Education Reform Works*. New Haven, CT: Yale University Press.

Confrey, J. (2012). Articulating a learning science foundation for learning trajectories in the CCSS-M. In L. R. Van Zoerst, J. J. Lo, & J. L. Kratky, (Eds.), *Proceedings of the 34th Annual Meeting of the North American Chapter of the International Group for the Psychology Mathematics Education* (pp. 2–20). Kalamazoo, MI: Western Michigan University.

Confrey, J., Maloney, A., Nguyen, K., Lee, K., Panorkou, N., Corley, D., Gibson, T. (n.d.). TurnOnCCMath.net Learning Trajectories for the K-8 Common Core Math Standards. Retrieved July 31, 2015, from https://www.turnonccmath.net/

Confrey, J., Maloney, A. P., Nguyen, K. H., Mojica, G., & Myers, M. (2009). Equipartitioning/splitting as a foundation of rational number reasoning using learning trajectories. In M. Tzekaki, M. Kaldrimidou, & H. Sakonidis (Eds.), *Proceedings of the 33rd Conference of the Psychology of Mathematics Education* (Vol. 2, pp. 345–352). Thessaloniki, Greece: PME.

Confrey, J., & Smith, E. (1995). Splitting, covariation, and their role in the development of exponential functions. *Journal for Research in Mathematics, 26*, 26–86.

Corcoran, T., Mosher, F. A., & Rogat, A. (2009). Learning progressions in science: An evidence-based approach to reform. New York, NY: Columbia University, Teachers College: Center on Continuous Instructional Improvement, Consortium for Policy Research in Education. Retrieved from http://www.cpre.org/images/stories/cpre_pdfs/lp_science_rr63.pdf

Council of Chief State School Officers. (2010). *Common Core State Standards (Mathematics): National Governors Association Center for Best Practices*. Washington, DC.

Cramer, K., & Post, T. (1993). Connecting research to teaching proportional reasoning. *Mathematics Teacher, 86*(5), 404–407.

Cramer, K., Post, T., & Currier, S. (1993). Learning and teaching ratio and proportion: Research implications. In D. Owens (Ed.), *Research Ideas for the Classroom* (pp. 159–178). New York: Macmillan Publishing Company.

Cramer, K., & Wyberg, T. (2009). Efficacy of different concrete models for teaching the part-whole construct for fractions. *Mathematical Thinking and Learning, 11*(4), 226–257.

Da Ponte, J. P., & Chapman, O. (2003). Mathematics teachers' knowledge and practices. In A. Gutiérrez & P. Boero (Eds.), *Handbook of Research on the Psychology of Mathematics Education Past, Present and Future* (pp. 461–488). Rotterdam, The Netherlands: Sense Publishers.

Darling-Hammond, L., Wei, R. C., & Andree, A., (2010). *How High-achieving Countries Develop Great Teachers*, Research Brief. Stanford, CA: Stanford Center for Opportunity Policy in Education.

Desimone, L. M. (2009). Improving impact studies of teachers' professional development: toward better conceptualizations and measures. *Educational Researcher, 38*(3), 181–199.

Desimone, L. M., Porter, A. C., Garet, M., Yoon, K. S., & Birman, B. (2002). Does professional development change teachers' instruction? Results from a three-year study. *Educational Evaluation and Policy Analysis, 24*(2), 81–112.

Dougherty, B., Lannin, J., Chval, K., & Jones, D. (2013). *Putting Essential Understanding of Multiplication and Division into Practice in Grades 3–5*. NCTM.

Driscoll, M. (1999). *Fostering Algebraic Thinking: A Guide for teachers Grades 6–10*. Portsmouth, NH: Heinemann.

Dweck, Carol. (2006). *Mindset: The New Psychology of Success*. New York: Ballantine Books.

Dweck, C. (2008). *Mindsets and Math/Science Achievement*. New York: Carnegie Corporation of New York Institute for Advanced Study.

Elashhab, G. A. (1978). Division of fractions—discovery and verification. *School Science and Mathematics, 78*(2), 159–162. http://doi.org/10.1111/j.1949-8594.1978.tb09334.x

Elliot, A., & Dweck, C. (2005). *Handbook of Competence and Motivation*. New York: Guilford Press.

English, Lyn. (2006). Mathematical modeling in the primary school: Children's construction of a consumer guide. *Educational Studies in Mathematics, 63*(3), 303–323.

Fernandez, C., Cannon, J., & Chokshi, S. (2003). A US–Japan lesson study collaboration reveals critical lenses for examining practice. *Teaching and Teacher Education, 19*(2), 171–185.

Fernandez, C., & Yoshida, M. (2004). *Lesson Study: A Case of a Japanese Approach to Improving Instruction through School-based Teacher Development*. Mahwah, NJ: Lawrence Erlbaum.

Flores, A., & Priewe, M. D. (2013). Orange you glad I *did* say "fraction division"? *Mathematics Teaching in the Middle School, 19*(5), 288–293.

Garet, M. S., Porter, A. C., Desimone, L., Birman, B. F., & Yoon, K. S. (2001). What makes professional development effective? Results from a national sample of teachers. *American Educational Research Journal, 38*(4), 915–945.

Glasersfeld, E. von. (1990). Chapter 2: An exposition of constructivism: Why some like it radical. *Journal for Research in Mathematics Education. Monograph, 4*, 19–210. http://doi.org/10.2307/749910

Goldin, G., & Shteingold, N. (2001). Systems of representations and the development of mathematical concepts. In A. A. Cuoco & F. R. Curcio (Eds.), *The Roles of Representations in School Mathematics* (pp. 1–23). Reston, VA: National Council of Teachers of Mathematics.

Gravemeijer, K. (1999). How emergent models may foster the constitution of formal mathematics. *Mathematical Thinking and Learning, 1*(2), 155–177.

Greenes, C. E., & Findell, C. (1999). Developing students' algebraic reasoning abilities. In Lee V. Stiff (Ed.), *Developing Mathematical Reasoning in Grades K–12, 1999 Yearbook of the National Council of Teachers of Mathematics (NCTM)*, (pp. 127–137). Reston, VA: NCTM.

Grossman, P., Hammerness, K., & McDonald, M. (2009). Redefining teaching, re-imagining teacher education. *Teachers and Teaching: Theory and Practice, 15*(2), 273–289.

Hiebert, J., & Grouws, D. A. (2007). The effects of classroom mathematics teaching on students' learning. In F. K. Lester (Ed.), *Second Handbook of Research on Mathematics Teaching and Learning* (pp. 371–404). Charlotte, NC: Information Age.

Hiebert, J., Morris, A. K., Berk, D., & Jansen, A. (2007). Preparing teachers to learn from teaching. *Journal of Teacher Education, 58*(1), 47–61.

Hill, H. C., Rowan, B., & Ball, D. L. (2005). Effects of teachers' mathematical knowledge for teaching on student achievement. *American Educational Research Association, 42*(2), 371–406.

Hill, H. C., Sleep, L., Lewis, J. M., Ball, D. L. (2007). Assessing teachers' mathematical knowledge what knowledge matters and what evidence counts. In F. Lester (Ed.), *Handbook of Research on Mathematics Teaching and Learning* (pp. 111–156). Reston, VA: NCTM.

Hong, L. T. (1993). *Two of Everything*. Morton Grove, IN: Albert Whitman & Company.

Hufferd-Ackles, K., Fuson, K. C., & Sherin, M. G. (2004). Describing levels and components of a math-talk learning community. *Journal for Research in Mathematics Education, 35*(2), 81–116.

Hunt Institute. (2012). *Advance America: A Commitment to Education and the Economy, Issue Briefs*. Prepared for the 2012 Governors Education Symposium. Retrieved from http://www.hunt-institute.org/knowledge-library/articles/2012-5-24/2012-governors-education-symposium-briefs/

Jacobs, V. R., Lamb, L. L. C., & Philipp, R. A. (2010). Professional noticing of children's mathematical thinking. *Journal for Research in Mathematics Education, 41*(2), 169–202.

Kazemi, E., & Franke, M. L. (2004). Teacher learning in mathematics: Using student work to promote collective inquiry. *Journal of Mathematics Teacher Education, 7*(3), 203–235.

Kazemi, E., & Hubbard, A. (2008). New directions for the design and study of professional development attending to the coevolution of teachers' participation across contexts. *Journal of Teacher Education, 59*(5), 428–441.

Kent, A., & McMonagle. (2002). Using representational context to support multiplicative reasoning. In *Making Sense of Fractions, Ratio and Proportions*. NCTM Yearbook. (Eds.) Bonnie Litwiller, and Bright, G.W. Reston, VA.

Krich, P. (1964). Meaningful vs. mechanical method, teaching division of fractions by fractions. *School Science and Mathematics, 64*(8), 697–708. http://doi.org/10.1111/j.1949-8594.1964.tb17033.

Lamon, S. J. (2007). Rational numbers and proportional reasoning: Toward a theoretical framework for research. In F. K. Lester (Ed.), *Second Handbook of Research on Mathematics Teaching and Learning* (pp. 629–667). Charlotte, NC: Information Age; Reston, VA: National Council of Teachers of Mathematics.

Lamon, S. (2001). Presenting and representing: From fractions to rational numbers. In A. Cuoco & F. Curcio (Eds.), *The Roles of Representation in School Mathematics, 2001 Yearbook* (pp. 146–165). Reston, VA: National Council of Teachers of Mathematics.

Lampert, M. (2009). Learning teaching in, from, and for practice: What do we mean? *Journal of Teacher Education, 61*(1–2), 21–34.

Lave, J., & Wenger, E. (1990). *Situated Learning: Legitimate Peripheral Participation*. Cambridge, UK: Cambridge University Press.

Leinwand, S. (2014). *Principles to Actions: Ensuring Mathematical Success for All*. Reston, VA: National Council of Teachers of Mathematics.

Lesh, R., Cramer, K., Doerr, H., Post, T., & Zawojewski, J. (2003). Using a translation model for curriculum development and classroom instruction. In R. Lesh & H. Doerr (Eds.), *Beyond Constructivism: Models and Modeling Perspectives on Mathematics Problem Solving, Learning, and Teaching.* Mahwah, NJ: Lawrence Erlbaum Associates.

Lesh, R., & Doerr, H. M. (Eds.). (2003). *Beyond Constructivism: Models and Modeling Perspectives on Mathematics Problem Solving, Learning, and Teaching.* Mahwah, NJ: Lawrence Erlbaum Associates.

Lesh, R., & Fennewald, T. (2013). Introductions to part I modeling: What is it? Why do it? In R. Lesh, P. L. Galbraith, C. R. Haines, & A. Hurford (Eds.), *Modeling Students' Mathematical Modeling Competencies* (pp. 5–10). New York: Springer.

Lesh, R., Landau, M., & Hamilton, E. (1983). Conceptual models in applied mathematical problem solving research. In R. Lesh & M. Landau (Eds.), *Acquisition of Mathematics Concepts & Processes* (pp. 263–343). New York: Academic Press.

Lesh, R., Post, T., & Behr, M. (1987). Representations and translations among representations in mathematics learning and problem solving. In C. Janvier (Ed.), *Problems of Representation in the Teaching and Learning of Mathematics* (pp. 33–40). Hillsdale, NJ: Erlbaum.

Lesh, R., & Zawojewski, J. (2007). Problem solving and modeling. In F. K. Lester, Jr. (Ed.), *Second Handbook of Research on Mathematics Teaching and Learning: A Project of the National Council of Teachers of Mathematics* (Vol. 2, pp. 763–804). Charlotte, NC: Information Age Publishing.

Lewis, C. (2002). *Lesson Study: A Handbook of Teacher-Led Instructional Change.* Philadelphia, PA: Research for Better Schools.

Lewis, C., Perry, R., & Hurd, J. (2004). A deeper look at lesson study. *Educational Leadership,* February 2004, *61*(5), 18–22.

Lewis, C., Perry, R., & Murata, A. (2006). How should research contribute to instructional improvement? The case of lesson study. *Educational Researcher, 35*(3), 3–14.

Livy, S., Muir, T., & Maher, N. (2012). How do they measure up? Primary pre-service teachers' mathematical knowledge of area and perimeter. *Mathematics Teacher Education & Development, 14*(2), 91–112.

Lobato, J., & Ellis, A. B. (2010). Essential understandings: Ratios, proportions, and proportional reasoning. In R. M. Zbiek (Series Ed.), *Essential Understandings.* Reston, VA: National Council of Teachers of Mathematics (NCTM).

Loucks-Horsley, S., Hewson, P., Love, N., & Stiles, K. (1998). *Designing Professional Development for Teachers of Science and Matheamtics.* Thousand Oaks, CA: Corwin Press.

Ma, L. (1999). *Knowing and Teaching Elementary Mathematics: Teachers' Understanding of Fundamental Mathematics in China and the United States.* Mahwah, NJ: Lawrence Erlbaum Associates.

Marble, S. T. (2006). Learning to teach through lesson study. *Action in Teacher Education, 28*(3), 86–96.

Marshall, A. M., Superfine, A. C., & Canty, R. S. (2010). Star students make connections. *Teaching Children Mathematics, 17*(1), 38–47.

McDonald, M., Kazemi, E., & Kavanagh, S. S. (2013). Core practices and pedagogies of teacher education: A call for a common language and collective activity. *Journal of Teacher Education, 64*(5), 378–386.

McMeen, G. H. (1962). Division by a fraction—a new method. *The Arithmetic Teacher, 9*(3), 122–126.

Middleton, J., & Spanias, P. (1999). Motivation for achievement in mathematics: Findings, generalizations, and criticisms of the research. *Journal for Research in Mathematics Education, 30*(1), 65–88.

Mishra, P., & Koehler, M. J. (2006). Technological pedagogical content knowledge: A framework for teacher knowledge. *Teachers College Record, 108*(6), 1017–1054.

Moss, J., & Case, R. (1999). Developing children's understanding of the rational numbers: A new model and an experimental curriculum. *Journal for Research in Mathematics Education, 30*(2), 122–47.

Moss, J., & Case, R. (2000). Developing children's understanding of the rational numbers: A new model and an experimental curriculum. *Journal for Research in Mathematics Education, 30*, 122–147. Reston, VA: NCTM.

Moyer P. S., Bolyard J., & Spikell M. (2002). What are virtual manipulatives? *Teaching Children Mathematics, 8*(6), 372–377.

Murata, A., & Takahashi, A. (2002). Vehicle to connect theory, research, and practice: How teacher thinking changes in district-level lesson study in Japan. In D. Mewborn, P. Sztajn, D. White, H. Wiegel, R. Bryant, & K. Noony (Eds.), *Proceedings of the Annual Meeting of the North American Chapter of the International Group for the Psychology of Mathematics Education.* Athens, GA: PME.

National Council of Teachers of Mathematics. (1989). *Curriculum and Evaluation Standards for School Mathematics.* Reston, VA: Author.

National Council of Teachers of Mathematics. (1991). *Professional Standards for Teaching Mathematics.* Reston, VA: Author.

National Council of Teachers of Mathematics. (2000). *Principles and Standards for School Mathematics.* Reston, VA: Author.

National Council of Teachers of Mathematics. (2009). *Reasoning and Sense Making.* Reston, VA: Author.

National Council of Teachers of Mathematics. (2013). *Supporting the Common Core State Standards for Mathematics.* Retrieved from: http://www.nctm.org/ccssmposition/

National Council of Teachers of Mathematics. (2013). *Principles to Actions.* Reston, VA: NCTM.

National Governors Association Center for Best Practices & Council of Chief State School Officers. (2010). *Common Core State Standards for Mathematics.* Washington DC: NGACBP & CCSSO.

National Research Council. (2001). Adding it up: Helping children learn mathematics. In J. Kilpatrick, J. Swafford, & B. Findell (Eds.), *Mathematics Learning Study Committee, Center for Education, Division of Behavioral and Social Sciences and Education.* Washington, DC: National Academy Press.

Niess, M. L., & Walker, J. M. (2010). Guest editorial: Digital videos as tools for learning mathematics. *Contemporary Issues in Technology and Teacher Education, 10*(1). Retrieved from http://www.citejournal.org/vol10/iss1/mathematics/article1.cfm

Otto, A. D., Caldwell, J., Lubinski, C. A., & Hancock, S. (2012). *Developing Essential Understanding of Multiplication and Division for Teaching Mathematics in Grades 3–5.* Essential Understanding Series. Reston, VA: National Council of Teachers of Mathematics.

Outhred, L., & Mitchelmore, M. (2000). Young children's intuitive understanding of rectangular area measurement. *Journal for Research in Mathematics Education, 31*(2), 144–167.

Partnership for 21st Century Skills. (2011). *Framework for 21st Century Learning.* Tucson, AZ: Author. Retrieved from http://www.p21.org/overview/skills-framework

Perry, R., & Lewis, C. (2003, April). *Teacher-initiated Lesson Study in a Northern California District.* Paper presented at the Annual Meeting of the American Educational Research Association, Chicago, IL.

Polya, G. (1957, 1945). *How to Solve It*, 2nd ed., Princeton University Press.

Popham, W. J. (2007). The lowdown on learning progressions. *Educational Leadership, 64*(7), 83–84.

Porter, A. C., Garet, M. S., Desimone, L. M., & Birman, B. F. (2003). Providing effective professional development: Lessons from the Eisenhower program. *Science Educator, 12*(1), 23–40.

Pothier, Y., & Sewada, D. (1983). Partitioning: The emergence of rational number ideas in young children. *Journal for Research in Mathematics Education, 14*(5), 307–317.

Rasmussen, C., & Marrongelle, K. (2006) Pedagogical content tools: Integrating student reasoning and mathematics into instruction. *Journal for Research in Mathematics Education, 37*(5), 388–420.

Reinke, K. (1997). Area and perimeter: Preservice teachers' confusion. *School Science and Mathematics, 97*(2), 75–77.

Ritchhart, R., Church, M., & Morrison, K. (2011). *Making Thinking Visible.* San Francisco: Jossey-Bass.

Ryan, J., & Williams, J. (2007). *Children's Mathematics 4-15: Learning from Errors and Misconceptions.* Buckingham, GBR: Open University Press.

Russo, A. (2004, July/August). School-based coaching: A revolution in professional development—or just the latest fad? *Harvard Education Letter, 20*(4).

Sahlberg, P. (2011). *Finnish Lessons: What can the World Learn from Educational Change in Finland?* Series on School Reform.

Schifter, D., & Fosnot, C. T. (1993). *Reconstructing Mathematics Education.* New York: Teachers College Press.

Schoenfeld, A. H. (1985). *Mathematical Problem Solving.* San Diego: Academic Press.

Schoenfeld, A. H. (1992). Learning to think mathematically: Problem solving, metacognition, and sense making in mathematics. In D. Grouws (Ed.), *Handbook of Research on Mathematics Teaching and Learning* (pp. 334–370). New York: MacMillan.

Schoenfeld, A. H. (1992). Learning to think mathematically: Problem solving, metacognition, and sense making in mathematics. In D. Grous (Ed.), *Handbook of Research on Mathematics Teaching and Learning* (pp. 334–370). New York: McMillan.

Schoenfeld, A. (2007). *Assessing Mathematical Proficiency.* New York: Cambridge University Press.

Schorr, R. Y., & Koellner-Clark, K. (2003). Using a modeling approach to analyze the ways in which teachers consider new ways to teach mathematics. *Mathematical Thinking and Learning, 5*(2), 191–210. doi:10.1080/10986065.2003.9679999.

Schorr, R. Y., & Lesh, R. (2003). A modeling approach for providing teacher development. In R. Lesh & H. Doerr (Eds.), *Beyond Constructivism: Models and Modeling Perspectives on Problem Solving, Learning, and Teaching* (pp. 141–158). Mahwah, NJ: Lawrence Erlbaum Associates.

Schoenfeld, A. H. (1985). *Mathematical Problem Solving.* Orlando, FL: Academic Press.

Seshaiyer, P., Suh, J. M., & Freeman, P. W. (2011). Unlocking the locker problem through technology. *Teaching Children Mathematics, 18*(5), 322–325.

Sharp, J., & Adams, B. (2002). Children's constructions of knowledge for fraction division after solving realistic problems. *The Journal of Educational Research, 95*(6), 333–347.

Sherin, M. G., & van Es, E. A. (2003). A new lens on teaching: Learning to notice. *Mathematics Teaching in the Middle School, 9*(2), 92–95.

Shulman, L. S. (1986). Those who understand: Knowledge growth in teaching. *Educational Researcher, 15*(2), 4–14.

Shulman, L. S. (1987). Knowledge and teaching: Foundations of the new reform. *Harvard Educational Review, 57*(1), 1–22.

Siebert, D., & Gaskin, N. (2006). Creating, naming, and justifying fractions. *Teaching Children Mathematics, 12*(8), 394–400.

Simon, M. (1995). Reconstructing mathematics pedagogy from a constructivist perspective. *Journal for Research in Mathematics Education, 26*(2), 114–145.

Smith, M. S., & Stein, M. K. (2011). *5 Practices for Orchestrating Productive Mathematical Discussions*. Reston, VA: National Council of Teachers of Mathematics.

Smith, M. S., & Stein, M. K. (2012). Selecting and creating mathematical tasks: From research to practice. In Glenda Lappan (Ed.), *Rich and Engaging Mathematical Tasks: Grades 5–9*. Reston, VA: National Council of Teachers of Mathematics.

Society for Industrial and Applied Mathematics (SIAM). *Moody's Mega Math Challenge website*. Retrieved from http://m3challenge.siam.org/

Sowder, J. T., Phillip, R. A., Armstrong, B. E., & Schappelle, B. P. (1998). *Middle-Grade Teachers' Mathematical Knowledge and Its Relationship to Instruction*. Albany, NY: State University of New York Press.

Stein, M. K., Engle, R. A., Smith, M. S., & Hughes, E. K. (2008). Orchestrating productive mathematical discussions: five practices for helping teachers move beyond show and tell. *Mathematical Thinking and Learning, 10*(4), 313–340.

Stein, M. K., Remillard, J., & Smith, M. (2007). How curriculum influences student learning. In F. Lester (Ed.), *Second Handbook of Research on Mathematics Teaching and Learning* (pp. 319–370). Charlotte, NC: Information Age.

Stein, M. K., Smith, M. S., Henningsen, M. A., & Silver, E. A. (2009). *Implementing Standards-Based Mathematics Instruction: A Casebook for Professional Development*. New York, NY: Teachers College Press, Columbia University.

Suh, J. M. (2007). Tying it all together: Building mathematics proficiency for all students. *Teaching Children Mathematics, 14*(3), 163–169.

Suh, J. M., Graham, S., Ferranone, T., Kopeinig, G., & Bertholet, B. (2011). Developing persistent and flexible problem solvers with a growth mindset. In D. J. Brahier (Ed.), *Motivation and Disposition: Pathways to Learning Mathematics* (pp. 169–184). NCTM Yearbook.

Suh, J., Seshaiyer, P., Leong, K., Freeman, P., Corcoran, M., Meints, K., & Wills, T. (2012). Fostering strategic competence for teachers through modeling rational numbers problem tasks. In L. R. Van Zoerst, J. J. Lo, & J. L. Kratky (Eds.), *Proceedings of the 34th Annual Meeting of the North American Chapter of the International Group for the Psychology Mathematics Education. Kalamazoo* (pp. 474–481). MI: Western Michigan University.

Suh, J. M. (2010). Leveraging cognitive technology tools to expand opportunities for critical thinking on data analysis and probability in elementary classrooms. *Journal of Computers in Mathematics and Science Teaching, 29*(3), 289–302. http://www.citejournal.org/vol10/iss1/mathematics/article1.cfm

Suh, J., & Seshaiyer, P. (2014). Developing strategic competence by teaching using the common core mathematical practices. *Annual Perspectives in Mathematics Education*, 77–87.

Suh, J. M., Seshaiyer, P., Moore, K., Green, M., Jewell, H., & Rice, I. (2013). Being an environmentally friendly package engineer. *Teaching Children Mathematics, 20*(4), 261–263.

Sztajn, P. (2011). Standards for reporting mathematics professional development in research studies. *Journal for Research in Mathematics Education, 42*(3), 220–236.

Trilling, B., & Fadel, C. (2009). *21st Century Skills: Learning for Life in Our Times*. San Francisco, CA: Jossey-Bass.

Van de Walle, J., Karp, K., & Bay-Williams, J. (2014). *Elementary and Middle School Mathematics: Teaching Developmentally*, 8th ed., London: Pearson Education Limited.

Wang-Iverson, P., & Yoshida, M. (2005). *Building Our Understanding of Lesson Study*. Philadelphia: Research for Better Schools.

Weiner, B. (2005). Motivation from an attributional perspective and the social psychology. In A. Elliot & C. Dweck (Eds.), *Handbook of Competence and Motivation* (pp. 73–84). New York: Guilford Press.

Woodward, J. (1999). *Self-Concept, Self-Esteem, and Attributional Issues in Secondary Math Classes*. Presented at the Pacific Coast Research Conference, San Diego.

Yeo, J. K. K. (2008). Teaching area and perimeter: Mathematics-pedagogical-content knowledge-in-action. Retrieved from https://repository.nie.edu.sg/handle/10497/14397

Zawojewski, J. S., & Lesh, R. (2003). A models and modeling perspective on problem solving. In R. Lesh & H. M. Doerr (Eds.), *Beyond Constructivism: Models and Modeling Perspectives on Mathematics Problem Solving, Learning, and Teaching* (pp. 317–336). Mahwah, NJ: Lawrence Erlbaum Associates.

Index

modeling operations with fractions,
   123–41;
using tools to prove their thinking, 124–26

validation, problem solving, 11
Venn diagram, 102
verbal reasoning, 14
vertical learning progression, 20–22;
   conceptual models and, 20–22
vertical teaming, 174
visible thinking:
   described, 13;

in mathematics, 59–62;
Modeling Math Mat, 82–85;
multiple representations and strategies,
   13–19;
Poster Proofs, 13;
problem solving and, 13;
strategies, 99–103, 189–91

Walker, J. M., 34
Wei, R. C., 171

Zawojewski, J. S., 39

About the Authors

Jennifer Suh is an associate professor in the Graduate School of Education, College of Education and Human Development, George Mason University. Dr. Suh teaches mathematics methods courses in the Elementary Education Program and mathematics leadership courses for the Mathematics Specialist Masters and PhD Programs. She directs the Center for Outreach in Mathematics Professional Learning and Educational Technology (COMPLETE), a joint center between the College of Education and the College of Science. Her research focuses on: implementing lesson study to develop pedagogical mathematics knowledge across the continuum from preservice teachers to mathematics teacher leaders; building children's development of mathematical meaning through math modeling and representational fluency; promoting equitable access to twenty-first century skills through problem-based learning, encouraging creativity, critical thinking, communication and collaboration for diverse student populations. Through formal and informal educational outreach, Dr. Suh enjoys working with schools, communities, teachers and parents to show how math can be useful in solving real-world problems and be enjoyable to teach and learn. Dr. Suh lives in Virginia with her husband Tim and two sons, Jeremy and Zachary.

Padmanabhan Seshaiyer is a professor of mathematical sciences and serves as the director of the STEM Accelerator Program and the Center for Outreach in Mathematics Professional Learning and Educational Technology (COMPLETE) at George Mason University in Fairfax, Virginia. During the last decade, he has initiated and directed a variety of educational programs including graduate and undergraduate research, K-12 outreach, teacher professional development, and enrichment programs to foster the interest of students and teachers in mathematical modeling and STEM at all levels. He is also actively involved in multiple global initiatives and training programs that engage students, teachers and faculty to develop innovative STEM-based solutions to real-world problems. Engaging teachers and students through inquiry-based, hands-on learning by doing approaches in making mathematics meaningful to solve real-world problems has always been an integral part of his work. Dr. Seshaiyer lives in Virginia with his wife Revathy and two daughters, Pradyuta and Prasidha.